Nonprofit Resources

Second Edition

A Companion to Nonprofit Governance

Victor Futter and Lisa A. Runquist

Editor-In-Chief
Victor Futter

Acting Editor-in-Chief
Lisa A. Runquist

Managing Editors

Victoria B. Bjorklund	Lizabeth A. Moody
Evelyn Brody	Norman I. Silber
Daniel L. Kurtz	Peter Swords
Pamela Mann	Stanley S. Weithorn
Jill Manny	J. Warren Wood, III

Printed in the United States of America.

ISBN: 10: 1-59031-426-3
ISBN: 13: 978-1-59031-426-5

Library of Congress Cataloging-in-Publication Data

Nonprofit resources : a companion to Nonprofit governance and management / editor-in-chief, Victor Futter. — 2nd ed.
   p. cm.
 Includes bibliographical references and index.
 ISBN-13: 978-1-59031-426-5 (pbk. : alk. paper)
 ISBN-10: 1-59031-426-3 (pbk. : alk. paper)
1. Nonprofit organizations—Law and legislation—United States—Bibliography.
2. Nonprofit organizations—Management—Bibliography.
I. Futter, Victor, 1919-2005. II. Nonprofit governance and management.

KF1388.A1N66 2007
658'.048—dc22
                                        2006038648

Discounts are available for books ordered in bulk. Special consideration is given to state and local bars, CLE programs, and other bar-related organizations. Inquire at ABA Publishing, American Bar Association, 321 North Clark Street, Chicago, Illinois 60610.

For a complete list of ABA publications, visit www.ababooks.org.

10 09 08 07   5 4 3 2 1

Dedication

This edition of Nonprofit Resources is dedicated to its editor-in-chief, Victor Futter, who died in 2005.

At his passing, Victor was a special counsel to the dean and a professor who taught courses on nonprofit law and corporate governance at Hofstra University School of Law. He previously had a distinguished career in private practice, served as the general counsel at Fairleigh Dickinson University, and also had taught at Columbia University Law School.

Victor grew up in New York and graduated with honors from Columbia Law School in 1942. After the Second World War he began his legal career at Sullivan & Cromwell and then spent many years at the corporation that is now known as Honeywell International, retiring in 1984 as vice president and secretary. He also served as counsel to the law firm, which has become Sills Cummis.

Victor always exhibited great intellectual curiosity, energy, and practical wisdom. He didn't merely serve on boards and in leadership positions—he insisted on motion and accomplishment. He revitalized the activities of the Columbia College Alumni Association when he became its president. He sustained and expanded the work of the Greenwich House after he joined its Board. Under the auspices of the American Society of Corporate Secretaries, he developed and chaired a nonprofit luncheon group whose regular meetings enlightened and informed attorneys specializing in counseling nonprofit groups. He played an active part in American Law Institute projects.

His association with the American Bar Association went considerably further than serving as the general editor of *Nonprofit Governance* (with managing editors Judith A. Cion and George W. Overton) and this companion volume, *Nonprofit Resources.* Victor also took on senior leadership positions in the ABA, chairing the Senior Lawyer's Division and the Association's Experience Editorial Board. In 1999 he was named to the ABA's Board of Governors.

Victor's insatiable drive led him to barrage friends and associates with articles, notes, comments, editorial comments, bold ideas, and practical suggestions. In print and in correspondence he probed, reacted, and invited the exchange of ideas. "Is there such a thing as a duty of obedience?" "Shouldn't there be an ombudsman in every corporation to improve communication along the organizational chain?" "Don't you think too many groups qualify for the nonprofit exemption?" "Isn't legal education producing too many technicians and not enough statesmen these days?" He went out of the way to offer help and advice so often that expressions of interest that would seem "extraordinary" coming from others became quite routine coming from Vic. Vic urged us to keep paying attention to important questions.

Neither the initial volume nor this updated version would have appeared without his dedication to this project. His participation in the later stages of this project, in particular, is sorely missed. And if Vic had remained in good health a bit longer, no doubt this volume would have appeared sooner.

All of us who have contributed to this volume treasure our recollection of this wonderful and gifted man—unfailingly insightful, enthusiastic, good-natured, courteous, and forever willing to pitch in for the good of the legal profession and the public interest.

Norman I. Silber
on behalf of the editors

Contents

Introductory Note

Nonprofit Resources is a compilation of helpful references on a range of topics in the nonprofit field. It is not intended as a comprehensive guide or bibliography such as that done by The National Center on Philanthropy and the Law at N.Y.U. School of Law, which can be accessed at www.law.nyu.edu/ncpl/search. Rather, because of the glut of books on the nonprofit world, we have tried to pick a variety of references that we think will be useful and provide a running start on any given topic. We hope our readers will thus be able to avoid the necessity of painstakingly pursuing a digest or index of periodicals, cases, or statutes.

We have sought to distinguish this book from other bibliographies by arranging the references topically rather than alphabetically. References beneath each topic are divided into four categories: bibliography (printed references such as books, journal articles, and brochures); case law; statutory and other authority; and Internet sites. In addition, under "Internet Resources," we have added a number of prominent resources available through the Internet. We believe that this book will prove to be a valuable supplement to *Nonprofit Governance and Management*.

For ease of reference, we have included most of the references listed at the end of each chapter of *Nonprofit Governance and Management* and have supplemented these with additional resources.

This work is basically the accomplishment of our Managing Editors, each of whom has taken responsibility for the sections listed below:

- Internet Resources; Internet   Pamela Mann
- Accountability through Attorney General Peter Swords
- Business Judgment Rule through Cy Pres J. Warren Wood, III
- Directors through Foundations   Daniel L. Kurtz
- Fund Raising through General   Lizabeth A. Moody
- Gifts-Restrictions, etc. through   Evelyn Brody
  Intermediate Sanctions
- Investment through Registration   Victoria B. Bjorklund
  (except Political Activities);
  International
- Religious Organizations   Lisa A. Runquist
  and Political Activities
- Restrictions on Fund Raising   Stanley S. Weithorn
  through Strategic Alliances
- Strategic Planning through Volunteers   Norman I. Silber

In addition, Jill Manny reviewed the entire manuscript to be certain that we have not omitted any crucial item.

The Managing Directors have made radical changes in this second edition:

- A list of Important Publications has been added;

- A list of Periodicals has been added;

- In due deference to modern technology, "Internet Resources" has been moved to the front of the book;

- In some cases, subheadings have been added to the Table of Contents, particularly to make the distinction between private foundations and public charities;

- Works that are not readily accessible have been eliminated;

- The first edition had 56 topical headings; the second edition has 92, or 80% more; and

- The first edition contained some 628 entries; the second edition—while maintaining its selectivity, and even though it deleted several entries found in the first edition—has more than 1,629 entries, or 159% more, and this does not include the List of Important Publications, the List of Helpful Periodicals, or the Internet Resources. In some cases where an entry appears more than once, it has been counted as many times as it appears.

I am especially thankful to Victoria Bjorklund, Evelyn Brody, Jill Manny, and Lisa A. Runquist for their interest in this work and their care, diligence, and expertise in reviewing it.

Our thanks to Genevieve Canseco, Production Editor at the American Bar Association for her contributions to the editing and printing of this Reference Guide.

I would be derelict indeed if we did not thank Christine Sullivan who has very ably and imaginatively assisted Victoria Bjorklund in her efforts.

Finally, my thanks to my secretary, Michelle TumSuden who, without complaint, has typed and retyped several drafts of this document.

We welcome the suggestions of our readers concerning items that should be added to, deleted from, or re-categorized in future editions.

Victor Futter
Editor-in-Chief

Editor's Note

After Victor's untimely death, which resulted in a significant delay in getting this book to press, it was apparent that some additional updating needed to be done to reflect new materials that had been published since his last draft. It has been my privilege to work with the other editors, most importantly, Jill Manny and her staff, as well as my associate, Patrick B. Sternal, to finalize this volume.

Vic, I hope you are pleased with the result.

Lisa A. Runquist
Acting Editor-in-Chief

List of Important Publications

Betsy B. Adler, Rules of the Road: A Guide to the Law of Charities in the U.S. (Council on Foundations 1999).

American Bar Association, Guidebook for Directors of Nonprofit Corporations (2d ed. ABA 2002).

American Bar Association, Revised Model Nonprofit Corporation Act (ABA 1988). (Also online and 2006 exposure draft listed on p. 11.)

American Law Institute, Principles of Corporate Governance: Analysis and Recommendations (ALI 1992).

American Law Institute, Principles of the Law of Nonprofit Organizations—Discussion Draft (ALI 2006).

American Law Institute, Restatement (Third) of the Law of Trusts (The Prudent Investor Rule) (ALI 1992).

American Law Institute, Restatement (Third) of the Law of Trusts (ALI 2003).

Better Business Bureau, Wise Giving Alliance; Standards for Charitable Solicitations (Better Business Bureau 2002).

Victoria B. Bjorklund, James J. Fishman, & Daniel L. Kurtz, New York Nonprofit Law and Practice (Lexis Publications 1997 and annual supplements).

Jody Blazek, Tax Planning and Compliance for Tax-Exempt Organizations: Forms, Checklists, Procedures (3d ed. Wiley 1999 and 2003 Cumulative Supplement).

William G. Bowen, Inside the Boardroom: Governance by Directors and Trustees (John Wiley & Sons 1994).

Evelyn Brody ed., Property-Tax Exemption for Charities: Mapping the Battlefield (Urban Institute Press 2002).

Nicholas P. Cafardi & Jaclyn Sabean Cherry, Tax Exempt Organizations (LexisNexis 2003).

Zecheriah Chafee, Jr., *The Internal Affairs of Associations Not for Profit,* 43 Harv. L. Rev. 993 (1930).

Ronald Chester, George G. Bogert, & George T. Bogert, Trusts and Trustees, §§ 411–470 (Charitable Trusts) (3d rev. ed. 2005).

Charles T. Clotfelter & Thomas Ehrlich, ed., Philanthropy and the Nonprofit Sector in a Changing America (Indiana University Press, 1999).

John D. Colombo & Mark A. Hall, The Charitable Tax Exemption (Westview Press 1995).

GREGORY L. COLVIN, FISCAL SPONSORSHIP: SIX WAYS TO DO IT RIGHT (San Francisco Study Center 1993).

COMMISSION ON PRIVATE PHILANTHROPY AND PUBLIC NEEDS ("Filer Commission"), RESEARCH PAPERS (five volumes) (U.S. Treasury Department 1997).

TRACY DANIEL CONNORS ed., THE NONPROFIT HANDBOOK: MANAGEMENT (3d ed. Wiley 2001).

ALEXIS DETOCQUEVILLE, DEMOCRACY IN AMERICA (1849, Knopf Edition 1966).

JOHN A. EDIE, HOW TO CALCULATE THE PUBLIC SUPPORT TEST (2d ed. Council on Foundations 1998).

JOHN A. EDIE & JANE C. NOBER, BEYOND OUR BORDERS: A GUIDE TO MAKING GRANTS OUTSIDE THE UNITED STATES (3d ed. Council on Foundations 2002).

EDITH L. FISCH, CHARITIES AND CHARITABLE FOUNDATIONS (1974).

JAMES J. FISHMAN & STEPHEN SCHWARZ, NONPROFIT ORGANIZATIONS: CASES AND MATERIALS (3d ed. Foundation Press 2006).

JAMES J. FISHMAN & STEPHEN SCHWARZ, TAXATION OF NONPROFIT ORGANIZATIONS (Foundation Press 2003).

WILLIAM MEADE FLETCHER, CYCLOPEDIA OF THE LAW OF PRIVATE CORPORATIONS (Thompson-West supplemented through 2002).

MARION R. FREMONT-SMITH, FOUNDATIONS AND GOVERNMENT (Russell Sage Foundation 1965).

MARION R. FREMONT-SMITH, GOVERNING NONPROFIT ORGANIZATIONS: FEDERAL AND STATE LAW AND REGULATION (Belknap Press of the Harvard University Press 2004).

VICTOR FUTTER ed., NONPROFIT GOVERNANCE AND MANAGEMENT (American Bar Association and American Society of Corporate Secretaries 2002).

JOHN W. GARDNER, FORWARD TO BRIAN O'CONNOR, AMERICA'S VOLUNTARY SPIRIT (Foundation Center 1983).

MARTIN HALL & CAROLYN M. OSTEEN, HARVARD MANUAL ON THE TAX ASPECTS OF CHARITABLE GIVING (8th ed., Harvard University Press 1999).

Regina E. Herzlinger, *Effective Oversight: A Guide for Nonprofit Directors,* HARV. BUS. REV., July–Aug. 1994 at 52.

FRANCIS R. HILL & DOUGLAS M. MANCINO, TAXATION OF EXEMPT ORGANIZATIONS (Warren, Gorham & Lamont 2002).

BRUCE R. HOPKINS, CHARITY, ADVOCACY, AND THE LAW: HOW NONPROFITS CAN USE CHARITABLE DOLLARS TO AFFECT PUBLIC POLICY LAWFULLY (Wiley 1993 and Supplement 1995).

BRUCE R. HOPKINS, THE LAW OF TAX-EXEMPT ORGANIZATIONS (8th ed. John Wiley & Sons 2003).

Internal Revenue Service Exempt Organizations Continuing Professional Education (CPE) Technical Instruction Program, available at <http://www.irs.gov/charities/article/0,,id=96441,00.html>.

ANDREW M. JOHNSTON, ed., CONTEMPORARY CORPORATE FORMS, 2nd Edition, supplemented through 2002 (Aspen 1997).

DARRYLL JONES, STEPHEN J. WILLIS, DAVID M. BRENNER, & BEVERLEY MORAN, CHARITIES AND OTHER EXEMPT ORGANIZATIONS (Thompson-West 2003).

BARBARA L. KIRSCHTEN, NONPROFIT CORPORATION FORMS HANDBOOK (West Group 2002).

DANIEL L. KURTZ, BOARD LIABILITY: GUIDE FOR NONPROFIT DIRECTORS (Moyer Bell Limited 1988).

DOUGLAS MANCINO, TAXATION OF HOSPITALS AND HEALTH CARE ORGANIZATIONS (Warren, Gorham & Lamont 2000).

Lizabeth Moody, *The Who, What and How of the Revised Model Nonprofit Corporation Act* 15 KY. L J. (1989).

HOWARD OLECK & CAMI GREEN, PARLIAMENTARY LAW AND PRACTICE FOR NONPROFIT ORGANIZATIONS (2d ed. ALI-ABA 1991).

HOWARD OLECK & MARTHA STEWART, NONPROFIT CORPORATIONS, ORGANIZATIONS AND ASSOCIATIONS (6th ed. supplemented through 1998, Prentice Hall).

MARILYN E. PHELAN, NONPROFIT ENTERPRISES: CORPORATIONS, TRUSTS AND ASSOCIATIONS (Thompson-West 2000, supplemented through 2000).

MARILYN E. PHELAN, NONPROFIT ENTERPRISES: LAW AND TAXATION (Callaghan, also has annual loose-leaf updates) (2003).

MARILYN E. PHELAN & ROBERT DESIDERIO, NONPROFIT ORGANIZATIONS LAW AND POLICY (Thompson-West 2003).

WALTER W. POWELL ed., THE NONPROFIT SECTOR: A RESEARCH HANDBOOK (Yale University Press 1987).

LISA A. RUNQUIST, THE ABCS OF NONPROFITS (American Bar Association 2005).

AVIAM SAIFER, LAW AND THE COMPANY WE KEEP (Harvard University Press 1995).

LESTER M. SALAMON ed., THE STATE OF NONPROFIT AMERICA (Brookings Institution Press 2002).

LESTER M. SALAMON, THE INTERNATIONAL GUIDE TO NONPROFIT LAW (Wiley 1997).

SCOTT, NUTSHELL ON NONPROFIT LAW (Thompson-West 2003).

JACK SIEGEL, A DESKTOP GUIDE FOR NONPROFIT DIRECTORS, OFFICERS, AND ADVISORS: AVOIDING TROUBLE WHILE DOING GOOD (John Wiley & Sons, Inc. 2006).

NORMAN I. SILBER, A CORPORATE FORM OF FREEDOM (Westview 2001).

Jeffrey A. Sonnenfeld, *What Makes a Great Board Great,* HARV. BUS. REV., Sept. 2002, p. 106.

RICHARD STEINBERG & WALTER W. POWELL eds., THE NONPROFIT SECTOR: A RESEARCH HANDBOOK (2d ed., Yale University Press 2006).

Gary J. Stern, et al., The Drucker Foundation Self-Assessment Tool (2d rev. ed. Jossey-Bass 1998).

U.S. Department of Treasury, Commission on Private Philanthropy and Public Needs: Research Papers (Filler Commission, 1977) (hard copy reprint available from W.S. Hein).

2005 Grantmaker's Salary and Benefits Report (Council on Foundations 2005).

List of Helpful Periodicals

CCH Exempt Organization Reporters (Commerce Clearing House, 1971 and monthly supplements).

Chronicle of Philanthropy.

Foundation Notes & Commentary published by the Council on Foundations.

Internal Revenue Service's annual *Exempt Organizations Continuing Professional Education Technical Interaction Textbook* ("ECPE Text"), (available on-line at www.irs.gov and reprinted by Tax Analysts of Washington, D.C. and by CCH).

Monday Developments (InterAction Newsletter).

Paul Streckfus' E.O. Tax Journal.

Philanthropy News Digest (PND), monthly email newsletter from the Foundation Center.

Taxation of Exempts.

The Exempt Organization Tax Review.

The Nonprofit Times.

NVSQ: Nonprofit & Voluntary Sector Quarterly.

NML: Nonprofit Management & Leadership.

Internet Resources

ABA Revised Model Nonprofit Corporation Act (1987), <http://www.muridae.com/nporegulation/documents/model_npo_corp_act.html>; ABA Proposed Model Nonprofit Corporation Act (3d edition) (February 2006 Exposure Draft), <http://meetings.abanet.org/webupload/commupload/CL580000/sitesofinterest_files/MNCAexposuredraft.doc>.

Alliance for Nonprofit Management (devoted to improving the management and governance capacity of nonprofits), <http://www.allianceonline.org>.

American Association of Fundraising Counsel (promotes the need for professional and ethical standards of practice and influences the creation of laws governing philanthropy), <http://www.aafrc.org>.

American Institute of Philanthropy (a watchdog service that evaluates nonprofits against certain criteria and publicizes these evaluations to help donors make informed giving decisions), <http://www.charitywatch.org>.

Associated Grantmakers (a regional association of grantmakers whose mission is to support the practice and expansion of effective philanthropic giving), <http://www.agmconnect.org>.

Association of Fundraising Professionals (formerly the National Society of Fundraising Executives; offers educational programs and programs to improve the fund-raising profession), <http://www.afpnet.org>.

Association of Information and Image Management (AIIM) (connects users with suppliers who can help them apply document and content technologies to improve their internal processes), <http://www.aiim.org>.

Association of Professional Researchers for Advancement (conducts research on prospective donors, answers frequently asked questions about prospective research, and contains lists on fundraising and nonprofit issues), <http://www.aprahome.org>.

Association of Records Managers and Administrators (ARMA) (provides education, research and networking opportunities to information management professionals), <http://www.arma.org>.

Association of Small Foundations (provides information and assistance to small philanthropy foundations), <http://smallfoundations.org>.

Better Business Bureau (BBB) Wise Giving Alliance (formed with the merger of the National Charities Information Bureau and the Council of Better Business Bureaus Foundation and its Philanthropic Advisory Service; collects and distributes information on hundreds of nonprofit organizations that solicit nationally or have national or international program services), <http://give.org>.

BoardSource (formerly the National Center for Nonprofit Boards; is a resource for practical information, tools and best practices, training, and leadership development for board members of non-profit organizations worldwide), <http://www.boardsource.org>.

California Department of Justice, Registry of Charitable Trusts (offers information and assistance in evaluating solicitations from charities and commercial fund-raisers), <http://ag.ca.gov/charities>.

Charity Channel (established in 1992 as a volunteer-driven online community of voluntary-sector professionals; provides access to forums and e-newsletters), <http://charitychannel.com>.

Charity Lobbying in the Public Interest (information about lobbying done by charitable organizations), <http://www.clpi.org>.

Charity Navigator (evaluates financial information relating to large charities), <http://www.charitynavigator.org>.

Charleston Principles (developed by the National Association of Attorneys General and the National Association of State Charities Officials to address Internet solicitations), <http://www.nasconet.org>.

The Chronicle of Philanthropy (a news source for charity leaders, fund raisers, grantmakers, and other people involved in the phil-anthropic enterprise), <http://www.philanthropy.com>.

Corporate Governance (focuses on corporate governance topics in the for-profit area), <http://www.corpgov.net>.

Council on Foundations (helps foundation staff, trustees, and board members in their day-to-day grantmaking activities), <http://www.cof.org>.

Dot Org Media (a content publishing and syndication service that offers a free e-mail newsletter, web content, and special reports on selected topics such as online advocacy, fundraising, and Internet presence), <http://www.dotorgmedia.org>.

Forum of Regional Association of Grantmakers (a national network of local leaders and organizations across the United States that sup-ports effective charitable giving), <http://www.givingforum.org>.

The Foundation Center (database of information concerning pri-vate foundations, serving grantseekers, grantmakers, researchers, policymakers, the media, and the general public), <http://www.fdncenter.org>.

Foundation News and Commentary (news and commentary related to foundations), <http://www.foundationnews.org>.

Free Management Library (a free community resource, providing basic and practical information about business, management, and organizations), <http://www.managementhelp.org>.

Gilbert Center (provides assistance in the area of communication, par-ticularly to new projects and innovations), <http://www.gilbert.org>.

GuideStar, national database of nonprofit organizations (database of financial information, informational tax returns filed by not-for-profit organizations, posts copies of Form 990), <http://www.guidestar.org>.

Hauser Center for Nonprofit Organizations at Harvard University (an interdisciplinary research center at Harvard University seeking to illuminate the role that the sector plays in society, changed now to Network for Good—see below), <http://www.ksg.harvard.edu/hauser/>.

Independent Sector (organization committed to promoting, strengthening, and advancing the nonprofit and philanthropic community; prepares materials about new legislation, developments in nonprofit world; holds conferences), <http://www.independentsector.org>.

Indiana University Center on Philanthropy (contains information on philanthropy through programs on research, teaching, public service, and public affairs), <http://www.philanthropy.iupui.edu>.

The Innovation Network (a national nonprofit dedicated to building the evaluation capacity of nonprofits, so they can better serve their communities), <http://www.innonet.org>.

Institute for Global Ethics (promotes ethical behavior in industries, institutions, and nations) <http://www.globalethics.org>.

Institute for Not-for-Profit Management, Columbia University Business School (offers graduate programs that help students develop effective management and leadership techniques for nonprofit organizations), <http://www.gsb.columbia.edu/execed/INM/index.html>.

Internal Revenue Service (includes tax information for individuals, businesses, charities and nonprofits, government entities, and tax professionals), <http://www.irs.gov>.

International Center for Not-for-Profit Law (ICNL) (assists in creating and improving laws and regulatory systems that permit, encourage, and regulate the nonprofit, nongovernmental (NGO) sector in countries around the world), <http://www.icnl.org>.

Internet Nonprofit Center (summarizes state registration and reporting requirements and posts model forms, including Uniform Registration Statement), <http://www.nonprofits.org>.

Jossey-Bass, Inc. (publishes a wide range of books on the nonprofit sector), <http://www.josseybass.com>.

Lawyers' Alliance for New York (provides pro bono legal services to New York nonprofits; publishes manuals, holds seminars), <http://www.lany.org>.

Leader to Leader Institute, (formerly Peter F. Drucker Foundation for Nonprofit Management), <http://www.pfdf.org>.

The League of Women Voters (provides information on civic participation and current public policy issues such as election reform, campaign finance reform, and health care), <http://www.lwv.org>.

Mandel Center for Nonprofit Organizations (a multidisciplinary center for education, research, and community service, also offers graduate programs for nonprofit leaders and managers), <http://www.cwru.edu/mandelcenter>.

Maryland Association of Nonprofit Organizations (provides services to assist nonprofits in implementing ethical and accountability standards), <http://www.standardsforexcellence.org>.

Maryland Secretary of State, <http://www.sos.state.md.us>.

National Association of Corporate Directors (publishes information and holds seminars relating to board leadership issues), <http://www.nacdonline.org>.

National Association of State Charity Officials (NASCO), <http://www.nasconet.org>.

National Center for Charitable Statistics (reporting of data on the nonprofit sectors, provides software for online filing of Form 990), <http://www.nccs.urban.org>.

National Center for Social Entrepreneurs (strategize with nonprofits way to improve their services and carry out their missions), <http://www.missionmoneymatters.org>.

National Center on Philanthropy and the Law at New York University School of Law (educational programs addressing the legal issues affecting the nonprofit sector and providing an integrated examination of the legal doctrines related to the activities of charitable organizations), <http://www.law.nyu.edu/ncpl/>.

National Center on Philanthropy and Law—N.Y.U. School of Law's Comprehensive Nonprofit Law Bibliography, < http://www.law.nyu.edu/ncpl/libframe.html>.

National Council of Nonprofit Associations (membership organization providing training and technical assistance for nonprofit sector), <http://www.ncna.org>.

National Conference of Commissioners on Uniform State Laws, <http://www.nccusl.org/Update/>.

National Executive Service Corps (offers a broad range of consulting and advising services on Board problems and all aspects of the operations of nonprofit organization), <http://nesc.org >.

National Network of Grantmakers (provides publications, job lists, resource links, and more to funders, practitioners, and grantseekers), <http://www.nng.org>.

Network for Good (provides resources for nonprofit organizations to reach new audiences and resources for donors and volunteers), <www.networkforgood.org>.

New York Regional Association of Grantmakers (NYRAG), (provides programs and resources to support effective grantmaking in the New York City metropolitan area), <http://www.nyrag.org>.

Nonprofit Coordinating Committee of New York (NPCC), (acts as a chamber of commerce for New York nonprofit organizations, providing information on a variety of issues of concern to nonprofit organizations, educational seminars for its members, and advocacy on legislative and regulatory issues of concern to nonprofits), <http://www.npccny.org/>.

Nonprofit Resource Center (a list of links to websites of interest to nonprofits), <http://www.not-for-profit.org>.

Nonprofit Risk Management Center (provides assistance and resources related to risk management for community-serving nonprofit organizations. These include technical assistance, software, and consulting help), <http://www.nonprofitrisk.org>.

Nonprofit Times (Weekly trade publication for nonprofit organizations and fundraisers), <http://www.nptimes.com>.

N Power NY (Nonprofit technology needs), <http://www.npowerny.org>.

NPO Public Disclosure Site (provides information and resources concerning federal laws on public inspection and federal tax returns), < http://www.muridae.com/publicaccess/>.

OMB Watch (oversees and tracks the substantive issues that are reviewed by the White House Office of Management and Budget (OMB); these include regulations, the budget, information collection and dissemination, proposed legislation, and testimony by federal agencies.), <http://www.ombwatch.org>.

One Northwest (a nonprofit organization that provides technology resources and expertise to environmental groups in the Pacific Northwest), <http://www.onenw.org>.

Planned Giving Design Center (helps charitable organizations create strategic alliances with legal, tax, and financial services professionals in their communities by offering technical content and planning resources on the topic of charitable gift planning and taxation free of charge), <http://www.pgdc.net>.

TechSoup.org (offers technology hardware, software, and assistance to nonprofits), <http://www.techsoup.org>.

Uniform Management of Institutional Funds Act (1972) and Uniform Prudent Management of Institutional Funds Act (2006); Uniform Trust Code (2000, with amendments), <http://www.nccusl.org>.

Urban Institute Center on Nonprofits & Philanthropy, <http://www.urban.org/center/cnp/index.cfm>.

U.S. International Grantmaking (provides information on facilitating international grantmaking), <http://www.usig.org>.

Wall Watchers' Ministry Watch, database of largest church and parachurch ministries in the U.S., <http://www.ministrywatch.com>.

Yale Program on Nonprofit Organizations (an international center for multidisciplinary studies of philanthropy, voluntarism, and nonprofit organizations), <http://ponpo.som.yale.edu/>.

Resources by Topic

Accountability

Bibliography

Evelyn Brody, *Accountability and Public Trust,* in THE STATE OF AMERICA'S NONPROFIT SECTOR (Lester B. Salamon, ed., Brookings Institute Press and the Aspen Institute 2002).

Evelyn Brody, *The Limits of Charity Fiduciary Law,* 57 MD. L. REV. 1400 (1998).

Laura Brown Chisolm, *Accountability by Nonprofit Organizations and Those Who Create Them: The Legal Framework,* 6 NONPROFIT MANAGEMENT & LEADERSHIP 141 (1995).

Laura Brown Chisolm, *Sinking the Think Tanks Upstream: The Use and Misuse of Tax Exemption Law to Address the Use and Misuse of Tax-Exempt Organizations by Politicians,* 51 U. of PITT. L. REV. 577 (1990).

Carolyn Cordery & Mary Zajkowski, *Charity Accountability and Transparency—An International View,* CHARTERED ACCT. J. (Nov. 2005) at 54.

James Fishman, *Improving Charitable Accountability,* MD L. REV. 218 (2003).

Joel L. Fleishman, *Philanthropy and Outcomes: Dilemmas in the Quest for Accountability,* in PHILANTHROPY AND THE NONPROFIT SECTOR IN A CHANGING AMERICA (Charles T. Clotfelter & Thomas Ehrlich eds., Indiana U. Press 1999).

Susan Gary, *Regulating the Management of Charities: Trust Law, Corporate Law and Tax Law,* 21 U. HAW. L. REV. 593 (1999).

GILBERT GAUL & NEIL BOROWSKI, FREE RIDE: THE TAX EXEMPT ECONOMY (Andrews Mcmeel Publisher 1993).

Harvey J.Goldschmid, *The Fiduciary Duties of Nonprofit Directors and Officers: Paradoxes, Problems and Proposed Reforms*, 23 J. CORP. L. 631 (1998).

Thomas L. Greaney & Kathleen M Boozang, *Mission, Margin, and Trust in the Nonprofit Health Care Enterprise*, 5 YALE J. HEALTH POL'Y L. & ETHICS 1 (2005).

David C. Hammack, *Accountability and Nonprofit Organizations: A Historical Perspective*, 6 NONPROFIT MANAGEMENT AND LEADERSHIP 127 (1995).

Fisher Howe, *Nonprofit Accountability*, NONPROFIT WORLD, November/December 2000.

Joint Committee on Taxation, Study of Present Law Taxpayer Confidentiality and Disclosure Provisions as Required by Section 3802 of the Internal Revenue Service Restructuring and Reform Act of 1998, Volume II: Study of Disclosure Provisions Relating to Tax Exempt Organizations (2000).

Robert A. Katz, *Can Principal-Agent Models Explain Charitable Gifts and Organizations*, 2000 WIS. L. REV. 1 (2000).

Kevin P. Kearns, *The Strategic Management of Accountability in Nonprofit Organizations: An Analytic Framework*, 54 PUB. ADMIN. REV. 185 (1994).

BERIT LAKEY, NONPROFIT GOVERNANCE: STEERING YOUR ORGANIZATION WITH AUTHORITY AND ACCOUNTABILITY (BoardSource 2004).

Geoffrey Manne, *Agency Costs and the Oversight of Charitable Organizations*, 1999 WIS. L. REV. 227 (1999).

Ellen W. McVeigh & Eve R. Borenstein, *The Changing Accountability Climate and Resulting Demands for Improved "Fiduciary Capacity" Affecting the World of Public Charities*, 31 WM. MITCHELL L. REV. 119 (2004).

William Meehan & Les Silverman, *For Charities, Performance Is the New Ethic*, LEADER TO LEADER (Fall 2001 at 13).

Panel on the Nonprofit Sector: Strengthening the Transparency, Governance, and Accountability of Charitable Organizations: A Final Report to Congress and the Nonprofit Sector (Independent Sector ed., 2005).

Panel on the Nonprofit Sector: Supplement: Strengthening the Transparency, Governance, and Accountability of Charitable Organizations: A Final Report to Congress and the Nonprofit Sector (Independent Sector ed., 2006).

Susan Phillips & Karine Levasseur, *The Snakes and Ladders of Accountability: Contradictions Between Contracting and Collaboration for Canada's Voluntary Sector*, 47 CAN. PUB. ADMIN. 451 (2004).

Dana Brakman Reiser, *Enron.org: Why Sarbanes-Oxley Will Not Ensure Comprehensive Nonprofit Accountability,* 38 U.C. DAVIS L. REV. 205 (2004).

Mark Sidel, *The Nonprofit Sector and the New State Activism,* 100 Mich L. Rev. 1312 (2002).

NORMAN I SILBER, A CORPORATE FORM OF FREEDOM; THE EMERGENCE OF THE NONPROFIT SECTOR (Westview 2001).

GARY J. STERN, et al., THE DRUCKER FOUNDATION SELF-ASSESSMENT TOOL: PARTICIPANT WORKBOOK (2d rev. ed., Jossey-Bass 1998).

GARY J. STERN, et al., THE DRUCKER FOUNDATION SELF-ASSESSMENT TOOL: PROCESS GUIDE (2d rev. ed., Jossey-Bass 1998).

Peter Swords, *Nonprofit Accountability: The Sector's Response to Government Regulation,* 23 EXEMPT ORG. TAX REV. 417 (1999).

PETER SWORDS & HARRIET BOGRAD, NONPROFIT ACCOUNTABILITY: REPORT AND RECOMMENDATIONS, NONPROFIT COORDINATING COMM. OF N.Y., INC. (1997).

Case Law

Aramony v. United Way, 28 F. Supp. 147 (S.D.N.Y. 1998).

Internet Sites

Panel on the Nonprofit Sector: Strengthening Transparency, Governance, [and] Accountability of Charitable Organizations, (2005), <http://www.nonprofitpanel.org/final/Panel_Final_Report.pdf>.

Accounting

Bibliography

ABRAHAM J. BRILOFF, MORE DEBTS THAN CREDITS: THE BURNT INVESTOR'S GUIDE TO FINANCIAL STATEMENTS (HarperCollins 1976).

HERRINGTON J. BRYCE, THE NONPROFIT BOARD'S ROLE IN ESTABLISHING FINANCIAL POLICIES (The National Center for Nonprofit Boards 1996).

COOPERS & LYBRAND, FINANCIAL REPORTING AND CONTRIBUTIONS: A DECISION MAKING GUIDE TO FASB NOS. 116 AND 117 (1995). [No longer in print.]

COOPERS & LYBRAND, FINANCIAL REPORTING AND CONTRIBUTIONS: GUIDANCE FOR IMPLEMENTATION OF FASB NOS. 116 AND 117 (1994). [No longer in print.]

MARY E. FOSTER, et al., 2001 MILLER NOT-FOR-PROFIT REPORTING: GAAP PLUS TAX, FINANCIAL, AND REGULATORY REQUIREMENTS (Harcourt Professional Publishing 2006).

ROY FOULKE, PRACTICAL FINANCIAL STATEMENT ANALYSIS (McGraw-Hill 1961).

C. WILLIAM GARNER, ACCOUNTING AND BUDGETING IN PUBLIC AND NONPROFIT ORGANIZATIONS: A MANAGER'S GUIDE (Jossey-Bass 1991).

MALVERN J. GROSS, JR., et al., FINANCIAL AND ACCOUNTING GUIDE FOR NOT-FOR-PROFIT ORGANIZATIONS (7th ed. Wiley 2005).

MALVERN J. GROSS, JR., et al., FINANCIAL AND ACCOUNTING GUIDE FOR NOT-FOR-PROFIT ORGANIZATIONS, 2006 SUPPLEMENT (7th ed.Wiley 2006).

RICHARD E. LARKIN & MARIE DiTOMMASO: WILEY NOT-FOR-PROFIT ACCOUNTING FIELD GUIDE 2003 (Wiley 2003).

JOSEPH RAZEK, et al., INTRODUCTION TO GOVERNMENTAL AND NOT-FOR-PROFIT ACCOUNTING (5th ed Prentice Hall 2004).

EARL A. SPILLER JR. with PHILLIP T. MAY, FINANCIAL ACCOUNTING; BASIC CONCEPTS (5th ed. Richard D. Irwin 1990.)

JOHN WILD, et al., FINANCIAL STATEMENT ANALYSIS: THEORY, APPLICATION AND INTERPRETATION, (9th ed., McGraw-Hill/Irwin 2007).

EARL WILSON, et al., ACCOUNTING FOR GOVERNMENT AND NONPROFIT ENTITIES, (14th ed. McGraw, Hill 2007).

MICHAEL R. YOUNG, ed., ACCOUNTING IRREGULARITIES AND FINANCIAL FRAUD (3d ed. CCH 2006).

Affinity Cards

Bibliography

Affinity Card Income Not UBTI, 29 TAX ADVISER 10 (1998).

Fred Stokeld, *IRS Memo Tells Area Managers to Stop Litigating Affinity Card, Mailing List Cases,* 28 EXEMPT ORG. TAX REV. 18 (2000).

Antitrust

Bibliography

Olivia S. Choe, *Case Comment, A Missed Opportunity: Nonprofit Antitrust Liability in Virginia Vermiculite, Ltd. v. Historic Green Springs, Inc.*, 113 YALE L.J.533 (2003).

Peter J.Hammer, *Antitrust, Health Care Quality and the Courts*, 102 COLUM. L. REV. 545 (2002).

Teresa D.Harrison, *Hospital Mergers: Who Merges with Whom?*, 38 APPLIED ECONOMICS 637 (2006).

Michael Klausner & Jonathan Small, *Failing to Govern? The Reality of Nonprofit Boards*, STAN. SOC. INNOVATION REV., Spring 2005, at 42.

Peter James Kolovos, *Note, Antitrust Law and Nonprofit Organizations: The Law School Accredition Case*, 71 N.Y.U.L. REV. 689 (1996).

Tara Norgard, *How Charitable Is the Sherman Act?*, 83 MINN. L. REV. 1515 (1999).

Dana Brakman Reiser, *Symposium: Who Guards the Guardians?: Monitoring and Enforcement of Charity Governance: There Ought to Be a Law: The Disclosure Focus of Recent Legislative Proposals for Nonprofit Reform*, 80 CHI.-KENT L. REV. 559 (2005).

William C. Rivenbark & Paul W. Menter, *Building Results-Based Management Capacity in Nonprofit Organizations*, PUB. PERFORMANCE and MGMT. REV., Mar. 2006, at 255.

ELIOT SPITZER, NEW YORK ATTORNEY GENERAL, A GUIDE TO MERGERS AND CONSOLIDATIONS OF NOT-FOR-PROFIT CORPORATIONS UNDER ARTICLE 9 OF THE NEW YORK NOT-FOR-PROFIT CORPORATION LAW (2004).

Colburn S.Wilbur, *Self-Evaluation*, FOUND. NEWS & COMMENTARY, May/June 2005, at 45.

Case Law

American Soc'y of Mech. Eng'r, Inc. v. Hydrolevel Corp., 456 U.S. 556 (1982).

California Dental Association v. Federal Trade Commission, 526 U.S. 756 (1999).

United States v. Brown University, 5 F.3d 658 (3d. cir. 1993).

United States v. Rockford Mem'l Corp., 898 F.2d 1278, (7th Cir. 1990), *cert. denied*, 498 U.S. 920.

Assessment

Bibliography

PETER F. DRUCKER & GARY J. STERN, DRUCKER FOUNDATION SELF-ASSESSMENT TOOL (Drucker Foundation and Jossey-Bass, Inc. 1999).

ANTHONY J. GAMBINO & THOMAS J. REARDON, FINANCIAL PLANNING AND EVALUATION FOR THE NONPROFIT ORGANIZATION (Inst. of Management Accountants 1981).

HARRY P. HATRY, ELAINE MORLEY, & ELISA VINSON, OUTCOME MEASUREMENT IN NONPROFIT ORGANIZATIONS: CURRENT PRACTICES AND RECOMMENDATIONS (Independent Sector 2001).

THOMAS P. HOLLAND & MYRA BLACKMON, MEASURING BOARD EFFECTIVENESS (National Center for Nonprofit Boards 2000).

ROB REIDER, IMPROVING THE ECONOMY, EFFICIENCY, AND EFFECTIVENESS OF NOT-FOR-PROFITS: CONDUCTING OPERATIONAL REVIEWS (John Wiley & Sons 2001).

Internet Sites

Leader to Leader Institute, (formerly Peter F. Drucker Foundation for Nonprofit Management), <http://www.pfdf.org>.

Statutory and Other Authority

Revised Model Nonprofit Corporation Act § 1.70, 8.10 (1988).

Association

(See also: Clubs, Discrimination, and Membership)

Bibliography

Evelyn Brody, *Entrance, Voice and Exit: The Constitutional Bounds of the Right of Association,* 35 U.C. DAVIS L. REV. 821 (2002).

Kristen Colletta & Darya Kapulina, *Note, Employment Discrimination and the First Amendment: Case Analysis of Catholic Charities,* 23 HOFSTRA LAB. & EMP. L. J. 189 (2005).

Thomas Emerson, *Freedom of Association and Freedom of Expression,* 74 YALE L. J. 1.1 (1964).

Richard A. Epstein, *The Constitutional Perils of Moderation: The Case of the Boy Scouts* 74, S. CAL. L. REV. 119 (2000).

Steven K. Green, *"A Legacy of Discrimination"? The Rhetoric and Reality of the Faith-Based Initiative: Oregon as a Case Study,* 84 OR. L. REV. 725 (2005).

AMY GUTMANN, ed., FREEDOM OF ASSOCIATION (Princeton University Press 1998).

Melissa McClellan, *Note, Faith and Federalism: Do Charitable Choice Provisions Preempt State Nondiscrimination Employment Law,* 61 WASH. & LEE L. REV. 1437 (2004).

Liam Seamus O'Malinn, *The Sanctity of Association: The Corporation and Individualism in American Life,* 37(1) SAN DIEGO L. REV. 101 (2000).

Recent Legislation: Local Government Law—Homeowner Association Regulation—Illinois Act Prevents Homeowner and Condominium Associations from Interfering with Residents' Ability to Fly American and Military Flags, 117 HARV. L. REV. 2047 (2004).

Erez Reuveni, *Note, On Boy Scouts and Anti-Discrimination Law: The Associational Rights of Quasi-Religious Organizations,* 86 B.U. L. REV. 109 (2006).

Case Law

Boy Scouts of America v. Dale, 530 U.S. 640 (2000).

New York State Club Association v. City of New York, 487 U.S. 1 (1988).

Roberts v. United States Jaycees, 468 U.S. 609 (1984).

Attorney General

Bibliography

EVELYN BRODY, THE LEGAL FRAMEWORK FOR NONPROFIT ORGANIZATIONS IN THE NONPROFIT SECTOR: A RESEARCH HANDBOOK (Walter Powell & Richard Steinberg eds., Yale Univ. Press 2d ed. 2006).

EVELYN BRODY, *Whose Public? Parochialism and Paternalism in State Charity Law Enforcement,* 79 IND. L. J. 937 (2004).

Ronald Chester, *Improving Enforcement Mechanisms in the Charitable Sector: Can Increased Disclosure of Information Be Utilized Effectively?,* 40 NEW ENG. L. REV. 447 (2006).

Michael S. DeLucia, *Attorney General Article: Charitable Trusts Unit,* N.H. B. J., Spring 2004, at 8.

James J. Fishman, *Improving Charitable Accountability,* 62 MD. L. R. 218 (2003).

MARION FREMONT-SMITH, GOVERNING NONPROFIT ORGANIZATIONS: FEDERAL AND STATE LAWS AND REGULATION (Belknap University Press of Harvard University Press 2004).

Jessica E. Jay, *Third-Party Enforcement of Conservation Easements*, 29 Vt. L. Rev. 757 (2005).

Jennifer L. Komoroski, *Note, The Hershey Trust's Quest to Diversify: Redefining the State Attorney General's Role When Charitable Trusts Wish to Diversify*, 45 Wm & Mary L. Rev. 1769 (2004).

David Villar Patton, *The Queen, The Attorney General, and the Modern Charitable Fiduciary: A Historical Perspective on Charitable Enforcement and Reform*, U. Fla. J. L. & Pub. Poly 131 (Spring 2000).

Mark Sidel, *The Nonprofit Sector and the New State Activism*, 100 Mich. L. Rev. 1312 (2002).

Margaret Soper, *The Protector of Charities: The Role of the Attorney General*, 2002 N.Z. L.J. 57.

Peter Swords & Harriet Bograd, Nonprofit Accountability: Report and Recommendations (Nonprofit Coordinating Comm. of N.Y., Inc. 1997).

Eliot Spitzer, New York Attorney General: A Guide to Mergers and Consolidations of Not-For-Profit Corporations Under Article 9 of the New York Not-For-Profit Corporation Law (2004).

Eliot Spitzer, New York Attorney General: Internal Controls and Financial Accountability for Not-For-Profit Boards (2004).

Eliot Spitzer, New York Attorney General: The Regulatory Role of the Attorney General's Charities Bureau (2003), available at <http://www.oag.state.ny.us/charities/role.pdf>.

John W. Vinson, *The Charity Oversight of the Texas Attorney General*, 35 St. Mary's L. J. 243 (2004).

Case Law

Bertram v. Berger, 274 N.E. 2d 667 (Ill. App. Ct. 1971).

Brown v. Mem'l Nat'l Home Found., 329 P.2d 118 (Cal. Ct. App. 1958).

Champ v. Poelker, 755 S.W. 2d 383 (Mo. Ct. App. 1988).

Ebon Found., Inc. v. Oatman, 498 S.E. 2d 728 (Ga. 1998).

In re Estate of Yablick, 526 A. 2d 1154 (N.J. Super. Ct. App. Div. 1987).

In the Matter of the Trust under the Will of Caroline Weld Fuller, 636 N.E. 2d 1333 (Mass. 1994).

Lefkowitz v. Lebensfeld, 417 N.Y.S. 2d 715 (App. Div. 1979), aff'd 415 N.E. 2d 919 (N.Y. 1980).

Nathan Littauer Hospital v. Spitzer, 734 N.Y.S. 2d 671(N.Y. Sup. Ct. Third Department, 2001).

Oberly v. Kirby, 592 A. 2d 445 (Del. 1991).

Pacific Home v. County of Los Angeles 264 P. 2d 539 (Cal. 1953).

People by Abrams v. NYS Federation of Police 590 N.Y.S. 2d 573 (3d Dep't. 1992).

St. Joseph's Hospital v. Bennett, 22 N.E. 2d 305 (N.Y. 1939).

Statutory and Other Authority

Revised Model Nonprofit Corp. Act §§ 1.70, 3.04(b)-(c), 8.10(a), 14.03-.04. 14.30 (c)(i).

Internet Sites

National Association of Attorneys General (contains information about the offices around the country, including addresses and phone numbers), <http://www.naag.org>.

New York State Attorney General (contains a subdivision about the Charities Bureau and the New York charities laws), <http://www.oag.state.ny.us>.

Audit Committee

Bibliography

John Brooks, Once in Golconda, A True Drama of Wall Street 1920-1938 (Wiley 1999).

Robert K. Jaedicke & Robert T. Sprocise, Accounting Flows: Income, Funds and Cash (Prentice Hall 1965).

Vincent M. O'Reilly, et al., Montgomery's Auditing, 12th Edition (Wiley 1998).

Carl Pacini, et al., *Internal Auditors and Charities: Combating the Threat of Terrorism*, 19 Internal Auditing 12 (2004).

Report and Recommendations of the Blue Ribbon Committee on Improving the Effectiveness of Audit Committees, 54 Bus. Law 1067 (May, 1999).

Lee Seidler, et al., The Equity Funding Papers: The Anatomy of a Fraud (Wiley 1977).

Karyn R. Vanderwarren, *Note, Financial Accountability in Charitable Organizations: Mandating an Audit Committee Function*, 71 Chi-Kent L. Rev. 963 (2002).

Thomas E. Vermeer, et al., *The Composition of Nonprofit Audit Committees*, Acct. Horizons, Mar. 2006, at 75.

Business Judgment Rule

Bibliography

Mark Fellows, *Note*, A *Business or a Trust?: Janssen v. Best & Flanagan and Judicial Review of For-Profit and Nonprofit Board of Directors Decisions*, 30 WM. MITCHELL L. REV. 1503 (2004).

DANIEL L. KURTZ, BOARD LIABILITY: GUIDE FOR NONPROFIT DIRECTORS 49-59 (Moyer Bell 1988).

Michael W. Peregrine & James R. Schwartz, *The Business Judgment Rule and Other Protections for the Conduct of Not-for-Profit Directors,* 33 J. HEALTH L. 455 (2000).

Denise Ping Lee, *Note, The Business Judgment Rule: Should It Protect Nonprofit Directors?,* 103 COLUM. L. REV. 925 (2003).

Lisa A. Runquist, *The Night the Sky Fell: Directors of Nonprofits Continue at Risk,* Vol. 15, No. 2 LAW NEWS 15 (Spring, 1999).

James G. Wiehl, *Roles and Responsibilities of Nonprofit Health Care Board Members in the Post-Enron Era,* 25 J. LEGAL MED. 411 (2004).

Case Law

Oberly v. Kirby, 592 A2d 445 (Del.1991).

Schever Family Foundation, Inc. v. 61 Associates 582 N.Y.S.2d 662 (App. Div. 1992).

Stern v. Lucy Webb Hayes Nat'l Training School for Deaconesses and Missionaries, (Sibley Hospital Case) 381 F. Supp. 1003 (D.C.1974).

Bylaws

Bibliography

Kevin E. Davis, *The Role of Nonprofits in the Production of Boilerplate,* 104 MICH. L. REV. 1075 (2006).

VICTOR, FUTTER ed. NONPROFIT GOVERNANCE AND MANAGEMENT, CHAP. 36, P. 485 (American Bar Association 2002).

D. BENSON TESDAHL, THE NONPROFIT BOARD'S GUIDE TO BYLAWS: CREATING A FRAMEWORK FOR EFFECTIVE GOVERNANCE (BoardSource 2003).

Charitable Contribution Deduction

Bibliography

William D. Andrews, *Personal Deductions in an Ideal Income Tax*, 86 HARV. L. REV. 309 (1972).

Ellen P. Aprill, *Churches, Politics and the Charitable Contribution Deduction*, 42 B.C. L. REV. 843 (2001).

Evelyn Brody, *Charities in Tax Reform: Threats to Subsidies Overt and Covert*, 66 TENN. L. REV. 687 (1999).

Johnny Rex Buckles, *The Community Income Theory of the Charitable Contributions Deduction*, 80 IND. L.J. 947 (2005).

Milton Cerny & Rebecca I. Rosenberg, *New Regulations on Apportionment of Charitable Deductions Between U.S—and Foreign-Source Income Aid U.S. Charities*, 45 EXEMPT ORG. TAX REV. 351 (2004).

John D. Colombo, *The Marketing of Philanthropy and the Charitable Contributions Deduction: Integrating Theories for the Deduction and Tax Exemption*, 36 WAKE FOREST L. REV. 657 (2001).

Harvey P. Dale, *Foreign Charities*, 48 TAX LAW 655 (1995).

DAVID M. DONALDSON AND CAROLYN M. OSTEEN, THE HARVARD MANUAL ON TAX ASPECTS OF CHARITABLE GIVING (8th ed. Office of Planned Giving, Harvard University 1999).

William A. Drennan, *Charitable Donations of Intellectual Property: The Case for Retaining the Fair Market Value Tax Deduction*, 2004 UTAH L. REV. 1045.

David G. Duff, *Tax Treatment of Charitable Contributions in Canada: Theory, Practice, and Reform*, 42 OSGOODE HALL L. J. 47 (2004).

Daniel Halperin, *A Charitable Contribution of Appreciated Property and the Realization of Built-In Gains*, 56 TAX L. REV. 1 (2002).

Martha W. Jordan, *Charitable Contributions of Preservation Easements—A Primer*, 101 J. TAX'N 236 (2004).

Lawrence P. Katzenstein, *Reformation of the Charitable Contribution Deduction: Areas for Reform*, 35 EXEMPT ORG. TAX REV. 33 (2002).

David T. Leibell & Daniel L. Daniels, *Practical Planning Strategies for Art and Collectibles*, EST. PLAN. (WGL), Mar. 2006, at 27.

Khrista M. McCarden, *The Deductibility of Contributions to Single-Member LLCs Owned by Tax-Exempt Organizations*, 49 EXEMPT ORG. TAX REV. 233 (2005).

Martin Nissenbaum, *Hurricane Katrina: Charitable Deduction Opportunities*, 37 TAX ADVISER 6 (2006).

Carolyn M. Osteen, *Charitable Contributions: State of the Art Techniques in Planned Giving,* 37 TAX MGMT. MEMO. (BNA) 147 (1996).

John Peloza & Piers Steel, *The Price Elasticities of Charitable Contributions: A Meta-Analysis,* 24 J. PUB. POL'Y & MARKETING 260 (2005).

David Pozen, *Remapping the Charitable Deduction,* CONN. LAW REV., Vol. 39 (Fall 2006) (available online via SSRN at http://ssrn.com/abstract=900061).

Allan J. Samansky, *Deductibility of Contributions to Religious Institutions,* 24 VA. TAX REV. 65 (2004).

Leo L. Schmolka, *Income Taxation of Charitable Remainder Trusts and Decedents' Estates: Sixty-Six Years of Astigmatism,* 40 TAX L. REV. 1 (1984).

AUSTIN WAKEMAN SCOTT & WILLIAM FRANKLIN FRATCHER, SCOTT ON TRUSTS § 348 (4th ed. Aspen 2000).

C. EUGENE STEUERLE, *Managing Charitable Giving in the Wake of Disaster in* SEPTEMBER 11, PERSPECTIVES FROM THE FIELD OF PHILANTHROPY 1 (Foundation Center 2002).

Gene Steuerle, *An Option To Increase Charitable Giving and Reduce Current Taxes,* 90 TAX NOTES (TA) 959 (2001).

Conrad Teitell, *Guide to Tax Benefits for Charitable Gifts: The Rules and Legal Authorities in a Nutshell,* TR & EST., June 2003, at CGS 16.

WEALTH & TAX ADVISORY SERVICES, INC., TAX ECONOMICS OF CHARITABLE GIVING 2005/2006 (WG&L 2005).

Stanley S. Weithorn, *"Tax Simplification"—Grave Threat to the Charitable Contribution Deduction: The Problem and a Proposed Solution,* DUKE L. J. (1967).

Stanley S. Weithorn, Charity and the Tax Reform Act of 1969: "What Hath Congress Wrought?" Contributions of Appreciated Property and Other Assorted Problems, University of Miami Law Center 5th Annual Institute on Estate Planning (1973).

Stanley S. Weithorn, Prospective Impact of Noncharitable Provisions of 1976 Tax Reform Act on Incentives for Charitable Giving, 1st Annual Notre Dame Institute of Giving, Foundations and Trusts (1976) and *Taxes Magazine* 1977.

Case Law

Addis v. Commissioner, 118 T.C. 528 (2002).

Alice Phelan Sullivan Corp. v. United States, 381 F.2d 399 (Ct. Cl. 1967).

United States v. American Bar Endowment, 477 U.S. 105 (1986).

Statutory and Other Authority

Internal Revenue Code, §§ 170, 6115.

Charitable Immunity

Bibliography

Canon Bradley & Dean Jarus, *The Dynamics of Change in Judicial Doctrine: The Abrogation of Charitable Immunity,* 13 LAW & SOCIETY REV. 969 (1979).

William J. Chriss, *House Bill 4 and Other New Legislation: Homeowners Insurance, Architects & Engineers, and Immunity for School & Charity Workers and Volunteer Firefighters,* 46 S. TEX. L. REV. 1201 (2005).

Edith L. Fisch, *Charitable Liability for Tort,* 10 VILL. L. REV. 71(1964).

Brenda Kimery, *Tort Liability of Nonprofit Corporations and Their Volunteers,* 33 TULSA L. J. 683 (1997).

Samantha Kluxen LaBarbera, *Note, Secrecy and Settlements: Is the New Jersey Charitable Immunity Act Justified in Light of the Clergy Sexual Abuse Crisis?,* 50 VILL. L. REV. 261 (2005).

Myles McGregor-Lowndes & Linh Nguyen, *Volunteers and the New Tort Law Reform,* 13 TORTS L.J. 41 (2005).

Note: The Quality of Mercy: Charitable Torts and Their Continuing Immunity, 100 HARV. LAW REV. 1382 (1987).

M. H. Ogilvie, *Vicarious Liability and Charitable Immunity in Canadian Sexual Torts Law,* OXFORD U. COMMONWEALTH L. J., Winter 2004, at 167.

Nathan A. Olin, *In Defense of Charities: A Case for Maintaining the Massachusetts Damages Cap for Certain Employment Discrimination Claims,* 28 W. NEW ENG. L. REV. 11 (2005).

Stefan Toepler & Jon B. Gould, *Charitable Sharing: A Tort Reform Proposal,* 23 J. POL'Y ANALYSIS & MGMT. 153 (2004).

Charles R. Tremper, *Compensation for Harm from Charitable Activity,* 76 CORNELL L. REV. 401 (1991).

Case Law

Brown v. Anderson County Hosp. Assn., 268 S.G. 479 (1977).

Feoffees of Heriot's Hospital v. Ross, 12 Cl, and Fin 507, 8 Eng. Rep. (1508).

Gilbert v. Corp. of Trinity House, 17 Q.B. 795 (1886).

Keene v. Brigham & Women's Hosptial, Inc., 786 N.E. 2d 824 (Mass. 2003).

McDonald v. Massachusets General Hospital, 120 Mass. 432 (1876).

Mersey Docks & Harbour Board Trustees v. Gibbs, 11 Eng. Rep. 1500 (1866).

President and Directors of Georgetown College v. Hughes, 130 F.2d 810 (D.C. Cir., 1942).

Stern v. Lucy Webb Hayes National Training School, 381 F. Supp. 1003 (D.D.C., 1974).

Statutory and Other Authority

Revised Model Nonprofit Corporations Act § 170.

Clubs

(See also: Associations and Discrimination)

Bibliography

Regina E. Herzlinger, *Effective Oversight: A Guide for Nonprofit Directors*, HARV. BUS. REV., July–Aug. 1994, at 52.

In Club Wars, Privacy and Choice Battle Freedom From Discrimination, BUS. L. TODAY, NOV.–DEC. 1994, AT 26.

Douglas Mancino & Frances R. Hill, *Social Clubs Face Special Rules for Unrelated Business Income*, 14 TAX'N EXEMPTS 152 (2003).

NATIONAL CLUB ASSOCIATION, FEDERAL TAX TREATMENT OF PRIVATE CLUBS (Club Director Reference Series 1993).

Note, State Power and Discrimination by Private Clubs: First Amendment Protection for Nonexpressive Associations, 104 HARV. L. REV. 1835 (1991).

Fred L. Somers, Jr., *Pivot or Perish*, CLUB DIRECTOR, April 1996, at 4.

Fred L. Somers, Jr., *Prolegomenon to a Right of Private Association*, PERSPECTIVE, June 1988, at 22 (National Club Association's magazine before its current incarnation as Club Director).

Fred L. Somers, Jr., *Protecting against Public Accommodation Legislation*, CLUB DIRECTOR, Sept. 1989, at 9.

Case Law

Board of Directors v. Rotary Club, 481 U.S. 537 (1987).

Borne v. Haverhill Golf Club, 791 N. E. 2d 903 (Mass. App. Ct.).

Boy Scouts of America v. James Dale, 530 U.S. 640 (2000).

EEOC v. Chicago Club, 86 F.3d 1423 (7th Cir. 1996).

Karedes v. Colella, 100 N.Y. 2d 45 (2003).

Louisiana Debating & Literary Assoc. v. City of New Orleans, 42 F.3d 1483 (5th Cir. 1995).

N.Y. State Club Assoc. v. City of New York, 487 U.S. 1 (1987).

Roberts v. U.S. Jaycees, 468 U.S. 609 (1984).

Statutory and Other Authority

I.R.C. § 501(c)(7).

Codes of Conduct

(See: Ethics)

Commerce Clause

Bibliography

Charles Nave, *Charitable State Registration and the Dormant Commerce Clause,* 31 Wm. Mitchell L. Rev. 227 (2004).

Case Law

American Charities for Reasonable Fundraising Regulation, Inc. v. Pinellas County, 32 F. Supp. 2d 1308 (M.D. Fla. 1998), *aff'd* in part, *vacated* and *rem'd* in part, 221 F.3d 1211 (11th Cir. 2000).

Camps Newfoundland / Owatonna Inc. v. Town of Harrison, 520 U.S. 564 (1997).

Chapman v. Commissioner of Revenue, 651 N.W. 2d 825 (Minn. 2002).

Commercial Activity

(See: Unrelated Business Income Tax)

Bibliography

John D. Colombo, *Commercial Activity and Charitable Tax Exemption*, 44 Wm. & Mary L. Rev. 487 (2002).

John D. Colombo, *Regulating Commercial Activity by Exempt Charities: Resurrecting the Commensurate-in-Scope Doctrine,* 39 Exempt Org. Tax Rev. 341 (2003).

Kenneth C. Eliasberg, *Charity and Commerce: Section 501 (c), (3)—How Much Unrelated Business Activity,* 21 TAX L. REV. 53 (1965).

Thomas L. Greaney and Kathleen M. Boozang, *Mission, Margin, and Trust in the Nonprofit Health Care Enterprise,* 5 YALE J. HEALTH POL'Y L. & ETHICS 1 (2005).

Baorong Guo, *Charity for Profit? Exploring Factors Associated with the Commercialization of Human Service Nonprofits,* 35 NONPROFIT & VOLUNTARY SECTOR Q. 123 (2006).

Frances R. Hill, *Targeting Exemption for Charitable Efficiency: Designing a Nondiversion Constraint* 56 SMU L. REV. 675 (2003).

Thomas Kelley, *Rediscovering Vulgar Charity: A Historical Analysis of America's Tangled Nonprofit Law,* 73 FORDHAM L. REV. 2437 (2005).

Jessica Pens & Alexander L.T. Reid, *Note: A Call for Reform of the Operational Test for Unrelated Commercial Activity in Charities,* 76 N.Y.U.L. REV. 1855 (2001).

Thomas C. Troger, *Quantity of Unrelated Business Consistent with Charitable Exemption—Some Clarification* 56 TAX NOTES 1075 (1992).

Burton A. Weisbrod, *The Pitfalls of Profits,* STAN. SOC. INNOVATION REV., Winter 2004, at 40.

Gary J. Young, *Federal Tax-Exemption Requirements For Joint Ventures Between Nonprofit Hospital Providers and For-Profit Entities: Form over Substance?,* 13 ANNALS HEALTH L. 327 (2004).

Committees

Bibliography

Revised Model Nonprofit Corporation Act §§ 825, 8.30(b).

Community Trusts

Bibliography

Johnny Rex Buckles, *The Community Income Theory of the Charitable Contributions Deduction,* 80 IND. L.J. 947 (2005).

Deborah G. Martin, *Nonprofit Foundations and Grassroots Organizing: Reshaping Urban Governance,* 56 PROF. GEOGRAPHER 394 (2004).

Debra Morris, *Charities and Community Interest Companies,* 51 EXEMPT ORG. TAX REV. 239 (2006).

David M. Van Slyke & Harvey K. Newman, *Venture Philanthropy and Social Entrepreneurship in Community Redevelopment,* 16 NONPROFIT MGMT. & LEADERSHIP 345 (2006).

Case Law

In re Application of the Community Service Society of New York, 713 N.Y.S. 2d 712 (N.Y. Cop. Div. 2000). Matter of Laura Spelman Rockefeller Memorial, et al., represented in New York Law Journal, Oct. 21, 1999.

Statutory and other Authority

Treas. Reg. 1.170A-9(e), (h).

Compensation

(See also: Intermediate Sanctions and Directors)

Bibliography

BOARDSOURCE, CHIEF EXECUTIVE COMPENSATION: A GUIDE FOR NONPROFIT BOARDS (BoardSource 1999).

CAROLYN KAY BRANCATO, et al., THE COMPENSATION COMMITTEE OF THE BOARD: BEST PRACTICES FOR ESTABLISHING EXECUTIVE COMPENSATION (Conference Board 2001).

BRUCE ELLIG, THE COMPLETE GUIDE TO EXECUTIVE COMPENSATION (McGraw-Hill 2001).

Peter Franklin, *Nonprofit Compensation and the Market*, 21 HAWAII L. R. 425 (1999).

Consuelo Lauda Kertz, *Executive Compensation Dilemmas in Tax-Exempt Organizations: Reasonableness, Comparability and Disclosure*, TUL. L. REV. 819 (1999).

JOSE PIERSON & JOSHUA MINTZ, ASSESSMENT OF THE CHIEF EXECUTIVE (BoardSource 2001).

The PM (Philanthropy Monthly) Annotated Investigative Report on United Way of Americas, THE PHILANTHROPY MONTHLY, DEC. 1991.

Report on Reforms to Improve the Tax Rules Governing Public Charities, pp. 14–15, Subcomm. On Oversight of House Comm. on Ways and Means, 103d Cong. 1994.

JEAN WRIGHT & JAY ROT, IRS EXEMPT ORGANIZATIONS CPE TECHNICAL INSTRUCTION PROGRAM TEXTBOOK, Ch. 1, "Reasonable Compensation" (1992).

Case Law

Board of Regents of the University of the State of New York, Report (1997) in The Committee to Save Adelphi et al. against Peter Diamandopoulos et al. This Report and the actions therein set forth was affirmed by the Appellate Division of the Supreme Court, Adelphi University v. Board of Regents of the State of New York, et al. 229 A.D. 2d 36, 652 N.Y.S. 2d 837 (1997).

Church of Scientology v. Commissioner, 823 F. 2d 1310 (9th Cir. 1987).

Mayson Mfg. Co. v. Commissioner, 178 F. 2d 115 (6th Cir. 1949).

United Cancer Council, Inc. v. Commissioner, 165 F. 3d 1173 (7th Cir. 1999).

Statutory and Other Authority

Internal Revenue Code §§ 162, 501(a), 501(c)(3), 4958.
Revised Model Nonprofit Corp. Act §§ 1.70, 8.10 (1988).

Condominiums

Bibliography

Note, The Rule of Law in Residential Associations, 99 HARV. L. REV. 472 (1985).

Recent Legislation: Local Government Law—Homeowner Association Regulation—Illinois Act Prevents Homeowner and Condominium Associations from Interfering with Residents' Ability to Fly American and Military Flags, 117 HARV. L. REV. 2047 (2004).

KEITH B. RONNEY, CONDOMINIUM DEVELOPMENT GUIDE: PROCEDURES, ANALYSIS, FORMS, Rev. Ed. (Warren, Gorham & Lamont 1983).

Conflicts of Interest

Bibliography

Michael Connelly, *The Sea Change in Nonprofit Governance: A New Universe of Opportunities and Responsibilities,* 41 INQUIRY 6 (2004).

Deborah A. DeMott, *Self-Dealing Transactions in Nonprofit Corporations,* 59 BROOK. L. REV. 131 (1993).

Mark Fellows, *Note, A Business or a Trust?: Janssen v. Best & Flanagan and Judicial Review of For-Profit and Nonprofit Board of Directors Decisions,* 30 WM. MITCHELL L. REV. 1503 (2004).

Marion R. Fremont-Smith, *Pillaging of Charitable Assets: Embezzlement and Fraud,* 46 EXEMPT ORG. TAX REV. 333 (2004).

William I. Innes, et al., *Selected Issues Regarding the Liability of Directors and Officers of Charitable and Nonprofit Corporations,* 19 PHILANTHROPIST 4 (2004).

DANIEL L. KURTZ & SARAH E. PAUL, MANAGING CONFLICTS OF INTEREST: A PRIMER FOR NONPROFIT BOARDS, (2d ed. BoardSource 2006).

Benjamin E. Ladd, *Note, A Devil Disguised As A Corporate Angel?: Questioning Corporate Charitable Contributions To "Independent" Directors' Organizations,* 46 WM. & MARY L. REV. 2153 (2005).

JANE C. NOBLER, COMPANY FOUNDATIONS AND THE SELF-DEALING RULES (COUNCIL ON FOUNDATIONS 2002).

Jane C. Nobler, *The Law On Conflicts: Part I: The Basics,* FOUNDATION NEWS & COMMENTARY, SUPPLEMENT 2005, at 2.

Jane C. Nobler, *Legal Brief: Conflicts of Interest, Part II: May the Foundation's Lawyer Serve as Trustee?,* FOUNDATION NEWS & COMMENTARY, SUPPLEMENT 2005, at 3.

Jane C. Nobler, *Legal Brief: Conflicts of Interest, Part III,* FOUNDATION NEWS & COMMENTARY, Sept./Oct. 2004, at 50.

Jane C. Nobler, *May the Foundation's Lawyer Serve as a Trustee?,* FOUNDATION NEWS & COMMENTARY, 2004, at 38.

Report to Congress and the NonProfit Sector on Governance, Transparency and Accountability (Panel on the Nonprofit Sector, Independent Sector ed., 2005).

Thomas Silk, *State SOX: Explanation of California's Charitable Integrity Act of 2004,* 46 EXEMPT ORG. TAX REV. 195 (2004).

Case Law

United States v. Ariamony, 88 F.3d 1369 (4th Cir. 1996), *cert. den.* 520 U.S.1239 (1999).

Statutory and Other Authority

Rev. Model Nonprofit Corporation Law § 8.31.

Co-Ops

Case Law

40 West 67th Street v. Pullman 790 N.E. 2d 1174 (N.Y. 2003).
Levandusky v. One Fifth Avenue Corp 75 N.Y. 2d 530 (First
  Department, 1990).

Corporate Sponsorships

Bibliography

Daryll K. Jones, *Advertisements and Sponsorships in Charitable
  Cyberspace: Virtual Reality Meets Legal Fiction,* 70 Miss. L. Rev.
  323 (2001).
Catherine E. Livingston and Amy R. Segal, *Tax-Exempt Organizations
  and the Internet,* Prac. Tax Law., Winter 2000, at 29.
Catherine E. Livingston and Amy R. Segal, *Tax-Exempt Organizations
  and the Internet (Part 2)*, Prac. Tax Law., Spring 2000, at 13.
Elizabeth M. Roberts, *Note, Presented to You by . . . : Corporate
  Sponsorship and the Unrelated Business Income,* 17 Va. Tax Rev.
  399 (1997).
LaVerne Woods, *Tax Treatment of Corporate Sponsorship Payments
  to Exempt Organizations: Final Regulations,* 97 J. Tax'n 174
  (2002).

Statutory and Other Authority

I.R.C. § 509(a)(2).

Cy Pres—Power to Vary

(See: Gifts—Restrictions, Purposes, and Cy Pres)

Directors

(See also: The Business Judgment Rule, Compensation, Governance,
  and Intermediate Sanctions)

Bibliography

AMERICAN BAR ASSOCIATION, REVISED MODEL NONPROFIT CORPORATION ACT (1989) AND PROPOSED MODEL NONPROFIT CORPORATION ACT, (3d ed. February 2006 Exposure Draft).

ABA COORDINATING COMMITTEE ON NONPROFIT GOVERNANCE, GUIDE TO NONPROFIT CORPORATE GOVERNANCE IN THE WAKE OF SARBANES-OXLEY (American Bar Association 2005).

AMERICAN LAW INSTITUTE, PRINCIPLES OF CORPORATE GOVERNANCE (1992) AND PRINCIPLES OF THE LAW OF NONPROFIT ORGANIZATIONS (Discussion draft, April 2006).

AMERICAN SOCIETY OF CORPORATE SECRETARIES, DIRECTOR: SELECTION, ORIENTATION, COMPENSATION, EVALUATION AND TERMINATION (American Society of Corporate Secretaries 1998).

AMERICAN SOCIETY OF CORPORATE SECRETARIES, LOGISTICAL ARRANGEMENTS FOR BOARD MEETINGS (American Society of Corporate Secretaries 1999).

AMERICAN SOCIETY OF CORPORATE SECRETARIES, MEETINGS OF THE BOARD OF DIRECTORS AND ITS COMMITTEES: A GUIDEBOOK (American Society of Corporate Secretaries 1985).

AMERICAN SOCIETY OF CORPORATE SECRETARIES, REVIEW OF BOARD PRACTICES BY BOARD OF DIRECTORS (American Society of Corporate Secretaries 1997).

JOHN ANDERSON, ART HELD HOSTAGE: THE BATTLE OVER THE BARNES COLLECTION (W. W. Norton & Company 2003).

ROBERT C. ANDRINGH & TED W. ENGSTROM, NONPROFIT BOARD ANSWER BOOK (BoardSource 2002).

David W. Barrett, *A Call for More Lenient Director Liability Standards for Small Charitable Nonprofit Corporations,* 71 IND. L.J. 967, 969 (1996).

JAMES C. BAUGHMAN, TRUSTEES, TRUSTEESHIP AND THE PUBLIC GOOD (Quorum Books 1987).

Bishop Estate Closing Agreement, 27 EXEMPT ORG. TAX REV. 174, 174-81 (2000).

BOARDSOURCE, THE SOURCE—TWELVE PRINCIPLES OF GOVERNANCE THAT POWER EXCEPTIONAL BOARDS (BoardSource 2005).

Evelyn Brody, *Charity Governance: What's Trust Law Got to Do with It?,* 80 CHI.-KENT L. REV. 641 (2005).

Evelyn Brody, *The Limits of Charity Fiduciary Law,* 59 MD. L. REV. 1400 (1998).

William A. Brown & Joel O. Iverson, *Exploring Strategy and Board Structure in Nonprofit Organizations,* 33 NONPROFIT & VOLUNTARY SECTOR Q. 377 (2004).

NICHOLAS P. CAFARDI & JACLYN FABEAN CHERRY, UNDERSTANDING NONPROFIT AND TAX EXEMPT ORGANIZATIONS (LexisNexis 2006).

Jaclyn A. Cherry, *Update, The Current State of Nonprofit Director Liability,* 37 DUQ. L. REV. 557, 562 (Summer 1999).

P.K. Chew, Director's and Office's Liability (Practising Law Institute 1999).

Committee on Corporate Laws, Corporate Director's Guidebook, (4th ed. American Bar Association, Section of Business Law 2004).

Ian Dawson & Alison Dunn, *Governance Codes of Practice in the Not-for-Profit Sector,* 14 Corp. Governance 33 (2006).

Duties of Charitable Trust Trusties and Charitable Corporation Directors, 2 Real Prop. Prob. & Tr. J. 545 (1967).

Mark Fellows, *Note, A Business or a Trust?: Janssen v. Best & Flanagan and Judicial Review of For-Profit and Nonprofit Board of Directors Decisions,* 30 Wm. Mitchell L. Rev. 1503 (2004).

James J. Fishman, *Standards of Conduct for Directors of Nonprofit Corporations,* 7 Pace L. Rev. 389 (1987).

Marion R. Fremont-Smith, Governing Nonprofit Organizations: Federal and State Law and Regulation (Belknap Press 2004).

Victor Futter, Advice to the Lovelorn or What Every Director from the For-Profit World Should Know About Nonprofit Organizations, 69 Annual Survey of Bankruptcy Law, 1999–2000 Edition (West Group 1999).

Harvey Goldschmid, *The Fiduciary Duties of Nonprofit Directors and Officers: Paradoxes, Problems and Proposed Reforms,* 23 Iowa J. Corp. L. 4, 631–653 (1998).

Guidebook for Directors of Nonprofit Corporations (George W. Overton & Jeannie Carmedelle Frey eds., American Bar Association 2d ed. 2002).

Fisher Howe, Welcome to the Board: Your Guide to Effective Participation (Jossey-Bass 1995).

Richard T. Ingram, Ten Basic Responsibilities of Nonprofit Boards (National Center for Nonprofit Boards, rev. ed. 2003).

William I. Innes, et al., *Selected Issues Regarding the Liability of Directors and Officers of Charitable and Nonprofit Corporations,* 19 Philanthropist 4 (2004).

Robert A. Katz, *Let Charity Directors Direct: Why Trust Law Should Not Curb Board Discretion Over a Charitable Corporation's Mission and Unrestricted Assets,* 80 Chi.-Kent L. Rev. 689 (2005).

Michael Klausner & Jonathan Small, *Failing to Govern? The Reality of Nonprofit Boards,* Stan. Soc. Innovation Rev., Spring 2005, at 42.

Daniel L. Kurtz, Board Liability: Guide for Nonprofit Directors (Moyer Bell Ltd. 1988).

Daniel L. Kurtz & Sarah E. Paul, Managing Conflicts of Interest: A Primer for Nonprofit Boards (BoardSource 2006).

Berit Lakey, Nonprofit Governance: Steering Your Organization with Authority and Accountability (BoardSource 2004).

Marie Malaro, A Legal Primer on Managing Museum Collections (Smithsonian Institute 1998).

Jill S. Manny, *Governance Issues for Nonprofit Religious Organizations,* 40 Cath. Law. 1 (Summer 2000).

Ellen W. McVeigh & Eve R. Borenstein, *The Changing Accountability Climate and Resulting Demands for Improved "Fiduciary Capacity" Affecting the World of Public Charities,* 31 Wm. Mitchell L. Rev. 119 (2004).

National Center for Nonprofit Boards, The Legal Obligations of Nonprofit Boards: A Guidebook for Board Members (NCNB 1997).

National Center for Nonprofit Boards, Ten Basic Responsibilities of Nonprofit Boards, (NCNB Revised 1996).

The Nonprofit Leadership Team (Jossey-Bass 2003).

Judith Grummon Nelson, Six Tips to Recruiting, Operating and Involving Nonprofit Board Members (NCNB 1991).

Brian O'Connell, The Board Member's Book (3d ed. The Foundation Center 2003).

John F. Olson & Josiah O. Hatch III, Director and Officer Liability: Indemnification and Insurance (West Group 1998).

Katherine M. O'Regan & Sharon M. Oster, *Does the Structure and Composition of the Board Matter? The Case of Nonprofit Organizations,* 21 J.L. Econ. & Org. 205 (2005).

Francie Ostrower, Trustees of Culture: Power, Wealth and Status on Elite Arts Boards (Univerity of Chicago Press 2003).

Report to Congress and the NonProfit Sector on Governance, Transparency and Accountability (Panel on the Nonprofit Sector, Independent Sector ed., 2005).

Restatement of the Law Third, Trusts, (ALI 2003).

Susan M. Scribner, Boards From Hell (Scribner & Associates 1999).

Patricia Siebart, *Corporate Governance of Nonprofit Organizations: Cooperation and Control,* 28 Int'l J. Pub. Admin. 857 (2005).

Norman I. Silber, *Symposium: Who Guards the Guardians?: Monitoring and Enforcement of Charity Governance: Nonprofit Interjurisdictionality,* 80 Chi.-Kent L. Rev. 613 (2005).

Thomas Silk, *Ten Emerging Principles of Governance of Nonprofit Corporations,* 43 Exempt Org. Tax Rev. 35 (2004).

Eliot Spitzer, New York Attorney General, *Internal Controls and Financial Accountability for Not-For-Profit Boards* (2004), available at http://www.oag.state.ny.us/charities/internal_controls.pdf.

Strengthening the Transparency, Governance, and Accountability of Charitable Organizations: A Final Report to Congress and the Nonprofit Sector (Panel on the Nonprofit Sector, Independent Sector ed., 2005).

Supplement: Strengthening the Transparency, Governance, and Accountability of Charitable Organizations: A Final Report to Congress and the Nonprofit Sector (Panel on the Nonprofit Sector, Independent Sector ed., 2006).

Symposium, *Bishop Estate Matter,* 21 U. HAW. L. REV. (2001).

ALAN D. ULLBERG & PATRICIA ULLBERG, MUSEUM TRUSTEESHIP (American Association of Museums 1981).

James G. Wiehl, *Roles and Responsiblities of Nonprofit Health Care Board Members in the Post-Enron Era,* 25 J. LEGAL MED. 411 (2004).

Case Law

Estate of Donner 82 N.Y. 2d 574 (1993).

Gilbert v. McLeod Infirmary 64 S.E. 2d 524 (S. Car. 1951).

Holt v. College of Osteopathic Physicians and Surgeons 61 Cal. 2d 750 (1964).

Howard Savings Institution v. PSCP, 190 A. 2d 39 (1961).

In re Caremark International Inc. Derivative Litigation Case 698 A.2d 959 (Del. Ch. 1996).

In the Matter of the Manhattan Eye, Ear and Throat Hosp. v. Spitzer, 715 N.Y.S.2d 575 (Sup. Ct. 1999).

Lynch v. John M. Redfield Found., 88 Cal. Rptr. 86 (Cal. Ct. App. 1970).

Matter of Jones 90 N.Y. 2d 41 (1997).

Matter of Rothko 43 N.Y. 2d 305 (1977).

Mile-O-Mo Fishing Club, Inc. v. Noble, 210 N.E.2d 12 (Ill. App. Ct. 1965).

George Pepperdine Found. v. Pepperdine, 271 P.2d 600 (Cal. Ct. App. 1954).

Scheuer Family Found., Inc. v. 61 Assocs., 582 N.Y.S.2d 662 (1992).

Stern v. Lucy Webb Hayes, 381 F.Supp. 1003 (D.D.C. 1974).

St. Joseph's Hospital v. Bennett 22 N.E. 2d 305 (N.Y. 1939).

Statutory and Other Authority

Rev. Model Nonprofit Corp. Act §§ 8.13, 8.30, 8.33, 8.41–8.42 (1988).

Directors' and Officers' Insurance

(See: Indemnification and Insurance)

Disaster Relief

Bibliography

Betsy Buchalter Adler & Barbara A. Rosen, *Disaster: Practices and Procedures for Charities Providing Relief After 9/11: A Case Study,* 96 J. TAX'N 297 (2002).

VICTORIA B. BJORKLUND, *Reflections on September 11 Legal Developments, in* SEPTEMBER 11: PERSPECTIVES FROM THE FIELD OF PHILANTHROPY 1 (Foundations Center 2002).

Milton Cerny & Michael W. Durham, *Tsunami: NGO Response: Now and the Future,* 47 EXEMPT ORG. TAX REV. 181 (2005).

Joint Comm. on Tax'n, *JCT Explanation of Katrina Emergency Tax Relief Act of 2005,* PAUL STRECKFUS' EO TAX J., Sept./Oct. 2005, at 155.

Robert A. Katz, *A Pig in a Python: How the Charitable Response to September 11 Overwhelmed the Law of Disaster Relief* 36 IND. L. REV. 251 (2003).

Catherine E. Livingston, *Disaster Relief Activities of Charitable Organizations,* 35 EXEMPT ORG. TAX REV. 153 (2002).

C. EUGENE STEUERLE, *Managing Charitable Giving in the Wake of Disaster, in* SEPTEMBER 11: PERSPECTIVES FROM THE FIELD OF PHILANTHROPY 1 (Foundation Center 2002).

Gene Steuerle, *Charities and Disaster Relief (Part One: The Problem of Selection),* 35 EXEMPT ORG. TAX REV. 49 (2002).

Gene Steuerle, *Charities and Disaster Relief (Third of Three Parts: Making Choices & Planning for the Future),* 35 EXEMPT ORG. TAX REV. 159 (2002).

Eric Thurman, *Performance Philanthropy,* 28 HARV. INT'L REV. 18 (2006).

Statutory and Other Authority

Internal Revenue Code § 139.
Victims of Terrorism Tax Relief Act, P.L. 107-134 (2002).

Discrimination

(See: Association, Clubs, and Public Policy)

Donor-Advised Funds

(See also: Private Foundations; Supporting Organizations) (Note: since the passage of H.R. 4, the Pension Protection Act of 2006, the provisions of the Internal Revenue Code governing donor-advised funds have been significantly revised and expanded. For a discussion of these revisions, see the 2006 publications listed below.)

Bibliography

Allfirst Charitable Gift Fund, Inc. Exemption Application Materials, republished in PAUL STRECKFUS' EO TAX JOURNAL, November/December 2002 AT 159.

EDWARD JAY BECKWITH, DAVID A. MARSHALL, JOHN A. EDIE, AND ROBERT EDGAR, ESTABLISHING AN ADVISED FUND PROGRAM: A SUMMARY OF LEGAL & MANAGEMENT ISSUES (Council on Foundations 1992).

Victoria B. Bjorklund, *Charitable Giving to a Private Foundation: The Alternatives, The Supporting Organization, and the Donor-Advised Fund,* EXEMPT ORG. TAX REV. (Jan. 2000).

Victoria B. Bjorklund, *Victoria Bjorklund Addresses Donor-Advised Fund Issues,* PAUL STRECKFUS' EO TAX J., Sept./Oct. 2004, at 13.

Debra E. Blum, *Tailor Made for Charity: Private-label Gift Funds are Growing in Popularity,* THE CHRONICLE OF PHILANTHROPY (May 2002).

Terrance S. Carter, *Donor-Restricted Charitable Gifts: A Practical Overview Revisited II*, 18 PHILANTHROPIST 121 (2004).

Choosing Among the Private Foundation, Supporting Organization and Donor-Advised Funds, text of presentation outline prepared by Victoria B. Bjorklund for ALI-ABA conference in Chicago, Illinois on May 29, 2003.

Charlotte Cloutier, *Donor-Advised Funds in the U.S.: Controversy and Debate*, 19 PHILANTHROPIST 85 (2005).

Common Operating Procedures for Donor-Advised Funds, CHARITABLE GIFT PLANNING NEWS (May 2002).

Control and Power: Issues Involving Supporting Organizations, Donor Advised Funds and Disqualified Person Financial Institutions, Topic G, Fiscal Year 2001 Exempt Organizations Continuing Professional Education Technical Instruction Program Textbook.

Council on Foundations, *Changes in Intermediate Sanctions for Donor-Advised Funds and Sponsoring Organizations,* available at www.cof.org (2006).

Council on Foundations, *Taxable Distributions for Donor-Advised Funds*, available at www.cof.org (2006).

Donor Control, Topic O, Fiscal Year 1999 Exempt Organizations Continuing Professional Education Technical Instruction Program Textbook.

Donor Directed Funds, Topic M, Fiscal Year 1996 Exempt Organizations Continuing Professional Education Technical Instruction Program Textbook.

Group Offers Draft Guidance on Pension Protection Act Provisions that Affect Charities, 2006 Tax Notes Today 207-13 (October 2006).

Joint Comm. Taxation: Discrimination of Renewal Proposals Contained in the Presidents's Fiscal Year 2001 Budget Proposal 238–244 (909-2-00, March 6, 2000).

Marni A. Larose, *Assets of Donor-Advised Funds Totaled $12.3 Billion Last Year, Survey Finds,* THE CHRONICLE OF PHILANTHROPY (May 2002).

Harvey Lipman, *Survey Finds Rapid Rise in Assets and Grants of Donor-Advised Funds,* THE CHRONICLE OF PHILANTHROPY (May 2001).

National Charitable Gift Fund Determination Letter, PAUL STRECKFUS' EO TAX JOURNAL March/April 2002, at 123ff.

Reconsidering the Foundation Rules, 82 TAX NOTES (TA) 257 (1999).

David A. Shelvin, *Donor-Advised Funds: The Applicability of Rule 12b-1 Fees and Trail Commissions,* EXEMPT ORG. TAX REV. (June 2001).

David A. Shelvin, *Recent Court Decisions Analyze the Rules Governing "Type 3" Supporting Organizations,* EXEMPT ORG. TAX REV. (January 2003).

Ron Shoemaker & Bill Brockner, *Public Charity Classification and Private Foundation Issues: Recent Emerging Significant Developments,* Topic P, Fiscal Year 2000 Exempt Organizations Continuing Professional Education Technical Instruction Program Textbook.

Simpson Thacher & Bartlett LLP,: *Provisions of Interest to Charitable Organizations and their Donors in H.R. 4, the Pension Protection Act of 2006,* available at http://www.stblaw.com (August 2006).

Gene Steuerle, *Charitable Endowments, Advised Funds & the Mutual Fund Industry, Part One: A New Democracy of Endowment Giving,* 82 TAX NOTES (TA) 129 (1999).

The American Gift Fund, PAUL STRECKFUS' EO TAX JOURNAL (June 1998).

The Oppenheimer Funds Legacy Program, PAUL STRECKFUS' EO TAX JOURNAL (February 2001).

Tompkins Community Charitable Gift Fund, Inc., PAUL STRECKFUS' EO TAX JOURNAL (April 2001).

Treasury Department, *General Extortion of the Administrator's Fiscal 2001 Revenue Proposals,* 105–106 (Feb. 2000).

Vanguard Charitable Endowment Program, PAUL STRECKFUS' EO TAX JOURNAL (May 1998).

Wealthnet Charitable Gift Fund, PAUL STRECKFUS' EO TAX JOURNAL (January/February 2003).

Statutory and Other Authority

I.R.C. §§ 170(f)(18), 508(f), 2055(e)(5), 2522(c)(5), 4943(e), 4958, 4966, 4967, 6033(k), all as provided by The Pension Protection Act of 2006, P.L. 109–280.

Donor Control: Restricted Gifts and Cy Pres

(See: Gifts—Restrictions, Purposes, and Cy Pres)

Dual Payments

Case Law

Sklar v. Commissioner 282 F.3d 610 (9th Cir. 2002).
United States v. American Bar Endowment 477 U.S. 105 (1986).

Statutory and Other Authority

I.R.C. §§ 170, 6115.

Educational Institutions

Bibliography

BENJAMIN BAEZ, AFFIRMATIVE ACTION, HATE SPEECH, AND TENURE; NARRATIVES ABOUT RACE, LAW AND THE ACADEMY (Routledge Farmer 2002).

Hazel G. Beh, *Downsizing Higher Education and Derailing Student Educational Objectives: When Should Students Claims for Program Closures Succeed?* 33 GA. L. REV. 155 (1998).

DEREK BOK & WILLIAM G. BOWEN, THE SLOPE OF THE RIVER (Princeton University Press 1998).

Rita Bornstein, Legitimacy in the Academic Academy; From Entrance to Exit (Prager 2003).

William G. Bowen & Sandra A. Levin, Reclaiming the Game: College Sports and Educational Values (Princeton University Press 2003).

William G. Bowen & James L. Shulman, The Game of Life: College Sports and Educational Values (Princeton University Press 2001).

David A. Brennen, *Race-Conscious Affirmative Action by Tax Exempt 501(c)(3) Corporations After Grutter and Gratz,* 77 St. John's Law Rev. 711 (2003).

Curtis Bridgeman, *Allegheny College Revisited: Cardozo, Consideration, and Formalism in Context,* 39 U.C. Davis L. Rev. 149 (2005).

Jackie Cavilia Allen, *Catholic School-State University Cooperation Termed Philanthropic Phenomenon,* 36 Momentum 34 (2005).

Milton Cerny & Catherine E. Livingston, *IRS Intermediate Sanctions: How They will Impact Colleges and Universities,* 25 J.C. & U.L. 865 (1999).

John D. Colombo, *Why Is Harvard Tax-Exempt? (And Other Mysteries of Tax Exemption for Private Educational Institutions),* 35 Ariz. L. Rev. 841 (1993).

Jill Goldenziel, *Blaine's Name in Vain?: State Constitutions, School Choice, and Charitable Choice,* 83 Denv. U. L. Rev. 57 (2005).

Jennifer B. Green, *Campus Tour: The IRS Is Coming to Your School, College, or University,* 46 Exempt Org. Tax Rev. 185 (2004).

Maximilian M. Haag, *Hedge Fund Investments of Private Foundations and Educational Endowments,* 50 Exempt Org. Tax Rev. 261 (2005).

Henry Hansmann, *Why Do Universities Have Endowments?* 19 J. Leg. Stud. 3 (1990).

Bertrand M. Harding, Jr., The Tax Law of Colleges and Universities (2d ed. Wiley 2001).

Christopher Jencks & Meredeth Phillips, The Black-White Test Score Gap (Brookings 1998).

Alexander Kern, The Law of Schools and Teachers in a Nutshell (3d ed. Thompson/West 2003).

Harriet M. King, *The Voluntary Closing of a Private College: A Decision for the Board of Trustees?* 32 S. Car. L. Rev. 547 (1981).

Philip Kintzele & William C. Hood, *Simplified, Accurate Tax Reporting for Scholarships and Fellowships,* 47 Exempt Org. Tax Rev. 169 (2005).

Alan Klaas, *Fund Faising in a Financial Crisis: Concordia University, River Forest, Illinois,* 5 Int'l J. Educ. Advancement 361 (2005).

Lynn Lu, *Flunking the Methodology Test: A Flawed Tax-Exemption Standard for Educational Organizations that "Advocate a Particular Position or Viewpoint,"* 29 N.Y.U. REV. L. & SOC. CHANGE 377 (2004).

CHARLES J. RUSSO & RALPH D. MAWDSKY, EDUCATION LAW (Law Journal Press 2003).

Allan J. Samansky, *Deductibility of Contributions to Religious Institutions,* 24 VA. TAX REV. 65 (2004).

JAMES L. SHULMAN & WILLIAM G. BOWEN, THE GAME OF LIFE (Princeton University Press 2001).

Edward A. Zelenski, *Are Tax "Benefits" Constitutionally Equivalent to Direct Expenditures,* 112 HARV. L. REV. 379 (1998).

Case Law

Calhoun Academy v. Commissioner, 94 T.C. 284 (1990).
Dartmouth College v. Woodward, 4 U.S. (4 Wheat.) 518 (1819).
Gratz v. Bollinger 539 U.S. 244 (2003).
Grutter v. Bollinger 539 U.S. 306 (2003).
United States v. Brown University 5 F. 3d 658(3d Cir. 1993).

Statutory and Other Authority

I.R.C. §§ 501(c)(3), 509(a)(1), and 170(b)(1)(A)(ii).
I.R.S. Form 1023, schedule B; 5578.
I.R.C. Rev. Proc. 75-50.
Proposed Examination Guidelines Regarding Colleges and Universities, 1993–2 IRB, p. 39 et seq.

Effective Boards

(See: Governance)

Employment Practices

Bibliography

Melissa Seifer Briggs, *Note, Exempt or Not Exempt: Mandated Prescription Contraception Coverage and the Religious Employer,* 84 OR. L. REV. 1227 (2005).

Case Note, Constitutional Law—First Amendment—California Supreme Court Upholds Compulsory Insurance Coverage of

Contraceptives over Establishment and Free Exercise Objections—Catholic Charities of Sacramento, Inc. v. Superior Court, 85 P.3d 67 (Cal. 2004), 117 HARV. L. REV. 2761 (2004).

Kristen Colletta & Darya Kapulina, *Note, Employment Discrimination and the First Amendment: Case Analysis of Catholic Charities,* 23 HOFSTRA LAB. & EMP. L. J. 189 (2005).

Richard L. Fox, *Practical Charitable Planning for Employee Stock Options,* EST. PLAN. (WGL), May 2005, at 3.

Laura Christine Henderson, *Comment, Equal Benefits, Unequal Burdens: How the Movement for Gay Rights in the Workplace is Affecting Religious Employers,* 55 CATH. U. L. REV. 227 (2005).

Melissa McClellan, *Note, Faith and Federalism: Do Charitable Choice Provisions Preempt State Nondiscrimination Employment Law,* 61 WASH. & LEE L. REV. 1437 (2004).

Nathan A Olin, *In Defense of Charities: A Case for Maintaining the Massachusetts Damages Cap for Certain Employment Discrimination Claims,* 28 W. NEW ENG. L. REV. 11 (2005).

WILLIAM J. QUIRK, HIRING HANDBOOK (Panel Publishers 1994).

JEREMY RIFKIN & ROBERT HEILBRONER, THE END OF WORK: THE DECLINE OF THE GLOBAL LABOR FORCE AND THE DAWN OF THE POST-MARKET ERA (G. P. Putnam's Sons 1995).

DAVID G. SAMUELS & HOWARD PIANCO, NONPROFIT COMPENSATION, BENEFITS AND EMPLOYMENT LAW (Wiley 2002).

Susan J. Stabile, *State Attempts To Define Religion: The Ramifications of Applying Mandatory Prescription Contraceptive Coverage Statutes to Religious Employers,* 28 HARV. J.L. & PUB. POL'Y 741 (2005).

Endowments

Bibliography

Evelyn Brody, *Charitable Endowments and the Democratization of Dynasty,* 39 ARIZONA L. REV. 873 (1997).

Financial Accounting Standards Board: Statement No. 117.

Maximilian M. Haag, *Hedge Fund Investments of Private Foundations and Educational Endowments,* 50 EXEMPT ORG. TAX REV. 261 (2005).

Henry Hansmann, *Why Do Universities Have Endowments?* 19 J. LEG. STUD. 3 (1990).

Jeanne M. Hauch, *The Role of Charitable and Educational Foundations in Corporate Control Transactions* 27 U.S.F. L. REV. 19 (1992).

Ronald R. Jordan & Katelyn L. Quynn, *Chapter 44 Nonprofit Investment Policies and Procedures* IN PLANNED GIVING: MANAGEMENT, MARKETING, AND LAW (Wiley 2004).

Terence Kelly, *Is Endowment Investment Income Subject to UBIT?,* 35 TAX ADVISER 272 (2004).

David T. Leibell & Daniel L. Daniels, *CRTs' and CLTs' Indirect Investment in University's Endowment Avoids UBTI,* 43 EXEMPT ORG. TAX REV. 171 (2004).

Gene Steuerle, *Charitable Endowments, Advised Funds & the Mutual Fund Industry, Part One: A New Democracy of Endowment Giving,* 82 TAX NOTES (TA) 129 (1999).

Gene Steuerle, *Charitable Endowments, Advised Funds & the Mutual Fund Industry, Part 2: Reconsidering the Foundation Rules,* 82 TAX NOTES (TA) 257 (1999).

Ethics

Bibliography

ABA COORDINATING COMMITTEE ON NONPROFIT GOVERNANCE, GUIDE TO NONPROFIT CORPORATE GOVERNANCE IN THE WAKE OF SARBANES-OXLEY (American Bar Association 2005).

ANTHONY ADAIR, CODE OF CONDUCT FOR NGO—A NECESSARY REFORM (INSTITUTE OF ECONOMIC AFFAIRS 1999).

BOARDSOURCE, THE SOURCE—TWELVE PRINCIPLES OF GOVERNANCE THAT POWER EXCEPTIONAL BOARDS (BoardSource 2005).

DEVELOPING AN ETHICS PROGRAM: A CASE STUDY FOR NONPROFIT ORGANIZATIONS (National Center for Nonprofit Boards).

Marilyn Laurie, *Best and Highest,* FOUNDATION NEWS & COMMENTARY, May/June 2005, at 50.

Nonprofit Organization Ethics, ASSOCIATION MANAGEMENT, April 1995.

Sylvia Shaz Shweder, *Note, Donating Debt to Society: Prosecutorial and Judicial Ethics of Plea Agreements and Sentences that Include Charitable Contributions*, 73 FORDHAM L. REV. 377 (2004).

Internet Sites

Maryland Association of Nonprofit Organizations, <www.standardsforexcellence.org>, has a standards for excellence program, a part of which is a code of ethics.

Feeder Corporations

Statutory and Other Authority

Internal Revenue Code §§ 502, 4943.

Financial

Bibliography

Steven Berger, Understanding Nonprofit Financial Statements (BoardSource 2003).

Evelyn Brody, *Charity Governance: What's Trust Law Got to Do with It?*, 80 CHI.-KENT L. REV. 641 (2005).

HERRINGTON J. BRYCE, FINANCIAL AND STRATEGIC MANAGEMENT FOR NONPROFIT ORGANIZATIONS (2d ed., Jossey-Bass 1992).

NICHOLAS P. CAFARDI & JACLYN FABEAN CHERRY, UNDERSTANDING NONPROFIT AND TAX EXEMPT ORGANIZATIONS (LexisNexis 2006).

JOHN PAUL DALSIMER, UNDERSTANDING NONPROFIT FINANCIAL STATEMENTS: A PRIMER FOR BOARD MEMBERS (National Center for Nonprofit Boards 1996).

FINANCIAL MANAGEMENT FOR NONPROFIT ORGANIZATIONS (Tracy D. Connors and Christopher T. Callaghan, eds., 1982).

PAUL FIRSTENBERG, THE 21ST CENTURY NON-PROFIT: REMAKING THE ORGANIZATION IN THE POST GOVERNMENT ERA (Foundation Center 1996).

Ted Flack & Christine Ryan, *Financial Reporting by Australian Nonprofit Organizations: Dilemmas Posed by Government Funders*, 64 AUSTL. J. PUB. ADMIN. 69 (2005).

MARY E. FOSTER, et al., MILLER NOT-FOR-PROFIT REPORTING 2006: GAAP, PLUS TAX, FINANCIAL, AND REGULATORY REQUIREMENTS (Harcourt Professional Publishing 2006).

John P. Giraudo, *Charitable Contributions and the FCPA: Schering-Plough and the Increasing Scope of SEC Enforcement,* 61 BUS. LAW. 135 (2005).

JO ANN HANKIN, ALAN G. SEIDNER, & JOHN T. ZIETLOW, FINANCIAL MANAGEMENT FOR NONPROFIT ORGANIZATIONS (Wiley 1998).

Christopher L. Jones & Andrea Alston Roberts, *Management of Financial Information in Charitable Organizations: The Case of Joint-Cost Allocations,* 81 ACCT. REV. 159 (2006).

Susan C. Kattellus, et al., *The Challenges of Cross-Disciplinary Work: Accounting and Financial Reporting for Governments and Nonprofits,* 17 J. PUB. BUDGETING ACCT. & FIN. MGMT. 152 (2005).

Ranjani Krishnan, et al., *Expense Misreporting in Nonprofit Organizations,* 81 ACCT. REV. 399 (2006).

BEVIS LONGSTRETH, MODERN INVESTMENT MANAGEMENT AND THE PRUDENT MAN RULE (Oxford University Press 1986).

JEROME B. MCKINNEY, EFFECTIVE FINANCIAL MANAGEMENT IN PUBLIC AND NONPROFIT AGENCIES (2d ed. 1995).

EDWARD J. MCMILLIAN, MODEL POLICIES AND PROCEDURES FOR NOT-FOR-PROFIT ORGANIZATIONS (Wiley 2003).

Panel on the Nonprofit Sector: Supplement: Strengthening the Transparency, Governance, and Accountability of Charitable Organizations: A Final Report to Congress and the Nonprofit Sector (Independent Sector ed., 2006).

DEBRA RUEGG, TERRY M. FRASER, ANNE L., HORODEN, & SUSAN KENNY STEVENS, BUDGETING YOUR WAY TO FINANCIAL STABILITY (Larson Allen Public Service Group 2003).

GERALD L. SCHMAEDICK, COST EFFECTIVENESS IN THE NONPROFIT SECTOR: METHODS AND EXAMPLES FROM LEADING ORGANIZATIONS (Quorum Books 1993).

C. Eugene Steuerle, *Expanded Information Reporting for Charitable Giving,* 49 EXEMPT ORG. TAX REV. 347 (2005).

Statutory and Other Authority

Uniform Management of Institutional Funds Act (1972).
Uniform Prudent Management of Institutional Funds Act (2006).

Form 990

Bibliography

ABA Section of Taxation, Committee on Exempt Organizations, Comments of ABA Tax Section on S.2020, PAUL STRECKFUS' EO TAX J., Mar./Apr. 2006, at 66.

ACCOUNTANTS FOR THE PUBLIC INTEREST, FILING NONPROFIT TAX FORMS: WHAT A DIFFERENCE UNDERSTANDING MAKES: GUIDES TO NONPROFIT MANAGEMENT (Accountants for the Public Interest 1994).

JODY BLAZEK, 990 HANDBOOK: A LINE-BY-LINE APPROACH (Wiley 2003).

General Accounting Office Report to the Chairman and Ranking Minority Members, Committee on Finance, U.S. Senate: Improvements Possible in Public, I.R.S. and State Oversight of Charities (U.S. General Accounting Office 2002).

Andrew S. Lang & Michael Sorrells, The IRS Form 990: A Window into Nonprofits (National Center for Nonprofit Boards 2001).

Peter Swords, Form 990: A Detailed Examination, Nonprofit Coordinating Committee of New York (Nonprofit Coordinating Committee of New York, Inc. 2003).

Peter Swords, How to Read the I.R.S. Form 990 & Find Out What It Means, (Nonprofit Coordinating Committee of New York, Inc. 2003).

Peter Swords, *Nonprofit Accountability: The Sector's Response to Government Regulation*, 25 Exempt Org. Tax Rev. 413 (1999).

Peter Swords, *The Form 990 as an Accountability Tool for 501(c)(3) Nonprofits*, 51 Tax Law 571 (1998).

Tax Compliance For Tax-Exempt Organizations (2005).

Statutory and Other Authority

Internal Revenue Code, Section 6033(a)(1), 6104.

Internet Sites

Guidestar, The National Database of Nonprofit Organizations (posts copies of Form 990), <http://www.guidestar.org>.

Internal Revenue Service, Form 990, available at <http://www.irs.gov/pub/irs-pdf/f990.pdf>.

Formation

Bibliography

Kathryn M. Vanden Beck, ed., Do It Right the First Time: Starting a Nonprofit Organization in Illinois (Nonprofit Financial Center 2003).

Evelyn Brody, *Agents Without Principles: The Economic Emergence of the Nonprofit and For Profit Organizational Forms*, 40 N.Y.U.L. Sch. L. Rev. 457 (1996).

Evelyn Brody, *Intellectual Dissonance in the Nonprofit Sector*, 41 Vill. L. Rev. 433 (1999)

Evelyn Brody, *The Limits of Charity Fiduciary Law*, 57 Md. L. Rev. 1400 (1998).

Nicholas P. Cafardi & Jaclyn Fabean Cherry, Understanding Nonprofit and Tax Exempt Organizations (LexisNexis 2006).

Carolyn C. Clark & Glen M. Troost, *Forming a Foundation: Trust vs. Corporation*, 32 Prob. & Prop. J. (May–June 1989).

JOHN A. EDIE, FIRST STEPS IN STARTING A FOUNDATION (5th ed. Council on Foundations 2002).

James J. Fishman, *The Development of Nonprofit Corporate Law and an Agenda for Reform,* 34 EMORY L. J. 619 (1985).

MARION R. FREMONT-SMITH, FOUNDATIONS AND GOVERNMENT: STATE AND FEDERAL LAW AND SUPERVISION, (Russell Sage Foundation 1965).

MARION R. FREMONT-SMITH, GOVERNING NONPROFIT ORGANIZATIONS: FEDERAL AND STATE LAWS AND REGULATION (Belknap Press of the Harvard University Press 2004).

Harry G. Henn & Michael George Pfeifer, *Nonprofit Groups: Factors Influencing Choice of a Form,* 11 WAKE FOREST L. REV. 181 (June 1975).

BRUCE HOPKINS, STARTING AND MANAGING A NONPROFIT ORGANIZATION: A LEGAL GUIDE (4th ed. Wiley 2004).

I.R.S. Publication 557.

I.R.S. Publication 4220: Applying for 501(c)(3) Tax Exempt Status (2003).

JANICE JOHNSON, TURNING VISION INTO REALITY: WHAT A FOUNDING BOARD SHOULD KNOW ABOUT STARTING A NONPROFIT (National Center for Nonprofit Boards 1999).

Kenneth L. Karst, *The Efficiency of the Charitable Dollar: An Unfilled State Responsibility,* 73 HARV. L. REV. 433 (1960).

John H. Largbein, *The Contractarian Basis of the Law of Trusts,* 105 YALE L. J. 625 (1995).

ANTHONY MANCUSO, HOW TO FORM A NONPROFIT ORGANIZATION (7th ed. NOLO PRESS 2005).

Carlyn S. McCaffrey, *When S Corps Meet Charities: Choice of Entity Considerations from an Income Tax Perspective,* 90 J. TAX'N 181 (1999).

Planning Tax-Exempt Organizations, in SHEPHARD'S McGRAW HILL TREATISE (Robert J. Desiderio & Scott A. Taylor, eds., updated annually in loose-leaf form, 1984).

Dana Brakman Reister, *Decision Makers Without Duties: Defining the Duties of Parent Corporations Acting as Sole Corporate Members in Nonprofit Health Care Systems,* 53 RUTGERS L. REV. 979 (2001).

RESTATEMENT OF THE LAW—THIRD, TRUSTS, (ALI 2003).

LISA A. RUNQUIST, ABCS OF NONPROFITS (American Bar Association 2005).

LEWIS M. SIMES, PUBLIC POLICY AND THE DEAD HAND (University Michigan School of Law 1955).

CARL ZOLLMANN, AMERICAN LAW OF CHARITABLE TRUSTS (The Bruce Publishing Company 1924).

Case Law

Brigham v. Peter Dent Brigham Hospital 124 F. 513 (1st Cir. 1904).

Help The Children, Inc. v. Commissioner, 28 T.C. 1128 (1957).

IHC Health Plans, Inc. v. Commissioner 325 F. 3d 1188 (10th Cir. 2003).

In the Matter of the Trust Under the Will of Caroline Weld Fuller 636 N.E. 2d 1333 (Mass. 1994).

Lynch v. Spilman, 431 P.2d 636 (Cal. 1987).

Morales v. Sevananda, 293 S.E. 2d 387 (Ga. App. 1982).

Moody v. Haas, 493 S.W. 2d 555 (Tex. App. 1973).

Nixon v. Lichtenstein, 959 S.W. 2d 854 (Mo. App. 1997).

Oberly v. Kirby, 592 A. 2d 445 (Del. Sup. Ct., 1991).

Queen of Angeles Hospital v. Younger, 136 Cal. Rptr. 36 (Cal. Ct. App. 1977).

Statutory and Other Authority

Revised Model Nonprofit Corp. Act §§ 1.25–6.22; 7.01–7.30 (1988).

Fundraising

Bibliography

AMERICAN ASSOCIATION OF FUNDRAISING COUNSEL, GIVING USA 2005 (AAFC 2005).

Thomas Bakewell, *Fund Raising When the Weather Is Foul: Are There Limits to Fund Raising During Times of Trouble?*, 5 INT'L J. EDUC. ADVANCEMENT 357 (2005).

DAVID G. BAUER, THE "HOW TO" GRANTS MANUAL: SUCCESSFUL GRANTSEEKING TECHNIQUES FOR OBTAINING PUBLIC AND PRIVATE GRANTS (4th ed. American Council on Education 1999).

BETTER BUSINESS BUREAU, NEW YORK GIVING GUIDE (Better Business Bureau 2005).

Laura K. Brown & Elizabeth Troutt, *Funding Relations between Nonprofits and Government: A Positive Example,* 33 NONPROFIT & VOLUNTARY SECTOR Q. 5 (2004).

DWIGHT BURLINGAME, ed., CRITICAL ISSUES IN FUND RAISING (John Wiley & Sons 1997).

MICHAEL E. BURNS, PROPOSAL WRITER'S GUIDE (Development & Technical Assistance Center 1989).

Rita Marie Cain, *Nonprofit Solicitation Under the Telemarketing Sales Rule,* 57 FED. COMM. L. J. 81 (2004).

MIM CARLSON, WINNING GRANTS STEP BY STEP: SUPPORT CENTERS OF AMERICA (John Wiley & Sons, Canada 1995).

Terrance S. Carter, *Looking a Gift Horse in the Mouth—Avoiding Liability in Charitable Fundraising,* available at http://www .charitylaw.ca (2004).

Center on Philanthropy at Ind. U., *Corporate Support for Charities: Research Finding and Fundraising Tips,* GIVING USA Q., Summer 2005, at 1.

SORAYA M. COLEY & CYNTHIA SCHEINBERG, PROPOSAL WRITING (Sage Publications 2000).

Errol Copilevitz, *There is a Place for the Nonprofit Community in the Regulatory Process,* FUND RAISING MANAGEMENT 64 (October, 1991).

SCOTT CUTLIP, FUND RAISING IN THE UNITED STATES: IT'S ROLE IN AMERICA'S PHILANTHROPY (Transaction Publishers 1990).

Owen Dyer, *New Fund-Raising Scheme Fuses Profit with Philanthropy,* 84 BULL. WORLD HEALTH ORG. 257 (2006).

Montgomery E. Engel, *Note, Donating "Blood Money": Fundraising for International Terrorism by United States Charities and the Government's Efforts to Constrict the Flow,* 12 CARDOZO J. INT'L & COMP. L. 251 (2004).

Leslie G. Espinoza, *Sharing the Quality of Mercy: Abandoning the Quest for Informed Charitable Giving,* 64 S. CAL. L. REV. 605 (1991).

FOUNDATION CENTER, THE FOUNDATION CENTER'S GUIDE TO PROPOSAL WRITING (4th ed. Foundation Center 2004).

FOUNDATION CENTER, FOUNDATION GIVING TRENDS (Foundations Today Series 2006).

MARION R. FREMONT-SMITH, GOVERNING NONPROFIT ORGANIZATIONS: FEDERAL AND STATE LAW AND REGULATION (Belknap Press of the Harvard University Press 2004).

Rita A. Fuerst, ed., *What Fundraisers Need to Know About State and Federal Regulation. How it Can Influence All Aspects of Their Work, in* 13 NEW DIRECTIONS FOR PHILANTHROPIC FUNDRAISING (Fall, 1996).

Robin R. Ganzert & Charles O. Mahaffey, *Spirit of Sarbanes-Oxley: Relevance of Nonprofit Governance on Planned Giving Fundraising Efforts, in* 2004 NATIONAL COMMITTEE ON PLANNED GIVING CONFERENCE PROCEEDINGS 541 (2004).

ELEANOR G. GILPATRICK, GRANTS FOR NONPROFIT ORGANIZATIONS: A GUIDE TO FUNDING AND GRANT WRITING (Praeger Publishers 1989).

JUDITH MIRICK GOOCH, WRITING WINNING PROPOSALS (Council for Advancement and Support of Education 1987).

KAY SPRINKEL GRACE, BEYOND FUNDRAISING: NEW STRATEGIES FOR NONPROFIT INNOVATION AND INVESTMENT (2nd ed. 2005 Wiley).

JAMES M. GREENFIELD, FUND RAISING FUNDAMENTALS: A GUIDE TO ANNUAL GIVING FOR PROFESSIONALS AND VOLUNTEERS (Wiley 1994).

MARK GUYER, A CONCISE GUIDE TO GETTING GRANTS FOR NONPROFIT ORGANIZATIONS (Nova Science Publishers 2003).

Holly Hall, Harvey Lipman, & Martha Voleg, *Charities' Zero-Sum Filing Game,* CHRON. PHILANTHROPY, May 18, 2000, p. 1.

MARY S. HALL, GETTING FUNDED: A COMPLETE GUIDE TO PROPOSAL WRITING (3d ed. Continuing Education Publications 1988).

ELLEN HARRIS, et al., *Fundraising Into the 1990's: State Regulation of Charitable Solicitation After* Riley, *in* TOPICS IN PHILANTHROPY (1989).

ROBERT F. HARTSOOK, NOBODY WANTS TO GIVE MONEY AWAY (ASR Philanthropic Publishing 2003).

CECILIA HOGAN, PROSPECT RESEARCH: A PRIMER FOR GROWING NONPROFITS (Jones & Bartlett, Sudbury 2003).

BRUCE HOPKINS, THE LAW OF FUND RAISING (3d ed. John Wiley & Sons, Inc. 2002).

Timothy L. Horner & Hugh H. Makens, *Nonprofit Symposium: Securities Regulation of Fundraising Activities of Religious and Other Nonprofit Organizations,* 27 STETSON L. REV. 473 (1997).

FISHER HOWE, THE BOARD MEMBER'S GUIDE TO FUND RAISING: WHAT EVERY TRUSTEE NEEDS TO KNOW ABOUT RAISING MONEY (Jossey-Bass 1997).

FISHER HOWE, WHAT EVERY BOARD MEMBER SHOULD KNOW ABOUT FUNDRAISING (Jossey-Bass 1995).

NORTON J. KIRITZ, PROGRAM PLANNING AND PROPOSAL WRITING (expanded version, The Grantsmanship Center 1988).

KIM KLEIN & STEPHANIE ROTH, ed., RAISE MORE MONEY: THE BEST OF THE GRASSROOTS FUNDRAISING JOURNAL (Chardon Press 2002).

Ely R. Levy & Norman I. Silber, *Nonprofit Fundraising and Consumer Protection: A Donor's Right to Privacy,* 15 STAN. L. & POL'Y REV. 519 (2004).

Catherine E. Livingston & Amy R. Segal, *Tax-Exempt Organizations and the Internet (Part 2),* PRAC. TAX LAW, Spring 2000, at 13.

JAMES GREGORY LORD, THE RAISING OF MONEY: THIRTY-FIVE ESSENTIALS EVERY TRUSTEE SHOULD KNOW (Third Sector Press 1983).

Douglas M. Mancino, *California Regulation of Out-of-State Charities,* 19 TAX'N EXEMPTS 243 (2006).

Susan M. Manwaring & Robert Hayhoe, *Proposed New Uniform Charitable Fundraising Act May Harmonize Fundraising Licensing Across Canada,* 50 EXEMPT ORG. TAX REV. 33 (2005).

Augusta Meacham, *To Call or Not to Call? An Analysis of Current Charitable Telemarketing Regulations,* 12 COMMLAW CONSPECTUS 61 (2004).

LYNN E. MINER & JEREMY T. MINER, PROPOSAL PLANNING AND WRITING, (3d ed. Greenwood Publishing Group 2003).

JUDITH NICHOLS, PINPOINTING AFFLUENCE IN THE 21ST CENTURY: INCREASING YOUR SHARE OF MAJOR DONOR DOLLARS (Bonus Books 2001).

TERESA OHENDAHL, CHARITY BEGINS AT HOME: GENEROSITY AND SELF-INTEREST AMONG THE PHILANTHROPIC ELITE (Basic Books 1990).

Michael W. Peregrine & James R. Schwartz, *A General Counsel's Guide to Accessing Restricted Gifts,* 29 EXEMPT. ORG. TAX REV. 27 (2000).

Haim Sandberg, *Where Do Your Pennies Go? Disclosing Commissions for Charitable Fundraising* (April 25, 2006). Available at SSRN: http://ssrn.com/abstract=898916.

Robin C. Satterwhite & Brent Cedja, *Higher Education Fund Raising: What Is the President to Do?,* 5 INT'L J. EDUC. ADVANCEMENT 333 (2005).

EDWARD SCHUMACHER, CAPITAL CAMPAIGNS: CONSTRUCTING A SUCCESSFUL FUND-RAISING DRIVE, (National Center for Nonprofit Books 2001).

JOHN SIMON, CHARLES POWERS, & JON GUNNEMANN, THE ETHICAL INVESTORS: UNIVERSITIES AND CORPORATE RESPONSIBILITY (Yale University Press 1972).

Jared Strauss, *Note, The Do-Not-Call List's Big Hang-up,* 10 RICH. J.L. & TECH. 27 (2004).

Christopher R. Sullivan, *Note, Get the Balance Right: Finding an Equilibrium Between Charitable Solicitation, Fraud, and the First Amendment in Illinois Ex. Rel. Madigan v. Telemarketing Associates, Inc.,* 538 U.S. 600 (2003), 31 WM. MITCHELL L. REV. 277 (2004).

Jeremy Thornton, *Nonprofit Fund-Raising in Competitive Donor Markets,* 35 NONPROFIT & VOLUNTARY SECTOR Q. 204 (2006).

MAL WARWICK, TEN STEPS TO FUNDRAISING SUCCESS (Jossey-Bass 2002).

Andrew Watts, *Fundraising Code: Volunteer Fundraising Is Now Protected by New Codes,* SOLIC. J. CHARITY & APP. SUPP.), Spring 2005, at 20.

Stanley S. Weithorn. *How Tax Planning Breakthroughs for Fund Raising Really Happen,* J. Tax'n Exempt Org. Vol. 3, No. 3, P. 5 (Fall 1991) published by Falkner and Gray.

GEORGE C. WORTH, FEARLESS FUND-RAISING FOR NON-PROFIT BOARDS (Rev. BoardSource 2003).

Case Law

American Charities for Reasonable Fundraising Regulation, Inc. v. Pinellas County 189 F. Supp. 2d 1319 (M.D. Fla., 2001).

American Target Advertising v. Giani 199 F.3d 1241 (10th Cir, 2000), *cert. denied* 531 U.S. 811 (2000).

Bella Lewinsky Dance Foundation v. Frohnmayer, 754 F. Supp 774 (C.D.Cal. 1991).

Carroll v. Blinken, 957 F. 2d 991(2d Cir., 1992).

Illinois ex. Rel. Madigan v. Telemarketing Associates 123 S.Ct. 1829 (2003).

Madigan v. Telemarketing Assoc., 123 S.Ct. 1829 (2003).

Maryland v. Joseph H. Munson Co. 467 U.S. 947 (1984).

Riley v. National Federation of the Blind of North Carolina, Inc., 487 U.S.781 (1988).

Village of Schaumberg v. Citizens for a Better Environment, 444 U.S. 620 (1980).

Telco Communications, Inc. v. Carbaugh 885 F.2nd 1225 (4st Cir. 1989).

Young v. New York City Transit Auth., 903 F.2d 146 (2d Cir. 1990), *cert. denied,* 498 U.S. 984 (1990).

Statutory and Other Authority

Internal Revenue Code §§ 17(a)(1), and f(8), 501 (c)(3), (13), (19), 509 (a)(1), 6113, 6115.

I.R.S. Forms: 8282, 8283, 990, 990-F, 990-T.

The Uniform Management of Institutional Funds Act.

General

Bibliography

Betsy Buchalter Adler, The Rules of the Road, A Guide to the Law of Charities in the United States (Council on Foundations 1999).

Jennifer Alexander, *The Impact of Devolution on Nonprofits: A Multiphase Study of Social Services Organizations,* Nonprofit Management and Leadership, Fall 1999, at 57.

Robert C. Anadtinga & Todd W. Engstrom, Nonprofit Board Answer Book (National Center for Nonprofit Boards 2001).

Rob Atkinson, *Altruism in Nonprofit Organizations,* 31 B.C. Law Rev. 501 (1990).

Avner Ben-Ner, *Who Benefits From the Nonprofit Sector? Reforming Law and Public Policy Toward Nonprofit Organizations,* 104 YALE L. J. 731 (1994).

Avner Ben-Ner, *Book review of "Who Benefits From the Nonprofit Sector? Reforming Law and Public Policy Toward Nonprofit Organizations,"* 104 YALE L. J. 731 (1994).

Avner Ben-Ner & Theresa Hoomissen, *The Governance of Nonprofit Organizations: Law and Public Policy,* 4 NONPROFIT MANAGEMENT LEADERSHIP 393 (1994).

JAMES T. BENNETT & THOMAS J. DiLORENZO, UNHEALTHY CHARITIES (Basic Books 1994).

JEFFERY M. BERRY, A VOICE FOR NONPROFITS (Brookings Institution Press 2003).

VICTORIA B. BJORKLUND, et al., NEW YORK NONPROFIT LAW AND PRACTICE (Lexis Publications 1997 and annual supplements).

R. BLANKEN & A. LIFF, FACING THE FUTURE: PREPARING YOUR ASSOCIATION TO THRIVE (American Society of Association Executives Foundation 1999).

DANIEL J. BOORSTIN, FROM CHARITY TO PHILANTHROPY (Harper & Row 1987).

Boston College Social Welfare Research Institute, Millionaires and the Millennium: New Estimates of the Forthcoming Wealth Transfer and the Prospects for a Golden Age of Philanthropy (1999), available at <http://www.bc.edu/swri>.

ROBERT O. BOTHWELL & ELIZABETH WIENER, TRENDS IN CORPORATE REPORTING ON PHILANTHROPIC EFFORTS, IN THE FUTURE OF THE NONPROFIT SECTOR. (Virginia Hodgkinson, Richard Lyman & Associates, eds., Jossey-Bass 1989).

WILLIAM G. BOWEN, THOMAS I. NYGREN, SARAH E. TURNER & ELIZABETH A. DUFFY, THE CHARITABLE NONPROFITS: AN ANALYSIS OF INSTITUTIONAL DYNAMICS AND CHARACTERISTICS (Jossey-Bass 1990).

ROBERT H. BREMNER, AMERICAN PHILANTHROPY (University of Chicago 1988).

ROBERT H. BREMNER, FROM THE DEPTHS: THE DISCOVERY OF POVERTY IN THE UNITED STATES (1956).

David A. Brennan, *The Power of the Treasury: Racial Discrimination, Public Policy and Charity in Contemporary Society,* 33 U.C. DAVIS L. REV. 389 (2000).

ELEANOR L. BRILLIANT, PRIVATE CHARITY AND PUBLIC INQUIRY: A HISTORY OF THE FILER AND PETERSON COMMISSIONS (Indiana University Press 2001).

Evelyn Brody, *Agents Without Principals: The Economic Convergence of the Nonprofit and For-Profit,* 40 N.Y. L. SCH. L. REV. 457 (1996).

Evelyn Brody, *Hocking the Halo: Implications of the Charities' Winning Briefs in Camps Newfoundland/Owatonna, Inc.* 27(2) STETSON L. REV. 433 (1997).

Evelyn Brody, *Institutional Dissonance in the Nonprofit Sector,* 41 VILLANOVA L. REV. 433 (1997).

Barbara K. Bucholtz, *Reflections on the Role of Nonprofit Associations in a Representative Democracy,* 7 CORNELL J. L. & PUB. POLICY 555 (1998).

LOUIS J. BUDD, ALTRUISM ARRIVES IN AMERICA IN THE AMERICAN CULTURE (Hennig Cohen ed., 1968).

CAPACITY FOR CHANGE: THE NON-PROFIT WORLD IN THE AGE OF DEVOLUTION (Dwight F. Burlingame et al., eds., Indiana University Center of Philanthropy 1996).

DAVID CANNADINE, DECLINE AND FALL OF BRITISH ARISTOCRACY, ch. 5 (Vintage 1999).

MIM CARLSON & DONAHUE, MARGARET: THE EXECUTIVE DIRECTOR'S SURVIVAL GUIDE: THINKING AS A NONPROFIT LEADER (Jossey-Bass 2003).

Zecheriah Chafee, Jr., *The Internal Affairs of Associations Not for Profit,* 43 HARV. L. REV. 993 (1930).

GERALD CELENTE, TRENDS 2000: HOW TO PREPARE FOR CHANGES OF THE 21ST CENTURY (Warner Brothers 1997).

CHRONICLE OF PHILANTHROPY—a biweekly publication.

Charles T. Clotfelter, *Symposium, What is Charity? Implications for Law and Policy, Tax-Induced Distortions in the Voluntary Sector,* 39 CASE W. RES. L. REV. 663 (1988–89).

CHARLES T. CLOTFELTER, WHO BENEFITS FROM THE NONPROFIT SECTOR? (Univ. of Chicago Press 1992).

CHARLES T. CLOTFELTER & THOMAS EHRLICH: PHILANTHROPY AND THE NONPROFIT SECTOR IN A CHANGING AMERICA (Indiana University Press 1999).

LILLY COHEN & DENNIS R. YOUNG, CAREERS FOR DREAMERS AND DOERS: A GUIDE TO MANAGEMENT CAREERS IN THE NONPROFIT SECTOR (The Foundation Center 1989).

COMMISSION IN PRIVATE PHILANTHROPY AND PUBLIC NEEDS (Filer Commission), (U.S. Treasury Department 1997).

CORPORATE PHILANTHROPY AT THE CROSSROADS (Dwight Burlingame & Dennis Young eds., 1996).

Nina J. Crimm, *Why All Is Not Quiet on the "Home Front" for Charitable Organizations,* 29 N.M. L. REV. 1 (1999).

Merle Curti, *American Philanthropy and the National Character,* 10 AMERICAN QUARTERLY 420, 420–37 (1958).

Alexis de Tocqueville, DEMOCRACY IN AMERICA (P. Bradley Edition, Alfred A. Knopf 1966).

Paul J. DiMaggio & Walter F. Powell, *The Iron Cage Revisited: Institutional Isomorphism and Collective Rationality in Organizational Fields,* 48 AMERICAN SOCIOLOGICAL REVIEW 147 (1983).

Peter F. Drucker, *The Age of Social Transformation,* ATLANTIC MONTHLY, November 1994, at 53.

PETER F. DRUCKER, MANAGING FOR THE FUTURE: THE 1990S AND BEYOND (Truman Talley Books/Dutton 1992).

PETER F. DRUCKER, MANAGING THE NONPROFIT ORGANIZATION (Collins 1992).

Marina Dundjerski, *Billion Dollar Growth at Big Funds*, CHRON. OF PHILANTHROPY, Feb. 24, 2000 at 1.

PAUL B. FIRSTENBERG, MANAGING FOR PROFIT IN THE NONPROFIT WORLD (The Foundation Center 1986).

PAUL B. FIRSTENBERG, THE 21ST CENTURY NONPROFIT: REMAKING THE ORGANIZATION IN THE POST-GOVERNMENT ERA (The Foundation Center 1996).

James J. Fishman, *The Development of Nonprofit Corporation Law and an Agenda for Reform,* 34 EMORY L.J. 617 (Summer & Fall 1985).

JAMES J. FISHMAN & STEPHEN SCHWARZ, NONPROFIT ORGANIZATIONS: CASES AND MATERIALS (Foundation Press, 2d ed. 2000).

MARION R. FREMONT-SMITH, GOVERNING NONPROFIT ORGANIZATIONS: FEDERAL AND STATE LAW AND REGULATION (Belknap Press of the Harvard University Press 2004).

MARION R. FREMONT-SMITH, PHILANTHROPY AND THE BUSINESS CORPORATION (Russell Sage Foundation 1972).

JOHN W. GARDNER, FOREWORD TO BRIAN O'CONNOR, AMERICA'S VOLUNTARY SPIRIT (Foundation Center 1983).

GILBERT M. GAUL & NEIL A. BOROWSKI, FREE RIDE: THE TAX EXEMPT ECONOMY (Andrews and McMeel 1993).

Kara A. Gilmore, *House Bill No. 1095: The New Nonprofit Corporation Law for Missouri*, 63 U. MO. K.C.L. REV. 633 (1995).

Harvey J. Goldschmid, *The Fiduciary Problems of Nonprofit Directors and Officers: Paradoxes, Problems and Proposed Reforms,* 23 J. CORP. L. 631 (1998).

SANDRA TRICE GRAY, EVALUATION WITH POWER: A NEW APPROACH TO ORGANIZATIONAL EFFECTIVENESS, EMPOWERMENT, AND EXCELLENCE (Independent Sector & Jossey-Bass 1997).

KEVIN M. GUTHRIE, THE NEW YORK HISTORICAL SOCIETY—LESSONS LEARNED FROM ONE NONPROFIT'S LONG-TERM STRUGGLE FOR SURVIVAL (Jossey-Bass 1996).

PETER DOBKIN HALL, INVENTING THE NONPROFIT SECTOR AND OTHER ESSAYS ON PHILANTHROPY, VOLUNTARISM, AND NONPROFIT ORGANIZATIONS (Johns Hopkins 1992).

PETER DOBKIN HALL, PRIVATE PHILANTHROPY AND PUBLIC POLICY: A HISTORICAL APPRAISAL (1992).

DAVID C. HAMMACK & DENNIS R. YOUNG, EDS., NONPROFIT ORGANIZATIONS IN A MARKET ECONOMY (Jossey-Bass 1993).

HENRY B. HANSMANN, THE OWNERSHIP OF ENTERPRISE (HARVARD UNIV. PRESS, 1996).

Henry B. Hansmann, *Reforming Nonprofit Corporation Law*, 129 U. PA. L. REV. 497 (1981).

Henry B. Hansmann, *The Role of Nonprofit Enterprise,* 89 YALE L.J. 835 (1980).

Henry B. Hansmann, *Symposium, What Is Charity? Implications for Law and Policy, The Evolving Law of Nonprofit Organizations: Do Current Trends Make Good Policy?*, 39 CASE W. RES. L. REV. 807 (1988–89).

Henry B. Hansmann, *Why Do Universities Have Endowments?*, 19 J. LEG. STUD. 3 (1990).

JAMES EDWARD HARRIS, THE NONPROFIT CORPORATION ACT OF 1993: CONSIDERING THE ELECTION TO APPLY THE NEW LAW TO OLD CORPORATIONS (Board of Trustees of the Univ. of Arkansas 1994).

H.D. HAZELTINE, INTRODUCTION TO ANGLO-SAXON WILLS (Dorothy Whitelock, ed., 1930 reprinted 1986).

REGINA E. HERZLINGER, *Can Public Trust in Nonprofits and Governments Be Restored?,* 74(2) HARV. BUS. REV. 97, (March, 1996).

ALAN G. HEVESY & IRA MILLSTEIN, NONPROFIT GOVERNANCE IN NEW YORK CITY (New York City Comptroller 2001).

GERTRUDE HIMMELFARB, POVERTY AND COMPASSION: THE MORAL IMAGINATION OF THE LATE VICTORIANS (Vintage 1991).

VIRGINIA A. HODGKINSON & MURRAY WELTZMAN, DIMENSIONS OF THE INDEPENDENT SECTOR (3d ed. 1989).

VIRGINIA A. HODGKINSON & RICHARD W. LYMAN, eds., THE FUTURE OF THE NONPROFIT SECTOR (Jossey-Bass 1989).

Michael C. Hone, *Symposium, What Is Charity? Implications for Law and Policy, Aristotle and Lyndon Baines Johnson: Thirteen Ways of Looking at Blackbirds and Nonprofit Corporations—The American Bar Association's Revised Model Nonprofit Corporation Act,* 39 CASE W. RES. L. REV. 751 (1888–89).

BRUCE R. HOPKINS, A LEGAL GUIDE TO STARTING AND MANAGING A NONPROFIT ORGANIZATION (2d ed. John Wiley & Sons 1993).

BRUCE R. HOPKINS, THE LAW OF TAX EXEMPT ORGANIZATIONS (8th ed. John Wiley & Sons 2003).

STAN HUTTON & FRANCES PHILLIPS, NONPROFIT KIT FOR DUMMIES (2d ed. For Dummies 2005).

LEON E. IRISH, GUIDELINES AND LAW AFFECTING CIVIC ORGANIZATIONS (2d ed. Open Society Institution 2004).

Jerald A. Jacobs, Introduction to American Bar Association Revised Model Nonprofit Corporation Act, (Prentice Hall Law & Business 1988).

Mary A. Jacobson, *Commentary to Recent Developments in Delaware Corporate Law: Nonprofit Corporations: Conversion to For-Profit Corporate Status & Nonprofit Corporation Members' Rights—Farahpour v. DCX, Inc.,* DE Law School of Widener Univ., 1995.

Kenneth L. Karst, *The Efficiency of the Charitable Dollar: An Unfilled State Responsibility,* 73 Harv. L. Rev. 433 (1960).

Leading for Innovation and Organizing for Results (Frances Hesselbein, Marshall Goldsmith, & Iain Somerville, eds., The Peter F. Drucker Foundation and Jossey-Bass 2001).

Kenneth D. Lewis, Jr., *Casenote & Comment, The Ramifications of Idaho's New Uniform Unincorporated Nonprofit Associations Act,* 31 Idaho L. Rev. 297 (1994).

Richard W. Lyman, What Kind of Society Should We Have? (Acumen Fund 2001).

Making the Nonprofit Sector in the United States: A Reader (David Harmach ed., Indiana University Press 1998).

Pamela A. Mann, Advising Nonprofit Organizations (Practising Law Institute 2002).

Kathleen D. McCarthy, Noblesse Oblige: Charity and Cultural Philanthropy in Chicago 1848–1929 (University of Chicago 1982).

Kathleen D. McCarthy, et al., The Nonprofit Sector in the Global Community (Jossey-Bass 1992).

Thomas Nagel, The Possibility of Altruism (Oxford 1970).

Waldemar A. Nielsen, The Third Sector: Keystone of a Caring Society (Acumen Fund 2001).

The Nonprofit Sector, A Research Handbook (Walter W. Powell, ed., Yale 1987 and Walter W. Powell and Richard Steinberg, eds., 2d ed., Yale 2006).

The Nonprofit Sector: A Research Handbook (Walter Powell and Richard Steinberg, eds. Yale University Press 2002).

Brian O'Connell, America's Voluntary Spirit: A Book of Readings (The Foundation Center 1983).

Teresa Odendahl, ed., America's Wealthy and the Future of Foundations (Foundation Center 1987).

Howard L. Oleck, Nonprofit Corporations, Organizations, and Associations (Prentice Hall, 5th ed. 1988).

Michael O'Neill, The Third America: The Emergence of the Nonprofit Sector in the United States (Jossey-Bass 1989).

The Organization of the Future (Frances Hesselbein, et al., eds., Jossey-Bass 1997).

Francis Ostrower, Why the Wealthy Give: The Culture of Elite Philanthropy (Princeton University Press 1997).

Robert Payton, et al., Philanthropy: Four Views (Transaction Press 1988).

Philanthropic Giving: Studies in Varieties and Goals (Richard Magat, ed., Oxford University Press 1989).

Robert D. Putnam, Bowling Alone (Simon & Schuster 2000).

The Responsibilities of Wealth (Dwight Burlingame ed., Indiana University Press 1992).

William P. Ryan, High Performance Nonprofit Organizations: Managing Upstream for Greater Profit (John Wiley & Sons 1998).

Albert M. Sacks, *The Role of Philanthropy: An Institutional View*, 46 Va. L. Rev. 516 (1960).

Lester M. Salamon, America's Nonprofit Sector: A Primer (The Foundation Center 1999).

Lester M. Salamon, The Emerging Nonprofit Sector: An Overview (St. Martin's Press 1996).

Lester M. Salamon, Partners in Public Service (Johns Hopkins University Press 1995).

Joseph A. Schumpeter, *Developments in the Law—Nonprofit Corporations,* 105 Harv. L. Rev. 1579 (1992).

Austin W. Scott & William F. Fratcher, IV, Scott on Trusts (4th ed. 1989).

Michael Seltzer, Securing Your Organization's Future: A Complete Guide to Fund Raising Strategies (rev. ed., The Foundation Center 2001).

Michael G. Sem, *Note, Szarzynski v. YMCA—Camp Minikani: Protecting Nonprofit Organizations from Liability under the Recreational Use Statute,* 184 Wis. L. Rev. 1209 (1995).

Lewis M. Simes, Public Policy and the Dead Hand (1955).

Hayden W. Smith, *Corporate Contributions to the Year 2000: Growth or Decline?, in* The Future of the Nonprofit sector: Challenges, Changes, and Policy Considerations (Virginia A. Hodgkinson and Richard W. Lyman eds., Jossey-Bass 1989).

Steven Smith & Michael Lipsky, Nonprofits for Hire: The Welfare State in the Age of Contracting (Harvard University Press 1995).

The State of Nonprofit America (Lester M. Salamon, ed., Brookings Institute Press and the Aspen Institute 2003).

The Systems Audit Group, Inc., Disaster Recovery Yellow Pages (Stephen Lewis ed. 1998).

Richard Titmuss, The Gift Relationship (1970).

Gary A. Tobin, American Jewish Philanthropy in the 1990s (Brandeis University Press 1995).

United Way of Pennsylvania, The Pennsylvania Non-Profit Handbook (Non-Profit Advocacy Network 1992).

VISION AND VALUES: RETHINKING THE NONPROFIT SECTOR IN AMERICA (Deborah Gardner, ed., The Nathan Cummings Foundation 1998).

LILLIAN G. WALD, THE HOUSE ON HENRY STREET (Dover Publications 1971).

AMOS G. WARNER, AMERICAN CHARITIES (1894).

WARREN WEAVER, PRE-CHRISTIAN PHILANTHROPY IN AMERICA'S VOLUNTARY SPIRIT AT 5 (Brian O'Connell 1983).

BURTON WEISBROD, THE NONPROFIT ECONOMY (Harvard University Press 1988).

MURRAY S. WEITZMAN, NADINE T. JALANDONI, LINDA M. LAMKIN, & THOMAS H. POLLACK, THE NEW NONPROFIT ALMANAC AND DESK REFERENCE (Independent Sector 2002).

THOMAS WOLF, MANAGING A NONPROFIT ORGANIZATION (Prentice Hall 1990).

DANIEL YERGIN & JOSEPH STANISLAW, THE COMMANDING HEIGHTS: THE BATTLE BETWEEN GOVERNMENT AND THE MARKETPLACE THAT IS REMAKING THE MODERN WORLD (Simon & Schuster Books 1998).

CARL ZOLLMANN, AMERICAN LAW OF CHARITIES (1924).

Internet Sites

BoardSource (formerly National Center for Nonprofit Boards, a resource for practical information, tools and best practices, training, and leadership development for board members of nonprofit organizations worldwide), <http://www.boardsource.org>.

The Business Roundtable (an association of CEOs committed to improving public policy), <http://www.brtable.org>.

The Chronicle of Higher Education (weekly news and job-information source for college and university faculty members, administrators, and staff), <http://www.chronicle.com>.

The Chronicle of Philanthropy (bi-weekly news source for charity leaders, fund raisers, and other people involved in the philanthropic enterprise), <http://www.philanthropy.com>.

Institute for Not-for-Profit Management, Columbia University Business School (offers graduate programs that help students develop effective management and leadership techniques for nonprofit organizations), <http://www.gsb.columbia.edu/exceed/INM/index.html>.

Internet Nonprofit Center (publishes the Nonprofit FAQ, a resource of information provided by participants in many online discussions about nonprofits and their work), <http://www.nonprofits.org>.

Mandel Center for Nonprofit Organizations, Case Western Reserve University (a multidisciplinary center for education, research, and community service, also offers graduate programs for nonprofit leaders and managers), <http://www.cwru.edu/mandelcenter>.

National Associations of Corporate Secretaries (includes efficient access to helpful information regarding its publications and seminars), <http://www.nacsonline.org>.

National Commission on Philanthropy and Civic Renewal, Giving Better, Giving Smarter: Renewing Philanthropy in America (1997), available at <http://www.hudson.org/ncpcr/report/report.html>.

Program on Non-Profit Organizations, The Yale Divinity School (an international center for multidisciplinary studies of philanthropy, voluntarism, and nonprofit organizations), <http://www.yale.edu/divinity/ponpo>.

Spencer Stuart (provides executive search and other human resources consulting services), <http://www.spencerstuart.com>.

Gifts—Restrictions, Purposes, and Cy Pres

Bibliography

Chris Abbinante, *Protecting "Donor Intent" in Charitable Foundations: Wayward Trusteeship and the Barnes Foundation,* 145 U. Pa. L. Rev. 665 (1997).

Am. L. Inst., Restatement of the Law of Trusts, Tentative Draft No. 3 (March 5) (approved by the membership May 2001).

Association of Fundraising Professionals, *How Much Donor Involvement Is Too Much?,* 2000, available at <www.nsfre.org/ethics> (excerpted from *Advancing Philanthropy* (November/December 2000)).

Rob Atkinson, *The Low Road to Cy Pres Reform: Principled Practice to Remove Dead Hand Control of Charitable Assets,* FSU College of Law, Public Law Research Paper No.176, available at <http://ssrn.com/abstract=845927> (2005).

Rob Atkinson, *Reforming Cy Pres Reform,* 44 Hastings L. J. 1111 (1993).

Rob Atkinson, *Unsettled Standing: Who (Else) Should Enforce the Duties of Charitable Fiduciaries?,* 23 J. Corp. L. 655 (1998).

Mary Grace Blasko, Curt S. Crossley, & David Lloyd, *Standing to Sue in the Charitable Sector,* 28 U. S. F. L. Rev. 37 (1993).

George G. Bogert & George T. Bogert, The Law of Trust and Trustees (2d rev. ed. 1991).

Evelyn Brody, *Charitable Endowments and the Democratization of Dynasty,* 39 Ariz. L. Rev. 873 (1997).

Evelyn Brody, *The Charity in Bankruptcy and Ghosts of Donors Past, Present, and Future,* 29 SETON HALL LEGIS. J. 471 (2005).

EVELYN BRODY, ENFORCEMENT: LEGAL STANDING AND PRIVATE REMEDIES, IN ACCOUNTABILITY: A CHALLENGE FOR CHARITIES AND FUNDRAISERS 7 (Putnam Barber ed., 2001).

Evelyn Brody, *Whose Public? Parochialism and Paternalism in State Charity Law Enforcement,* 79 IND. L.J. 937 (2004).

J.A. Bryant, Jr., *Extension of Charitable Trust Benefits to Persons Residing Outside Geographic Area Prescribed by Trust Instrument under Doctrines of Cy Pres or Equitable Deviation,* 68 A.L.R.3d 1049 (1976).

Mary Frances Butig, Gordon T. Butler, & Lynne M. Murphy, *Pledges to Nonprofit Organizations: Are They Enforceable and Must They Be Enforced?*, 27 U. S.F.L. REV. 47 (1992).

Ronald Chester, *Cy Pres or Gift Over: The Search for Coherence in Judicial Reform of Failed Charitable Trusts,* 23 SUFFOLK U. L. REV. 41 (1989).

Ronald Chester, *Grantor Standing to Enforce Charitable Transfers Under Section 405(2) of the Uniform Trust Code and Related Law: How Important is it and How Extensive Should it Be?* 37 REAL PROP. PROB. AND TR. J. 611 (2003).

Ronald Chester, *Modification and Termination of Trusts in the 21st Century: The Uniform Trust Code Leads a Quiet Revolution,* 35 REAL PROP. PROB. AND TR. J. 697 (2001).

Bruce D. Collins, *Charitable Intent*, INSIDE COUNSEL, Apr. 2006, at 100.

COMMITTEE ON COMMUNITY FOUNDATIONS LEGAL ADVISORY SUBCOMMITTEE, COUNCIL ON FOUNDATIONS, GUIDE TO DONOR INVOLVEMENT: BASIC CONSIDERATIONS AND BEST PRACTICES—A RESOURCE FOR COMMUNITY FOUNDATIONS (1996).

HARVEY P. DALE, THE BUCK TRUST (1987).

Joseph A. DiClerico, *Cy Pres: A Proposal for Change,* 47 B.U.L. REV. 153.

Joel C. Dobris, *The Death of the Rule Against Perpituities; or the RAP has No Friends: An Essay* 35 REAL PROP., PROB. & TR. J. 601 (2001).

Duties of Charitable Trust Trustees and Charitable Corporation Directors, 2 REAL PRO., PROB. & TR. J. 545 (1967).

John K. Eason, *Private Motive and Perpetual Conditions in Charitable Naming Gifts: When Good Names Go Bad*, 38 U.C. DAVIS L. REV. 375 (2005).

Mark Edelman, *Disaster Relief, Donor Intent, and Public Accountability, in* SEPTEMBER 11: PERSPECTIVES FROM THE FIELD OF PHILANTHROPY (2002).

David M. English, *The Uniform Trust Code (2000): Significant Provisions and Policy Issues,* 67 MO. L. REV. 143 (Spring 2002).

FINANCIAL ACCOUNTING STANDARDS BOARD ("ASB"), STATEMENT No. 117 (1993).

EDITH L. FISCH, et al. CHARITIES AND CHARITABLE FOUNDATIONS (1974).

Jennifer L. Franklin & David A. Shevlin, *Planning Considerations for Donors and Charities When Making and Accepting Gifts of Restricted Stock,* 35 EXEMPT. ORG. TAX REV. 141 (2002).

Marion R. Fremont-Smith, *Duties and Powers of Charitable Fiduciaries: The Law of Trusts and the Correction of Abuses,* 14 UCLA L. REV. 1041 (1966).

MARION R. FREMONT-SMITH, ORGANIZING NONPROFIT ORGANIZATIONS: FEDERAL AND STATE LAW AND REGULATION (Belknap Press of Harvard University Press 2004).

John T. Gaubatz, *Grantor Enforcement of Trusts: Standing in One Private Law Setting* 62 N.C.L.R. 905 (1984).

Iris J. Goodwin, *Donor Standing to Enforce Charitable Gifts: Civil Society vs. Donor Empowerment,* 58 VAND. L. REV. 1093 (2005).

HENRY HANSMANN, THE OWNERSHIP OF ENTERPRISE (1996).

Henry Hansmann, *The Role of Nonprofit Enterprise,* 89 YALE L. J. 385 (1980).

Henry Hansmann, *Why Do Universities Have Endowments?* 19 J. LEG. STUD., 3 (1990).

KENNETH T. HENSON, GRANT WRITING IN HIGHER EDUCATION: A STEP-BY-STEP GUIDE (Allyn & Bacon 2003).

Alex M. Johnson, Jr., *Limiting Dead Hand Control of Charitable Trusts: Expanding the Use of the Cy Pres Doctrine,* 21 U. HAW. L. REV. 353 (1999).

GEORGE W. KEETON, THE MODERN LAW OF CHARITIES (Pitman & Sons 1962).

COURTNEY S. KENNY, ENDOWED CHARITIES (1880).

Harriet M. King, *The Voluntary Closing of a Private College: A Decision for the Board of Trustees?* 32 S.C.L.R. 547 (1981).

Luis Kutner, *The Desecration of the Ferguson Monument Trust: The Need for Watchdog Legislation,* 12 DE PAUL L. REV. 217 (1962–1963).

Vanessa Laird, *Comment, Phantom Selves: The Search for a General Charitable Intent in the Application of the Cy Pres Doctrine,* 40 STAN. L. REV. (1988).

John H. Langbein, *The Contrarian Basis of the Law of Trusts,* 105 YALE L. J. 625 (1995).

James B. Lyon, *Considerations in Respecting Donor Intent,* TR. & EST., Sept. 1998, at 18.

Nancy A. McLaughlin, *Rethinking the Perpetual Nature of Conservation Easements,* 29 HARV. ENVTL. L. REV. 421 (2005).

Alan Newman, *The Intention of the Settlor Under the Uniform Trust Code: Whose Property Is It, Anyway?*, 38 Akron L. Rev. 649 (2005).

Francie Ostrower, *Donor Control and Perpetual Trusts: Does Anything Last Forever?, in* Philanthropic Giving: Studies in Varieties and Goals, 279 (Richard Magat ed. 1989).

Francie Ostrower, *The Role of Advisors to the Wealthy, in* America's Wealthy and the Future of Foundations 247 (Teresa Odendahl ed., 1987).

Michael W. Peregrine & James R. Schwartz, *A General Counsel's Guide to Accessing Restricted Gifts,* 29 Exempt Org. Tax Rev. 27 (July 2000).

Michael W. Peregrine & James R. Schwartz, *Nonprofit Corporate Law Developments in 2001,* 11 Health Law Reporter 272 (2002).

Rep. of [A.B.A.] Comm., *On Charitable Trusts, Duties of Charitable Trust Trustees and Charitable Corporation Directors,* 2 Real Prop., Prob and Tr. J. 545 (1967 Trust).

Restatement, Third Property § 6.2.

Restatement Third, Trusts §§ 28, 29, 63, 64, 65, 66, 67, 75, 76.

Julius Rosenwald, *Principles of Public Giving,* Atlantic Monthly, May 1929, reprinted in America's Voluntary Spirit 119 (Brian O'Connell ed., 1983).

Julius Rosenwald, The Trend Away from Perpetuities, Atlantic Monthly, Dec. 1930, at 749.

Louis M. Simes, Public Policy and the Dead Hand (Univ. Michigan Law School 1955).

John G. Simon, *American Philanthropy and the Buck Trust,* 12 U. S. F. L. Rev. 641 (1987).

Roger G. Sisson, *Relaxing the Dead Hand's Grip: Charitable Efficiency and the Doctrine of Cy Pres,* 74 Va. L. Rev. 635 (April 1988).

Jennifer L. White, *Note, When It's OK to Sell the Monet: A Trustee-Fiduciary-Duty Framework for Analyzing the Deaccessioning of Art to Meet Museum Operating Expenses,* 94 Mich. L. Rev. 1041 (1996).

Grant Williams, *Lawsuit in New York Could Affect Earmarked Funds at 500 Community Foundations,* Chron. Philanthropy, April 20, 2000, at 26.

Martin Morse Wooster, The Great Philanthropists and the Problem of Donor Intent (Capital Research Center 1994).

Howard M. Zaritsky, *Donor's Investment Strings Do Not Preclude Charitable Deductions*, Est. Plan. (WGL), Mar. 2005, at 56.

Case Law

Alco Gravure, Inc. v. Knapp Foundation., 479 N.E.2d 752 (N.Y. 1985).

Application of Community Serv. Soc'y of N.Y., 713 N.Y.S.2d 712 (App. Div. 2000).

Art Institute of Chicago v. Castle, 133 N.E. 2d 748 (Ill. App. 1956).

Attorney General v. Hahnemann Hospital et al., 494 N.E. 2d 1011 (Mass. 1986).

Board of Selectmen of Provincetown v. Attorney General 447 N.E. 2d 677 (Mass. App. 1983).

Brookline v. Barnes, 97 N.E. 2d 651 (Mass. 1951).

Brown v. Ryan, 788 N.E. 2d 1183 (Ill. App. 2003).

Cocke v. Duke University, 131 S.E. 2d 909 (N. Car. 1963).

Commonwealth v. Barnes Foundation, 159 A. 2d 500 (Pa. 1960).

Community Service Society v. The New York Community Trust 713 N.Y.S. 2d 712 (1st Dept. 2000).

Dabois v. Franciscan Health System, 679 N.E. 2d 1084 (Ohio, 1997).

Dartmouth College v. Woodward 17 U.S. (4 Wheat.) 518 (1819).

Davidson v. Duke University 194 S. E. 2d 761 (N.C. 1973).

Estate of Buck v. Marin Community Foundation, 35 Cal. Rptr. 2d 442 (Cal. App. 1994).

Estate of Estes, 523 N.W. 2d 863 (Mich. App. 1994).

Estate of Lind v. Northwestern University, 734 N.E. 2d 47 (Ill. App. 2000).

Estate of Violette De Mazia, 684 A. 2d 123 (Pa. Super. 1996).

Evans v. Abney, 396 U.S. 435 (1970).

Franklin Foundation v. Attorney General, 163 N.E. 2d 662 (1960).

Freme v. Walker 480 A. 2d 783 (Me. 1984).

Fulton v. Trustees of Boston College 361 N.E. 2d 1297 (Mass. 1977).

Girard Clarification Petition, 224 A. 2d 761 (1966).

Girard College Trusteeship, 138 A. 2d 844 (1958).

Girard Estate 27 Fiduc. 545 (1977).

Girard Will Case 127A. 2d 287 (1956), reversed Pennsylvania v. Board of Trusts 353 U.S. 230 (1957).

Herbert H. Lehman College Foundation v. Ricardo R. Fernandez, N.Y. App. Div., 1st Dept., 292 A.D. 2d 227 (2002).

Carl J. Herzog Foundation, Inc. v. University of Bridgeport, 699 A.2d 995 (Conn. 1997) (an objecting donor has no standing under the Uniform Management of Institutional Funds Act).

Hinkley Home Corp. v. Bracken, 152 A. 2d 325 (Conn. Super. 1959).

Holden Hospital Corp. v. Southern Illinois Hosp. Corp. 174 N.E. 2d 793 (Ill. 1961).

Holt v. College of Osteopathic Physicians and Surgeons 394 P. 2d 932 (Cal. 1964).

In re Estate of Buck, No. 23259 (Cal. Super. Ct. 1986), reprinted at 21 U.S.F.L. Rev. 691 (1987).

In re Estate of Eugene du Pont 663A. 2d 470 (Del. Ch. 1994).

In re Estate of Murdock, 884 P. 2d 749 (Kan. 1994).

In re Los Angeles County Pioneer Soc'y, 257 P.2d 1 (Cal. 1953).

In re Milton Hersey School Trust 807 A. 2d 324 (Pa. Comm. Ct, 2002).

In re Rood Estate v. Attorney General, 200 N.W. 2d 728 (Mich. App. 1972).

In the Matter of Estate of Othmer, 710 N.Y.S. 2d 848 (Surr. Ct., 2000).

In the Matter of the Estate of Edward B. Goehringer, 329 N.Y.S. 2d 516 (Surr. Ct., 1972).

In the Matter of the Estate of Robert R. Randall, 338 N.Y.S.2d 269 (Surr. Ct. 1972).

In the Matter of Multiple Sclerosis Service Organization of N.Y., 496 N.E.2d 861 (N.Y. 1986).

Jackson v. Phillips, 96 Mass. 539, 571 (1867).

James' Estate 199, A. 2d 275 (Pa. 1964).

Lacy Memorial Fund v. Norwest Bank Iowa 641 N.W. 2d 771 (Iowa 2002).

Meyer v. Jewish Home for the Aged of Rhode Island, C. A. No. 93-5374, 1994 R.I. Super, LEXIS 42 (1994).

Metropolitan Museum of Art v. Bank of Boston 1997 Comm. Super. Lexis 1408.

Morales v. Sevananda, 293S.E. 2d 387 (Ga. App. 1982).

Museum of Fine Arts v. Beland, 735 N.E. 2d 1248 (Mass. 2000).

Museum of the American Indian v. Huntington Free Library 610 N.Y.S. 2d 488 (1994).

National Foundation v. First National Bank of Catawba County, N.C. 288 F.2d 831 (4th Cir. 1961).

Oberly v. Kirby, 592 A.2d 445, 468 (Del. 1991).

Pacific Home v. County of Los Angeles, 41 Cal. 2d 844 (1953).

Persan v. Life Concepts, Inc., 738 So. 2d 1008 (Fla. App. 1999).

Queen of Angels Hospital v. Younger, 66 Cal. App. 3d 359 (Ct. App. 2d Dist. 1977).

Smithers v. St. Luke's-Roosevelt Hospital Center, 723 N.Y.S.2d 426 (App. Div. 2001).

Solomon v. Hall-Brooke Foundation, 619 A. 2d 863 (Conn. App. 1993).

St. Joseph's Hospital v. Bennett, 22 N.E.2d 305, 307 (N.Y. 1939).

Trustees of Dartmouth College v. Quincy 258 N.E.2d 745 (Mass. 1970).

United States v. Cerio 831 F. Supp. 530 (E.D., Va. 1993).

Warren v. Board of Regents, 544 S.E. 2d 190 (Ga. App. 2001).

Weir v. Howard Hughes Medical Institute, 407 A. 2d 1051 (Del. 1979).

Yale University v. Blumenthal, 621 A.2d 1304 (Conn. 1993).

Statutory and Other Authority

Uniform Management of Institutional Funds Act ("UMIFA") § 7 (1972).

Uniform Trust Code, Section 412.

Governance

Bibliography

A.B.A. Committee on Charitable Trusts, *Duties of Charitable Trust Trustees and Charitable Corporation Directors,* 2 REAL PROP. PROB. & TR. J. 545 (1967).

ABA COORDINATING COMMITTEE ON NONPROFIT GOVERNANCE, GUIDE TO NONPROFIT CORPORATE GOVERNANCE IN THE WAKE OF SARBANES-OXLEY (ABA 2005).

AMERICAN LAW INSTITUTE, PRINCIPLES OF CORPORATE GOVERNANCE, ANALYSIS AND RECOMMENDATIONS (ALI 1992).

AMERICAN LAW INSTITUTE, PRINCIPLES OF THE LAW OF NONPROFIT ORGANIZATIONS (Discussion Draft, April 2006).

AMERICAN LAW INSTITUTE, RESTATEMENT (THIRD) OF TRUSTS (THE PRUDENT INVESTOR RULE) (1990) AND RESTATEMENT (THIRD) OF TRUSTS (ALI 2003).

Alice Andre-Clark & Peter Frumkin, *Nonprofit Compensation and the Market,* 21 U. HAW. L. REV. 425 (1999).

Michael Anft & Grant Williams, *Redefining Good Governance*, CHRON. PHILANTHROPY, Aug. 19, 2004, at 6.

Avner Ben-Ner & Theresa Van Hoomissen, *The Governance of Nonprofit Organizations: Law and Public Policy,* 4 NONPROFIT MGMT. AND LEADERSHIP 393 (1994).

BETTER BUSINESS BUREAU, WISE GIVING ALLIANCE, PROPOSED STANDARDS FOR CHARITABLE SOLICITATIONS (Better Business Bureau 2001).

Stephen R. Block & Steven Rosenberg, *Toward an Understanding of Founder's Syndrome: An Assessment of Power and Privilege Among Founders of Nonprofit Organizations,* 12 NONPROFIT MGMT. AND LEADERSHIP 353 (2002).

BOARDSOURCE, THE SOURCE—TWELVE PRINCIPLES OF GOVERNANCE THAT POWER EXCEPTIONAL BOARDS (BoardSource 2005).

Harriet Bograd, *Alerting Nonprofit Boards to Financial Trouble: Variations on a Theme* (Yale PONPO Working Paper No. 226, 1995).

WILLIAM G. BOWEN, INSIDE THE BOARDROOM: GOVERNANCE BY DIRECTORS AND TRUSTEES (John Wiley & Sons 1994).

Brenda Boykin, *Note, The Nonprofit Corporation in North Carolina: Recognizing a Right to Member Derivative Suits,* 63 N.C.L. Rev. 999 (1985).

Dana Brakman Reiser, *There Ought to Be a Law: The Disclosure Focus of Recent Legislative Proposals for Nonprofit Reform,* 80 CHI.-KENT L. REV. 559 (2005).

Richard C. Breeden, *Giving It Away: Observations on the Role of the SEC in Corporate Governance and Corporate Charity,* 41 N.Y.L. SCH. L. REV. 1179 (1997).

Evelyn Brody, *The Limits of Charity Fiduciary Law,* 57 MD. L. REV. 1400 (1998).

EVELYN BRODY, ACCOUNTABILITY AND PUBLIC TRUST, IN THE STATE OF NONPROFIT AMERICA 471 (Lester M. Salamon ed., Brookings Institution Press and Aspen Institute 2002).

Evelyn Brody, *Agents Without Principals: The Economic Convergence of the Nonprofit and For-Profit Organizational Forms,* 40 N. Y. L. SCH. L. REV. 457 (1996).

Evelyn Brody, *Charity Governance: What's Trust Law Got to Do with It?,* 80 CHI.-KENT L. REV. 641 (2005).

Evelyn Brody, *Entrance, Voice and Exit: The Constitutional Bounds of the Right of Association,* 35 U. C. DAVIS L. REV. 821 (2002).

Evelyn Brody, *A Taxing Time for Bishop Estate: What Is the I.R.S. Role in Charity Governance?,* 21 U. HAW. L. REV. 537 (1999).

Evelyn Brody, *Whose Public? Parochialism and Paternalism in State Charity Law Enforcement,* 79 IND. LAW JOURNAL, 937 (2004).

JOHN CARVER, BOARDS THAT MAKE A DIFFERENCE: A NEW DESIGN FOR LEADERSHIP IN NONPROFIT AND PUBLIC ORGANIZATIONS (Jossey-Bass, 2d ed. 1997).

WILLIAM L. CARY & CRAIG B. BRIGHT, THE LAW AND THE LORE OF ENDOWMENT FUNDS (Ford Foundation 1969).

Zachariah Chafee, Jr., *The Internal Affairs of Associations Not for Profit,* 43 HARV. L. REV. 993 (1930).

Mark Chopko, *Emerging Liability Issues in Non-Profit Organizations: An Overview,* 8 CHARITY L. & PRAC. REV. 17 (2002).

Carolyn C. Clark & Glenn M. Troost, *Forming a Foundation: Trust vs. Corporation,* PROB. AND PROP. J., 32 (May–June 1989).

Michael Connelly, *The Sea Change in Nonprofit Governance: A New Universe of Opportunities and Responsibilities,* 41 INQUIRY 6 (2004).

TRACY DANIEL CONNORS, THE NONPROFIT MANAGEMENT HANDBOOK (John Wiley & Sons Inc. 1993).

Harvey P. Dale, *Nonprofit Directors and Officers-Duties and Liabilities for Investment Decisions in* 22ND NEW YORK UNIVERSITY CONFERENCE TAX PLAN 501(C)(3) ORG., Ch. 4 (1994).

Ian Dawson & Dunn Alison, *Governance Codes of Practice in the Not-for-Profit Sector,* 14 CORP. GOVERNANCE 33 (2006).

Ralph E. DeJong & Michael W. Peregrine, *Director Compensation Plans for Nonprofits: Addressing the Key Legal Issues,* 30 EXEMPT ORG. TAX REV. 29 (2000).

DETERMINING BOARD EFFECTIVENESS (The Conference Board 1999).

PETER F. DRUCKER, MANAGING THE NONPROFIT ORGANIZATION: PRINCIPLES AND PRACTICES (HarperCollins 1990).

Walter A. Effross, *Zen and the Art of Corporate Governance: Special Considerations in Counseling Spiritual/Religious Institutions,* 1 BUS. L. BRIEF 25 (2004).

Ira Mark Ellman, *Driven from the Tribunal: Judicial Resolution of Internal Church Disputes,* 69 CAL. L. REV. 1378 (1981).

FINANCIAL AND STRATIEGIC MANAGEMENT FOR NONPROFIT ORGANIZATIONS: A COMPREHENSIVE REFERENCE TO LEGAL, FINANCIAL, MANAGEMENT AND OPERATIONS RULES AND GUIDELINES FOR NONPROFITS (Jossey-Bass Nonprofit and Public Management Series 2000).

EDITH L. FISCH, CHARITIES AND CHARITABLE FOUNDATIONS (1974).

Jill E. Fisch, *Questioning Philanthropy from a Corporate Governance Perspective,* 41 N. Y. L. SCH. L. REV. 1091 (1997).

James J. Fishman, *The Development of Nonprofit Corporation Law and an Agenda for Reform,* 34 EMORY L. J. 617 (1985).

James J. Fishman, *Improving Charitable Accountability,* 62 MD. L. REV. 218 (2003).

James J. Fishman, *Standards of Conduct for Directors of Nonprofit Corporations,* 7 PACE L. REV. 389 (1987).

JOEL L. FLEISHMAN, PHILANTHROPY AND OUTCOMES: DILEMMAS IN THE QUEST FOR ACCOUNTABILITY, IN PHILANTHROPY AND THE NONPROFIT SECTOR IN A CHANGING AMERICA 172 (Charles T. Clotfelter & Thomas Ehrlich, eds., Indiana University Press 1999).

Julie L. Floch, *Not-for-Profit Governance: Too Much or Not Enough?,* CPA J., Jan. 2006, at 80.

MARION R. FREMONT-SMITH, GOVERNING NONPROFIT ORGANIZATIONS: STATE AND FEDERAL LAW AND REGULATION (Belknap Press of the Harvard University Press 2004).

Robin R. Ganzer & Charles O. Mahaffey, Spirit of Sarbanes-Oxley: Relevance of Nonprofit Governance on Planned Giving Fundraising Efforts, in 2004 National Committee on Planned Giving Conference Proceedings 541 (2004).

Susan N. Gary, *Regulating the Management of Charities: Trust Law, Corporate Law, and Tax Law,* 21 U. HAW. L. REV. 593 (1999).

JOHN S. GLASER, THE UNITED WAY SCANDAL: AN INSIDER'S ACCOUNT OF WHAT WENT WRONG AND WHY (John Wiley & Sons Inc. 1994).

Harvey J. Goldschmid, *The Fiduciary Duties of Nonprofit Directors and Officers: Paradoxes, Problems, and Proposed Reforms,* 23 J. CORP. L. 631 (1998).

Thomas L. Greaney, *Fourth Annual Health Law Colloquium: Oh, Darling! 40 Years Later: The Legacy of Darling v. Charleston Community Memorial Hospital and the Evolution of Hospital Liability: New Governance Norms and Quality of Care in Nonprofit Hospitals,* 14 ANNALS HEALTH L. 421 (2005).

Henry Hansmann, *Why Do Universities Have Endowments?,* 19 J. Leg. Stud. 3, 7 n. 15 (1990).

Deborah S. Hechinger & Marla J. Bobowick, *Boardroom: Governance Matters,* Foundation News & Commentary, July/Aug. 2005, at 39.

Regina E. Herzlinger, *Can Public Trust in Nonprofits and Governments Be Restored?,* Harv. Bus. Rev. March/April 1996, at 97.

Michael C. Hone, *Aristotle and Lyndon Baines Johnson: Thirteen Ways of Looking at Blackbirds and Nonprofit Organizations: The American Bar Association's Revised Model Nonprofit Corporation Act,* 39 Case W. Res. L. Rev. 751 (1998–1999).

Bruce R. Hopkins, Legal Guide to Starting and Maintaining a Nonprofit Organization (2d ed. John Wiley & Sons Inc. 1993).

Cyril O. Houle, Governing Boards Their Nature and Nurture (Jossey-Bass 1989).

Jerald A. Jacobs & Thomas E. Arend, *Drafting Proper Governance Documents,* Ass'n Mgmt., Apr. 1999, at 111.

Jerald A. Jacobs & David W. Ogden, Legal Risk Management for Associations: A legal Compliance for Volunteers and Employees of Trade and Professional Associations (American Psychological Association 1995).

Faith Stevelman Kahn, *Pandora's Box: Managerial Discretion and the Problem of Corporate Philanthropy,* 30 Sec. L. Rev. 223 (1998).

Laura Kalick, *Establishing Corporate Tax Compliance Programs for Complex Exempt Organizations,* 11 J. Tax'n Exempt Org. 147 (1999).

Kenneth L. Karst, *The Efficiency of the Charitable Dollar: An Unfulfilled State Responsibility,* 73 Harv. L. Rev. 433 (1960).

Consuelo Lauda Kertz, *Executive Compensation Dilemmas in Tax-Exempt Organizations: Reasonableness, Comparability, and Disclosure,* 71 Tul. L. Rev. 819 (1997).

Daniel L. Kurtz, Board Liability: Guide for Nonprofit Directors (Moyer Bell Limited 1988).

Berit Lakey, Nonprofit Governance: Steering Your Organization with Authority and Accountability (BoardSource 2004).

Paul C. Light, Making Nonprofits Work (Aspen Institute and Brookings Institution Press 2000).

Jill S. Manny, *Governance Issues for Non-Profit Religious Organizations,* 40 Cath. L. 1 (2000).

Ruth McCambridge, *Underestimating the Power of Nonprofit Governance,* 33 Nonprofit & Voluntary Sector Q. 346 (2004).

Melissa Middleton, Nonprofit Boards of Directors: Beyond the Governance Function, in The Nonprofit Sector: A Research Handbook 141 (Walter W. Powell ed., 1987).

Lizabeth A. Moody, *State Statutes Governing Directors of Charitable Corporations,* 18 U.S.F.L. REV. 749 (1984).

Mark H. Moore & L. David Brown, *Accountability, Strategy, and International Nongovernmental Organizations,* 30 NONPROFIT & VOLUNTARY SECTOR Q. 569 (2001).

J. Mueller, et al., *The Measurement of Responsible Governance and Management of NPOs in New Zealand: An Evaluation Tool for NPOs, Donors and Government,* CORP. GOVERNANCE: INT'L J. BUS. SOC'Y, Feb. 2005, at 159.

NONPROFIT CORPORATIONS COMMITTEE, GUIDEBOOK FOR DIRECTORS OF NONPROFIT CORPORATIONS, (George W. Overton & Jeannie Carmendelle Frey, eds., 2d ed. American Bar Association 2002).

NONPROFIT GOVERNANCE AND MANAGEMENT (Victor Futter, ed., ABA Section of Business Law 2002).

NONPROFIT LEADERSHIP AND MANAGEMENT (Jossey-Bass, Quarterly Journal)

BRIAN O'CONNELL, THE BOARD MEMBER'S BOOK: MAKING A DIFFERENCE IN VOLUNTARY ORGANIZATIONS (Center for Nonprofit Management 1985).

J.P. O'NEIL & S. BARNETT, COLLEGES AND CORPORATE CHANGE: MERGER, BANKRUPTCY AND CLOSURE (Conference-University Press 1980).

Philipp Pattberg, *The Institutionalization of Private Governance: How Business and Nonprofit Organizations Agree on Transnational Rules,* 18 GOVERNANCE 589 (2005).

Michael W. Peregrine, *Charitable Trust Laws and the Evolving Nature of the Nonprofit Hospital Corporation,* 30 J. HEALTH AND HOSP. L. 11 (1997).

Michael W. Peregrine & James R. Schwartz, *Key Nonprofit Corporate Law Developments in 2001,* 11 HEALTH LAW REPORTER 272 (February 14, 2002).

Dana Brakman Reiser, *Enron.org: Why Sarbanes-Oxley Will Not Ensure Comprehensive Nonprofit Accountability,* 38 U.C. DAVIS LAW REVIEW (Nov. 2004).

Report of the Blue Ribbon Commission on Board Evaluation: Improving Director Effectiveness (National Association of Corporate Directors 2001).

Report to Congress and the NonProfit Sector on Governance, Transparency and Accountability (Panel on the Nonprofit Sector, Independent Sector ed., 2005).

Judith R. Saidel, *Expanding the Governance Construct: Functions and Contributions of Nonprofit Advisory Groups,* 27 NONPROFIT AND VOLUNTARY SECTOR Q. 421 (1998).

Mark Sidel, *Symposium: Who Guards the Guardians? Monitoring and Enforcement of Charity Governance: The Guardians Guarding Themselves: A Comparative Perspective on Nonprofit Self-Regulation,* 80 CHI.-KENT L. REV. 803 (2005).

Patricia Siebart, *Corporate Governance of Nonprofit Organizations: Cooperation and Control,* 28 INT'L J. PUB. ADMIN. 857 (2005).

Norman I. Silber, *Nonprofit Interjurisdictionality,* 80 CHI.-KENT L. REV. 613 (2005).

Thomas Silk, *Corporate Scandals and the Governance of Nonprofit Corporations: What Every Director, Officer, and Advisor to Nonprofit Corporations in California Should Know About Corporate Responsibility Rules,* 38 EXEMPT ORG. TAX REV. 399 (2002).

Thomas Silk, *Rational Exuberance: An Exploration of the Adaptation by California's Charitable Sector to Changing Governance Standards: Notes from the Field,* 48 EXEMPT ORG. TAX REV. 271 (2005).

Thomas Silk, *Ten Emerging Principles of Governance of Nonprofit Corporations,* 43 EXEMPT ORG. TAX REV. 35 (2004).

Theda Skocpol, *Advocates Without Members: The Recent Transformation of American Civic Life, in* CIVIC ENGAGEMENT IN AMERICAN DEMOCRACY 461 (Theda Skocpol & Morris P. Fiorina, eds.) (1999).

STEVEN RATHGEB SMITH & MARTIN LIPSKY, NONPROFITS FOR HIRE: THE WELFARE STATE IN THE AGE OF CONTRACT (Harvard University Press 1993).

Jeffrey A. Sonnenfeld, *What Makes a Great Board Great,* HARV. BUS. REV. (Sept. 2002) p. 106.

Melissa Middleton Stone, *The Global Public Management Revolution: A Report on the Transformation of Governance,* 32 NONPROFIT AND VOLUNTARY SECTOR Q. 145 (2002).

STRENGTHENING THE TRANSPARENCY, GOVERNANCE, AND ACCOUNTABILITY OF CHARITABLE ORGANIZATIONS: A FINAL REPORT TO CONGRESS AND THE NONPROFIT SECTOR (Panel on the Nonprofit Sector, Independent Sector ed., 2005).

STRENGTHENING THE TRANSPARENCY, GOVERNANCE, AND ACCOUNTABILITY OF CHARITABLE ORGANIZATIONS: A SUPPLEMENT TO THE FINAL REPORT TO CONGRESS AND THE NONPROFIT SECTOR (Panel on the Nonprofit Sector, Independent Sector ed., 2006).

Alice M. Stuart, *Current Legal Trends Affecting Trustees and Directors of Nonprofit Corporations, in* TAKING TRUSTEESHIP SERIOUSLY: ESSAYS ON THE HISTORY, DYNAMICS AND PRACTICE OF TRUSTEESHIP (Richard C. Turner ed., 1995).

Henry C. Suhrke, *A Case Study in Governance: Massachusetts' Settlement with Boston University,* PHILANTHROPY MONTHLY, Oct. 1994, at 5.

RUSSY D. SUMARIWALLA & WILSON C. LEWIS, UNIFIED FINANCIAL REPORTING SYSTEM FOR NOT-FOR-PROFIT ORGANIZATIONS (Jossey-Bass 2000).

Charles R. Trempe, *Are Nonprofit Board Members Indecently Exposed?,* 22 U.S.F.L. REV. 857 (1988).

Karyn R. Vanderwarren, *Note, Financial Accountability in Charitable Organizations: Mandating An Audit Committee Function,* 77 CHI.-KENT L. REV. 963 (2002).

MURRAY S. WEITZMAN, THE NONPROFIT ALMANAC AND DESK REFERENCE: THE ESSENTIAL FACTS AND FIGURES FOR MANAGERS, RESEARCHERS, AND VOLUNTEERS (The Jossey-Bass Nonprofit and Public Management Series 2002) (Urban Inst. and Independent Sector).

DENNIS R. YOUNG & RICHARD STEINBERG, ECONOMICS FOR NONPROFIT MANAGERS (Foundation Center 1995).

ALVIN FREDERICK ZANDLER, MAKING BOARDS EFFECTIVE: THE DYNAMICS OF NONPROFIT GOVERNING BOARDS (Jossey-Bass 1999).

Case Law

Holt v. College of Osteopathic Physicians & Surgeons, 394 P.2d 932 (1964).

Matter of the Manhattan Eye, Ear & Throat Hospital v. Spitzer, 715 N.Y.S. 2d 575 (N.Y. Sup. Ct. 1999).

Nixon v. Lichtenstein, 959 S.W.2d 854 (Mo. App. 1997).

Oberly v. Kirby, 592 A.2d 445, 468 (Del. 1991).

Stern v. Lucy Webb Hayes Nat'l Training School for Deaconesses, 381 F. Supp. 1003 (D.C. 1974) (Sibley Hospital case).

From Capitol Hill

Joint Committee on Taxation Staff: Study of Present-Law Taxpayer Confidentiality and Disclosure Provisions as Required by Section 3802 of the Internal Revenue Service Restructuring and Reform Act of 1998, Volume II: Study of Disclosure Provisions Relating to Exempt Organizations (JCS-1-00, Jan. 28, 2000) (available at <www.house.gov/jct>).

U.S. Congress, Senate Finance Committee, Staff of U.S. Congress: Discussion Draft, Tax Exempt Governance Proposals. June 22, 2004, available at <http://finance.senate.gov/hearings/testimony/2004test/062204stfdis.pdf>.

From the I.R.S

Lawrence M. Brauer & Leonard J. Henzke, *Intermediate Sanctions (IRC 4958) Update,* I.R.S. EXEMPT ORG. CONTINUING PROF. EDUC. INSTRUCTION PROGRAM FOR FY 2003 § E (2002).

Lawrence M. Brauer, et al., *An Introduction to I.R.C. 4958,* I.R.S. EXEMPT ORG. CONTINUING PROF. EDUC. INSTRUCTION PROGRAM FOR FY 2002 § H (2001).

Debra Kawecki & Leonard Henzke, *Employment Tax Update—Review of Current Litigation,* I.R.S. EXEMPT ORG. CONTINUING PROF. EDUC. INSTRUCTION PROGRAM FOR FY 2003 § D (2002).

John Richards & Steve Fager, *Form 990*, I.R.S EXEMPT ORG. CONTINUING PROF. EDUC. INSTRUCTION PROGRAM FOR FY 2002 § G (2001).

Ward L. Thomas & Leonard J. Henzke, Jr., *Agency: A Critical Factor in Exempt Organizations and UBIT Issues*, I.R.S. EXEMPT ORG. CONTINUING PROF. EDUC. INSTRUCTION PROGRAM FOR FY 2002 § C (2001).

Health Care

From the I.R.S.

Lawrence M. Brauer, et al., *Update on Health Care*, I.R.S. EXEMPT ORG. CONTINUING PROF. EDUC. TECH. INSTRUCTION PROG. FOR FY 2002 § D (2001).

Tax-Exempt Health Care Organizations Community Board and Conflicts of Interest Policy, I.R.S. EXEMPT ORG. CONTINUING PROF. EDUC. TECH. INSTRUCTION PROG. FOR FY 1997 § C (1996).

Commentary

Gabriel O. Aitsebaomo, *The Nonprofit Hospital: A Call for New National Guidance Requiring Minimum Annual Charity Care to Qualify for Federal Tax Exemption*, 26 CAMPBELL L. REV. 75 (2004).

An Integrated Approach to Corporate Compliance: A Resource for Health Care Boards of Directors (Office of the Inspector General of the U.S. Departments of Health and Human Resources 2004).

Corporate Responsibility & Corporate Compliance, A Resource for Health Care Boards of Directors (Office of the Inspector of the U.S. Department of Health and Human Services 2003).

Richard C. Allen, *The Massachusetts Experience*, HEALTH AFF., Mar./Apr. 1997, at 85.

ANATOMY OF A MERGER: BJC HEALTH SYSTEM (Wayne M. Lerner ed., Health Administration Press 1997).

Craig E. Bain, et al., *The Methodist Hospital System: Tax Exemption and Charitable Responsibilities of Not-for-Profit Hospitals*, 16 ISSUES ACCT. EDUC. 67 (2004).

M. Gregg Bloche, *Health Policy Below the Waterline: Medical Care and the Charitable Exemption*, 80 MINN. L. REV. 299 (1995).

Robert A. Boisture & Douglas N. Varley, *State Attorneys General's Legal Authority to Police the Sale of Nonprofit Hospitals and HMOs*, 13 EXEMPT ORG. TAX REV. 227 (1996).

Chad Bowman, *AG Lannibes Probe of Catholic West after Charitable Trust Allegations by Union*, 9 BNA HEALTH LAW REPORTER, No. 40, 1565.

Jeffrey W. Brennan & Paul C. Cuomo, *The "Nonprofit Defense" in Hospital Merger Antitrust Litigation*, ANTITRUST, Spring 1999, at 13.

Bryant, L. Edward, Jr., *Responsibilities of Directors of Not-for-Profit Corporations Faced with Sharing Control with Other Nonprofit Organizations in Health Industry Affiliations: A Comment on Legal and Practical Realities*, 7 ANNALS HEALTH L. 139 (1998).

Jack Burns, *Note, Are Nonprofit Hospitals Really Charitable?: Taking the Question to the State and Local Level*, 29 IOWA J. CORP. L. 665 (2004).

Michael Chernew, et al., *Charity Care, Risk Pooling, and the Decline in Private Health Insurance*, AM. ECON. REV., 2005, at 209.

Laura B. Chisolm, *Symposium: Health Care and Tax Exemption: The Push and Pull of Tax Exemption Law on the Organization and Delivery of Health Care Services: Introduction*, 15 HEALTH MATRIX: J. L.-MED. 1 (2005).

Robert C. Clark, *Does the Nonprofit Form Fit the Hospital Industry?*, 93 HARV. L. REV. 1417 (1980).

Beverly Cohen, *The Controversy over Hospital Charges to the Uninsured—No Villains, No Heroes*, 51 VILL. L. REV. 95 (2006).

John D. Colombo, *The IHC Cases: A Catch-22 for Integral Part Doctrine, A Requiem for Rev. Ruling 69-545*, 34 EXEMPT ORG. TAX REV. 401 (2001).

John D. Colombo, *Health Care Reform and the Federal Tax Exemption: Rethinking the Issues*, 29 WAKE FOREST L. REV. 215 (1994).

John D. Colombo, *Symposium: Health Care and Tax Exemption: The Push and Pull of Tax Exemption Law on the Organization and Delivery of Health Care Services: The Failure of Community Benefit*, 15 HEALTH MATRIX: J. L.-MED. 29 (2005).

John D. Colombo, *The Role of Access in Charitable Tax Exemption*, 82 WASH. U. L.Q. 343 (2005).

John D. Colombo & Mark A. Hall, *The Future of Tax-Exemption for Nonprofit Hospitals and Other Health Care Providers*, 7 EXEMPT ORG. TAX REV. 395 (1993).

John F. Coverdale, *Preventing Insider Misappropriation of Not-for-Profit Health Care Provider Assets: A Federal Tax Law Prescription*, 73 WASH. L. REV. 1 (1998).

Molly Joel Coye, *The Sale of Good Samaritan: A View from the Trenches*, HEALTH AFF., Mar./Apr. 1997, at 102.

Peter Crampton, et al., *Does Community-Governed Nonprofit Primary Care Improve Access to Services? Cross-Sectional Survey of Practice Characteristics*, 35 INT'L. J. HEALTH SERVICES 465 (2005).

Nina J. Crimm, *Evolutionary Forces: Changes in For-Profit and Not-For-Profit Health Care Delivery Structures: A Regeneration of Tax Exemption Standards*, 37 B. C. L. REV. 1 (1995).

Nina J. Crimm, *Do Fiduciary Duties Contained in Federal Tax Law Effectively Promote National Health Care Policies and Practices*, 15 HEALTH MATRIX: J. L.-MED. 125 (2005).

James J. Fishman, *Checkpoints on the Conversion Highway: Some Trouble Spots in the Conversion of Nonprofit Health Care Organizations to For-Profit Status*, 23 J. CORP. L. 701 (1998).

Marion R. Fremont-Smith & Jonathan A. Lever, *State Regulation of Health Care Conversions and Conversion Foundations*, 9 B. N. A. HEALTH LAW REPORTER 714 (May 11, 2000).

FURROW, BARRY R., ET AL.: THE LAW OF HEALTH CARE ORGANIZATION AND FINANCE (4th ed. West 2001).

Marie Gantz, *Who Do You Trust? Comparing Data on Skilled-Nursing Facilities From the Internal Revenue Service and Health Care Financing Administration*, 28 NONPROFIT AND VOLUNTARY SECTOR Q. 476 (1999).

William F. Gaske & Rochelle Korman, *Joint Ventures Between Tax-Exempt and Commercial Health Care Providers*, 74 TAX NOTES 1575 (1997).

GRANTMAKERS IN HEALTH, ASSETS FOR HEALTH: FINDINGS FROM THE 2001 SURVEY OF NEW HEALTH FOUNDATIONS (2002).

Bradford H. Gray, *Conversion of HMOs and Hospitals: What's at Stake?*, HEALTH AFF., Mar./Apr. 1997, at 29.

Thomas L. Greaney, *Fourth Annual Health Law Colloquium: Oh, Darling! 40 Years Later: The Legacy of Darling v. Charleston Community Memorial Hospital and the Evolution of Hospital Liability: New Governance Norms and Quality of Care in Nonprofit Hospitals*, 14 ANNALS HEALTH L. 421 (2005).

Thomas L. Greaney & Kathleen M. Boozang, *Mission, Margin, and Trust in the Nonprofit Health Care Enterprise*, 5 YALE J. HEALTH POL'Y L. & ETHICS 1 (2005).

Peter J. Hammer, *Antitrust, Health Care Quality, and the Courts*, 102 COLUM. L. REV. 545 (2002).

Fred Hellenger, *Community Control and Pricing Patterns of Nonprofit Hospitals: An Antitrust Analysis*, 25 J. HEALTH POL. POL'Y. & L. 1051 (2000).

FRANCES R. HILL & DOUGLAS M. MANCINO, TAXATION OF EXEMPT ORGANIZATIONS (Tax Series, 2002).

H. CHESTER HORN, JR. & JAMES R. SCHWARTZ, HEALTH CARE ALLIANCES AND CONVERSIONS: A HANDBOOK FOR NONPROFIT TRUSTEES (Jossey-Bass 1999).

Jill R. Horwitz, *Why We Need the Independent Sector: The Behavior, Law and Ethics of Non-for-Profit Hospitals*, 50 UCLA L. REV. 1345 (2003).

Jill R. Horwitz & Marion R. Fremont-Smith, *The Common Law Power of the Legislature: Insurer Conversions and Charitable Funds,* 83 MILBANK Q. 225 (2005).

David A. Hyman, *Hospital Conversions: Fact, Fantasy, and Regulatory Follies,* 23 J. CORP. L. 741 (1998).

David A. Hyman, *The Conundrum of Charitability: Reassessing Tax Exemption for Hospitals,* 16 AM. J. HOSP. L. & MED. 327 (1990).

Melissa B. Jacoby & Elizabeth Warren, *Beyond Hospital Misbehavior: An Alternative Account of Medical-Related Financial Distress,* 100 NW. L. REV. 535 (2006).

Christopher M. Jedrey & Michael C. Fondo, *States Move to Limit Joint Ventures with For-Profit Health Care Providers,* 9 J. TAX'N. EXEMPT ORG. 3 (1997).

Nancy M. Kane, *Some Guidelines for Managing Charitable Assets from Conversions,* 16 HEALTH AFFAIRS 229 (March/April 1997).

Nancy M. Kane, et al., *Charitable Hospital Accountability: A Review and Analysis of Legal and Policy Initiatives,* 26 J. L. MED. & ETHICS 116 (1998).

Sarah Kaput, *Note, Expanding the Scope of Fiduciary Duties to Fill a Gap in the Law: The Role of Nonprofit Hospital Directors to Ensure Patient Safety,* 38 J. HEALTH L. 95 (2005).

Jack E. Karns, *Justifying the Nonprofit Hospital Tax Exemption in a Competitive Market Environment,* 13 WIDENER L. J. 383 (2004).

Robert C. Louthian, III, *The De-evolution of the Community Benefit Standard for Health Care Organizations,* 13J. TAX'N EXEMPT ORG. 118 (2001).

Douglas M. Mancino, *Final Physician Recruitment Ruling Provides Welcome Guidelines,* 87 J. TAX'N 50 (1997).

Douglas Mancino, *The Impact of Federal Tax Exemption Standards on Health Care Policy and Delivery,* 15 HEALTH MATRIX: J. L.-MED. 5 (2005).

DOUGLAS M. MANCINO, TAXATION OF HOSPITALS AND HEALTH CARE ORGANIZATIONS (Warren, Gorham & Lamont 2000).

Douglas M. Mancino & Frances R. Hill, Converting an Organization's Status from Nonprofit to For-Profit, 13 TAX'N EXEMPTS 155 (2002).

Gerald E. Matzke, *A Road Map from Nebraska,* HEALTH AFF., Mar./Apr. 1997, at 89.

Craig R. Mayton, *The View from Ohio,* HEALTH AFF., Mar./Apr. 1997, at 92.

Theresa McMahon, *Fair Value? The Conversion of Nonprofit HMO's,* 30 U.S.F.L. REV. 355 (1996).

Bruce McPherson, *Dialogue: Executive Compensation in Nonprofit Health Care Organizations,* 42 INQUIRY 110 (2005).

Bruce McPherson, *Dialogue: If Nonprofit Doesn't Mean "No Profit," How Much Is Enough in Health Care?,* 42 INQUIRY 211 (2005).

Harris Meyer, *Joint Ventures Between For-Profit and Not-For-Profit Health Care Companies,* HOSP. & HEALTH NETWORKS, June 5, 1996, at 36.

Harris Meyer, *Selling Not-For-Profit Hospitals to For-Profit Competitors,* HOSP. & HEALTH NETWORKS, June 5, 1996, at 22.

Linda B. Miller, *The Conversion Game: High Stakes, Few Rules,* HEALTH AFF., Mar./Apr. 1997, at 112.

NATIONAL HEALTH COUNCIL: STANDARDS OF ACCOUNTING AND FINANCIAL REPORTING FOR VOLUNTARY HEALTH AND WELFARE ORGANIZATIONS (4th ed. 1998).

Jack Needleman, *Nonprofit to For-Profit Conversions by Hospitals, Health Insurers, and Health Plans,* 114 PUB. HEALTH REP. 108 (1999).

Jack Needleman, et al., *Hospital Conversion Trends,* HEALTH AFF., Mar./Apr. 1997, at 187.

Paul T. O'Neill, *Charitable Immunity: The Time to End Laissez-Faire Health Care in Massachusetts Has Come,* 82 MASS. L. REV. 223 (1997).

Michael W. Peregrine, *Charitable Trust Laws and the Evolving Nature of the Nonprofit Hospital Corporation,* 30 J. HEALTH & HOSP. L. 11 (1997).

Michael W. Peregrine, *Physician Recruitment Ruling Offers Answers for Exempt Hospitals,* 16 EXEMPT ORG. TAX REV. 793 (1997).

Michael W. Peregrine, et al., *The Nonprofit Board's Duty of Loyalty in an "Integrated" World,* 29J. HEALTH & HOSP. L. 211 (1996).

Matthew Reiffer, *Antitrust Implications in Nonprofit Hospital Mergers,* 27 J. LEGIS. 187 (2001).

Dana Brakman Reiser, *Decision-Makers Without Duties: Defining the Duties of Parent Corporations Acting As Sole Corporate Members in Nonprofit Health Care Systems,* 53 RUTGERS L. REV. 979 (2001).

Damian P. Richard, *Case Note, Banner Health System v. Long: Controlling Nonprofit Healthcare Assets in the State of South Dakota,* 49 S.D.L.REV. 541 (2004).

Michael I. Sanders, *Health Care Joint Ventures Between Tax-Exempt Organizations and For-Profit Entities,* 15 HEALTH MATRIX: J. L.-MED. 83 (2005).

David Schactman, et al., *Public Policy Issues in Nonprofit Conversions: An Overview,* HEALTH AFF., Mar./Apr. 1997, at 9.

James R. Schwartz, *The California Model,* HEALTH AFF., Mar./Apr. 1997, at 96.

Yu-chu Shen & Glenn Melnick, *The Effects of HMO Ownership on Hospital Costs and Revenues: Is There a Difference Between For-Profit and Nonprofit Plans?,* 41 INQUIRY 255 (2004).

Donald Shriber, *State Experience in Regulating a Changing Health Care System,* HEALTH AFF., Mar./Apr. 1997, at 48.

Julie Silas, et al., *The Preservation of Charitable Health Care Assets,* HEALTH AFF., Mar./Apr. 1997, at 125.

NORMAN I. SILBER, A CORPORATE FORM OF FREEDOM: THE EMERGENCE OF THE MODERN NONPROFIT SECTOR (Westview Press 2001).

Lawrence E. Singer, *The Conversion Conundrum: The State and Federal Response to Hospitals' Changes in Charitable Status,* 23 AM. J. L. & MED. 221 (1997).

Lawrence Singer, *Gloria Jean Ate Catfood Tonight: Justice and the Social Compact for Health Care in America,* 36 LOY. U. CHI. L. J. 613 (2005).

Frank A. Sloan, *Commercialism in Nonprofit Hospitals,* 17 J. POL'Y ANALYSIS & MGMT. 234 (1998).

Pamela C. Smith, *An Empirical Investigation of For-Profit and Tax-Exempt Nonprofit Hospitals Engaged in Joint Ventures,* 29 HEALTH CARE MGMT. REV. 284 (2004).

Leah Snyder Batchis, *Comment, Can Lawsuits Help the Uninsured Access Affordable Hospital Care?: Potential Theories for Uninsured Patient Plaintiffs,* 78 TEMP. L. REV. 493 (2005).

A. L. (Lorry) Spitzer, *Executive Compensation in Nonprofit Health Care Organizations: Who's in Charge?,* 15 HEALTH MATRIX: J. L.-MED. 67 (2005).

Jennifer Wagner, *Case Note, Mahan v. Avera St. Luke's: Has the South Dakota Supreme Court Set a Precedent Allowing Nonprofit Hospitals the Right to Eliminate Competitors?,* 49 S.D.L.REV. 573 (2004).

DAVID M. WALKER, NONPROFIT, FOR-PROFIT, AND GOVERNMENT HOSPITALS: UNCOMPENSATED CARE AND OTHER COMMUNITY BENEFITS (United States Government Accountability Office 2005).

BURTON ALLEN WEISBROD, TO PROFIT OR NOT TO PROFIT: THE COMMERCIAL TRANSFORMATION OF THE NONPROFIT SECTOR (Cambridge University Press 1998).

Burton Allen Weisbrod & Myron J. Roomkin, *Managerial Compensation and Incentives in For-Profit and Nonprofit Hospitals,* 15 J. L. ECON. & ORG. 750 (1999).

Malcolm V. Williams & Saba S. Brelvi, *Profiling Foundations Created by Health Care Conversions,* HEALTH AFF., Mar./Apr. 2000, at 257.

Nancy Wolff & Mark Schlesinger, *Access, Hospital Ownership, and Competition Between For-Profit and Nonprofit Institutions,* 27 NONPROFIT AND VOLUNTARY SECTOR Q. 203 (1998).

Gary J. Young, *Federal Tax-Exemption Requirements For Joint Ventures Between Nonprofit Hospital Providers and For-Profit Entities: Form over Substance?,* 13 ANNALS HEALTH L. 327 (2004).

Case Law

Anclote Psychiatric Center, Inc. v. Commissioner, 76 T.C.M. 175 (1998) *aff'd* 190 F.3d 541 (11th Cir. 1999).

Caracci v. Commissioner, 118 T.C. No. 25 (May 22, 2002) (Sta-Home Health Agency).

Federated Pharmacy Services, Inc. v. Commissioner, 72 T. C. 687 (1979), *aff'd* 625F.2d 804 (8th Cir. 1980).

Harding Hospital v. Commissioner 505 F.2d1068 (6th Cir. 1974).

IHC Health Plans, Inc. v. Commissioner 325 F. 3d 1188 (10 Cir. 2003).

Nathan Littauer Hospital v. Spitzer (N.Y. Sup. Ct., Third Dept. 2003).

Plumstead Theater Society, Inc. v. Commissioner, 74 T.C. 1324 (1980).

Redlands Surgical Servs. v. Comm'r, 242 F.3d 904 (9th Cir. 2001).

St. David's Health Care System, Inc. v. United States, 349 F.3d 232 (5th Cir. 2003).

Sonora County Hospital v. Commissioner 46T.C.519 (1966) aff'd. 397F.2d814 (9th Cir. 1968).

History of Nonprofits

From the IRS

Alicia Meckstroth & Paul Arnsberger, *A 20-Year Review of the Nonprofit Sector,* 1975–1995, SOI Bull., Fall 1998, at 149.

Commentary

Philip Adler, Historical Origin of the Exemption from Taxation of Charitable Institutions, in Tax Exemptions on Real Estate: An Increasing Menace, Part I (1-84) (Westchester County Chamber of Commerce 1922).

Legal Instruments of Foundations 11 (F. Emerson Andrews ed., 1958).

Chauncy Belknap, *The Federal Income Tax Exemption of Charitable Organizations: Its History and Underlying Policy (1954),* reprinted as Appendix to John P. Persons, John J. Osborne, Jr., and Charles F. Feldman, Criteria for Exemption Under Section 501(c)(3), and in 4 Research Papers Sponsored by the Commission on Private Philanthropy and Public Needs and Filer Commission 2025 (U.S. Treasury Department 1977).

George R. Boyer, An Economic History of the English Poor Law 1750–1850 (Cambridge University Press 1990).

Evelyn Brody, *Of Sovereignty and Subsidy: Conceptualizing the Charity Tax Exemption,* 23 J. CORP. L. 585 (1998).

Evelyn Brody, *Charitable Endowments and the Democratization of Dynasty,* 39 ARIZ. L. REV. 873 (1997).

STEPHEN DIAMOND, EFFICIENCY AND BENEVOLENCE: PHILANTHROPIC TAX EXEMPTIONS IN 19TH CENTURY AMERICA, IN PROPERTY-TAX EXEMPTION FOR CHARITIES (Evelyn Brody ed., Urban Inst. Press 2002).

GEORGE DUKE, LAW OF CHARITABLE USES (R. W. Bridgman ed., London 1805).

JOHN A. EDIE, CONGRESS AND FOUNDATIONS: HISTORICAL SUMMARY, IN AMERICA'S WEALTHY AND THE FUTURE OF FOUNDATIONS (Teresa Odendahl ed., 1987).

CHARLES WILLIAM ELIOT, THE EXEMPTION FROM TAXATION OF CHURCH PROPERTY, AND THE PROPERTY OF EDUCATIONAL, LITERARY AND CHARITABLE INSTITUTIONS (1874).

MARION R. FREMONT-SMITH, FOUNDATIONS AND GOVERNMENT (Sage Foundation 1965).

MARION R. FREMONT-SMITH, GOVERNING NONPROFIT ORGANIZATIONS: STATE AND FEDERAL LAW AND REGULATION (Belknap Press of Harvard University Press 2004).

B. KIRKMAN GRAY, A HISTORY OF ENGLISH PHILANTHROPY: FROM THE DISSOLUTION OF THE MONASTERIES TO THE TAKING OF THE FIRST CENSUS 11 (1905).

PETER DOBKIN HALL, INVENTING THE NONPROFIT SECTOR (Johns Hopkins University Press 1992).

PETER DOBKIN HALL, A HISTORICAL OVERVIEW OF THE PRIVATE NONPROFIT SECTOR, IN THE NONPROFIT SECTOR A RESEARCH HANDBOOK 3 (Walter W. Powell ed., 1987).

MAKING THE NONPROFIT SECTOR IN THE UNITED STATES: A READER (David C. Hammack ed., Indiana University Press 1998).

ARTHUR HOBHOUSE, THE DEAD HAND: ADDRESSES ON THE SUBJECT OF ENDOWMENT AND SETTLEMENTS OF PROPERTY (1880).

William I. Innes, et al., *Selected Issues Regarding the Liability of Directors and Officers of Charitable and Nonprofit Corporations,* 19 PHILANTHROPIST 4 (2004).

GARETH JONES, HISTORY OF THE LAW OF CHARITY: 1532–1827 (Cambridge University Press 1969).

W. K. JORDAN, PHILANTHROPY IN ENGLAND: 1480–1660, A STUDY OF THE CHANGING PATTERN OF ENGLISH SOCIAL ASPIRATIONS (G. Allen & Unwin 1959).

Stanley N. Katz, Barry Sullivan, & C. Paul Beach, *Legal Change and Legal Autonomy: Charitable Trusts in New York, 1777–1893,* 3 L. & HIST. REV. 51 (1985).

GEORGE W. KEETON, THE MODERN LAW OF CHARITIES 1 (1962).

COURTNEY S. KENNEY, THE PRINCIPLES OF LEGISLATION WITH REGARD TO PROPERTY GIVEN FOR CHARITY OR OTHER PUBLIC USE 5 (1880) [this work is also known as KENNY ON ENDOWED CHARITIES].

Kathleen D. McCarthy, *The Gospel of Wealth: American Giving in* THEORY AND PRACTICE, IN PHILANTHROPIC GIVING: STUDIES IN VARIETIES AND GOALS 46 (Richard Magat, ed., 1989).

Howard S. Miller, The Legal Foundations of American Philanthropy 1776–1844 (State Historical Society of Wisconsin 1961).

Lizabeth Moody, *The Who, What and How of the Revised Model Nonprofit Corporation Act* 15 KY. L. J. (1989).

Liam Séamus O'Melinn, *The Sanctity of Association: The Corporation and Individualism in American Law,* 37 SAN DIEGO L. REV. 101 (2000).

DAVID OWEN, ENGLISH PHILANTHROPY, 1660–1960 (Belknap Press 1964).

David V. Patton, *The Queen, the Attorney General, and the Modern Charitable Fiduciary: A Historical Perspective on Charitable Enforcement Reform,* 11 U. FLA. J.L. & PUB. POL'Y. 131 (2000).

PHILANTHROPY IN AMERICA: A COMPREHENSIVE HISTORICAL ENCYCLOPEDIA (Dwight F. Burlingame ed., ABC-Clio 2004).

Michael D. Phillips & Magda B. Szabo, *Captive Insurance Companies in a Tax-Exempt Setting,* 19 TAX'N EXEMPTS 232 (2006).

William P. Quigley, *Reluctant Charity: Poor Laws in the Original Thirteen States,* 31 U. RICH L. REV. 111 (1997).

DANIEL ROSE, THE AMERICAN PHILANTHROPIC TRADITION, 18 EXECUTIVE SPEECHES 1 (2004).

NORMAN I. SILBER, A CORPORATE FORM OF FREEDOM; THE EMERGENCE OF THE MODERN NONPROFIT SECTOR (Westview 2001).

A. W. B. SIMPSON, A HISTORY OF THE LAND LAW 10–11 (2d ed. Oxford University Press 1986).

Ethan G. Stone, *Adhering to the Old Line: Uncovering the History and Political Function of the Unrelated Business Income Tax,* 54 EMORY L.J. 1475 (2005).

Thomas A. Troyer, *1969 Private Foundations Law: Historical Perspective on Its Origins and Underpinnings,* EXEMPT ORG. TAX REV., (2000).

TAKING TRUSTEESHIP SERIOUSLY: ESSAYS ON THE HISTORY, DYNAMICS AND PRACTICE OF TRUSTEESHIP (Richard C. Turner ed., Indiana University Center on Philanthropy 1995).

John W. Vinson, *The Charity Oversight of the Texas Attorney General,* 35 ST. MARY'S L.J. 243 (2004).

WHITEFORD, FERDINAND M.: THE LAW RELATING TO CHARITIES: ESPECIALLY WITH REFERENCE TO THE VALIDITY AND CONSTRUCTION OF CHARITABLE BEQUESTS AND CONVEYANCES (1878).

Adam Yarmolinsky & Marion R. Fremont-Smith, *Preserving the Private Voluntary Sector: A Proposal for a Public Advisory Commission on Philanthropy, in* 5 Research Papers Sponsored by the Commission on Private Philanthropy and Public Needs 2857 (U.S. Treasury Department 1977).

Carl Zollmann, AMERICAN LAW OF CHARITIES (1924).

Case Law

Late Corporation of the Church of Jesus Christ of the Latter-Day Saints v. United States, 10 S. Ct. 792, 810 (1890) (exercise of prerogative cy pres, which no longer exists in this country).

Trustees of Philadelphia Baptist Association v. Hart's Executors, 17 U.S. (1 Wheat.) 1, 38–39 (1819); *but see* Vidal v. Girard's Executor, 43 U.S. (2 How.) 127 (1844) (effectively repealing *Hart* after the discovery of evidence that charitable trusts existed at common law, that is, without regard to English statutes).

Trustees of Dartmouth College v. Woodward, 17 U.S. (4 Wheat.) 518 (1819) (holding the charter of a charitable corporation inviolate, in the absence of a reserve clause, from state alteration under the Contracts Clause of the Constitution).

Indemnification and Insurance

Bibliography

David James Brush, *The Constitutionality of the Charitable Immunity and Liability Act of 1987,* 40 BAYLOR L. REV. 657 (1988).

Mark Chopko, *Emerging Liability Issues in Non-Profit Organizations: An Overview,* 8 CHARITY L. & PRAC. REV. 17 (2002).

DAVID M. GISHE & VICKI E. FISHMAN, DIRECTORS AND OFFICERS LIABILITY INSURANCE OVERVIEW (2000).

JOSIAH O. HATCH III & JOHN F. OLSON, DIRECTOR AND OFFICER LIABILITY: INDEMNIFICATION AND INSURANCE (Clark Boardman Company 1992).

GERALD A. JACOBS & DAVID W. OGDEN, LEGAL RISK MANAGEMENT FOR ASSOCIATIONS: A LEGAL COMPLIANCE GUIDE FOR VOLUNTEERS AND EMPLOYEES OF TRADE AND PROFESSIONAL ASSOCIATIONS (American Psychological Association 1995).

DANIEL L. KURTZ, BOARD LIABILITY: A GUIDE FOR NONPROFIT DIRECTORS (Client Distribution Services 1988).

DANIEL L. KURTZ, THE DUTIES AND LIABILITIES OF OFFICERS AND DIRECTORS, INCLUDING A REVIEW OF INDEMNIFICATION AND INSURANCE, IN NON-PROFIT ORGANIZATIONS 263 (J. Small & D. Kurtz eds., 1986).

Alfred R. Light, *Conscripting State Law to Protect Volunteers: The Odd Formulation of Federalism in "Opt-out" Preemption,* 10 SETON HALL J. SPORTS L. 9 (2000).

Elizabeth M. Mills, *The Economic Family Doesn't Live Here Anymore: Self-Insurance Alternatives for Tax-Exempt Organizations and New Issues,* 35 EXEMPT ORG. TAX REV. 303 (2002).

NATIONAL CENTER FOR NONPROFIT BOARDS, RECOMMENDATIONS OF THE NONPROFIT SECTOR RISK AND INSURANCE TAX FORCE (NCNB 1989).

Charles R. Tremper, *Compensation for Harm from Charitable Activity,* 76 CORNELL L. REV. 401 (1991).

CHARLES R. TREMPER, RECONSIDERING LEGAL LIABILITY AND INSURANCE FOR NONPROFIT ORGANIZATIONS (Law College Education Services 1989).

Cases

Andy Warhol Found. for the Visual Arts v. Fed. Ins. Co., 189F.3d. 208 (2d Cir. 1999).

John v. John, 450 N.W.2d 795 (Wis. 1989), cert. den. 498 U.S. 814 (1990).

Information Flow

Bibliography

Richard S. Maurer, *Director Information Systems: The Advance Information Package, Minutes and Corporate Reports, in* HANDBOOK FOR CORPORATE DIRECTORS (R.R. Donnelley & Sons 1985).

John Mountjoy, *Information Flow to Directors, in* THE CORPORATE SECRETARY AND THE BOARD OF DIRECTORS: A COMPREHENSIVE GUIDEBOOK (American Society of Corporate Secretaries 1987).

Integral Part Doctrine

Bibliography

John D. Colombo, *The IHC Cases: A Catch-22 for Integral Part Doctrine, A Requiem for Rev. Ruling 69-545,* 34 EXEMPT ORG. TAX REV. 401 (2001).

Case Law

Cuddeback v. Commissioner 84 T.C.M. 623 (2002).

IHC Health Plans, Inc. v. Commissioner 325 F. 3d 1188 (10th Cir. 2003).
Nellie Callahan Scholarship Fund v. Commissioner 73 T.C. at 637.
Roe Found. Charitable Trust v. Commissioner T.C. Memo 1989-566.

Intermediate Sanctions

(See also: Compensation and Directors)

From the IRS

Lawrence M. Brauer & Leonard J. Henzke, *"Automatic" Excess Benefit Transactions under IRC 4958,* I.R.S. EXEMPT ORG. CONTINUING PROF. EDUC. TECH. INSTRUCTION PROG. for FY 2004 chap. 4 (2003).

Lawrence M. Brauer, et al., *An Introduction to I.R.C. 4958,* I.R.S. EXEMPT ORG. CONTINUING PROF. EDUC. TECH. INSTRUCTION PROG. FOR FY 2002 § H (2001).

Steven T. Miller, *Rebuttable Presumption Is Key to Easy Intermediate Sanctions Compliance,* 91 TAX NOTES 1735 (2001).

Commentary

Evelyn Brody, *Administrative Troubles for the Intermediate Sanctions Regime,* 92 TAX NOTES 423 (2001).

Evelyn Brody, *A Taxing Time for Bishop Estate: What Is the I.R.S. Role in Charity Governance?* 21 U. HAW. L. REV. 537 (1999).

Peter L. Faber, *Final Intermediate Sanctions Regulations Solve Some Problems But Not Others,* 35 EXEMPT ORG. TAX. REV. 295 (2002).

Deirdre Dessingue Halloran & Mark Chopko, *Catholic Conference Comments on Intermediate Sanctions,* 16 EXEMPT ORG. TAX REV. 107 (1997).

Robert Hayhoe, *Canadian Federal Budget Introduces Intermediate Sanctions (Section 170—Charitable Deduction),* 44 EXEMPT ORG. TAX REV. 185 (2004).

BRUCE R. HOPKINS, THE LAW OF INTERMEDIATE SANCTIONS: A GUIDE FOR NONPROFITS (John Wiley & Sons 2003).

FRANCES R. HILL & DOUGLAS M. MANCINO, TAXATION OF EXEMPT ORGANIZATIONS (Warren Gorham & Lamont 2002).

H.R. Report No. 506, 104th Cong., 2d Sess. 59 (1996).

Darryll Jones, *The Scintilla of Individual Profit: In Search of Private Inurement and Excess Benefit,* 19 VA. TAX REV. 575 (2000).

David H. Kirk, *Self-Dealing and the Lobster Pot of Joint Ventures,* 49 EXEMPT ORG. TAX REV. 221 (2005).

Michael S. Kutzin, *Comparing the Intermediate Sanctions to the Excise Tax on Self-Dealing,* 13 TAX'N EXEMPTS 242 (2002).

Catherine E. Livingston, NACUBO ADVISORY REPORT 2002-01: IRS PUBLISHES FINAL RULES ON INTERMEDIATE SANCTIONS (2002).

Robert C. Louthian III, *IRS Assesses Automatic Excise Tax Against Church Officials' Transgressions,* 17 TAX'N EXEMPTS 31 (2005).

Steven T. Miller, *Rebuttable Presumption Is Key to Easy Intermediate Sanctions Compliance,* 91 TAX NOTES (TA) 1735 (2001).

J. J. Pickle, *Federal Regulation of the Nonprofit World: From Congressional Oversight to Intermediate Sanctions,* in NEW DIRECTIONS PHILANTHROPIC FUNDRAISING, 1997, at 7.

Burgess J.W. Raby & William L. Raby, *Private Inurement, Private Benefit, UCC, and Intermediate Sanctions,* 82 TAX NOTES 1979 (1999).

Report on Reforms to Improve the Tax Rules Governing Public Charities, Subcomm. on Oversight of House Comm. on Ways and Means, 103d Cong. 17 2d Sess., (1994).

Mychel Russell-Ward, *Joint Ventures Beware: Discrepancies Exist in Penalties for Inurement and Private Benefit Scenarios. (Section 4958—Intermediate Sanctions),* 45 EXEMPT ORG. TAX REV. 95 (2004).

Elizabeth Schwinn, *Falling Through the Cracks: IRS Pursues Few Corrupt Charities Despite Tough Federal Law,* CHRONICLE OF PHILANTHROPY, *Nov. 14, 2002, at 1.* In the same issue by the same author: *A Controversial Provision Requires Charities to Tell IRS About Misdeeds of Top Officials; How '96 Law on Financial Abuses Has Been Applied by IRS in Four Cases; Charity Gets Help From IRS in Dealing With Missing Funds.*

Henry C. Suhrke, *Intermediate Sanctions Regulations and the Aggressive Reach of Bureaucracy,* PHILANTHROPY MONTHLY, Sept. 1998, at 2.

T. J. Sullivan, Kathleen Nilles, Ralph DeJong, Bernadette Broccolo, & Michael Peregrine, *Temporary Intermediate Sanctions Regulations,* 31 EXEMPT ORG. TAX REV. 177 (Feb. 2001).

Michael Folz Wexler & Alvin J. Geske, *The Private Benefit Rule and Interaction of Excess Benefit Transaction Taxes with Revocation,* 104 J. TAX'N 304 (2006).

Carolyn D. Wright, *IRS Assesses Intermediate Sanctions Against the Bishop Estate Incumbent Trustees,* 31 EXEMPT ORG. TAX REV. 155 (2001).

Case Law

Caracci v. Commissioner of Internal Revenue, 118 T.C. 379 (2002), rev.'d 456 F.3d 444 (5th Cir. 2006).

Statutory and Other Authority

I.R.C. §§ 501(c)(3) and 501(c)(4) (private inurement), 4941 (private foundation self-dealing), 4958 (intermediate sanctions on excess benefits to insiders of public charities), 4962, 6033(b)(11)(12).

International

Bibliography

Betsy Buchalter Adler, Victoria Bjorklund et al., Comments in Response to IRS Announcement 2003-29 Regarding International Grantmaking and International Activities by Domestic 501(c)(3) Organizations, ABA Tax Section, July 18, 2003.

Victoria B. Bjorklund & Jennifer I. Goldberg, *How a Private Foundation Can Use "Friends of" Organizations*, 48 INTERNATIONAL DATELINE, insert, August 1998.

Victoria B. Bjorklund & Jennifer I. Goldberg, *Conducting Overseas Site Visits*, 3 INTERNATIONAL JOURNAL OF NOT-FOR-PROFIT LAW, insert, December 2000.

VICTORIA B. BJORKLUND & JOANNA E. PRESSMAN, CROSS-BORDER PHILANTHROPY, NONPROFIT LAW: A COMPLETE GUIDE (Civic Research Institute 2005).

Chang, Joannie, et al., *Cross Border Charitable Giving*, 31 U.S.F.L. REV. 563 (1997).

Harvey P. Dale, *Foreign Charities*, 48 TAX LAW, 655 (1995).

Edgardo Ramos, Timothy R. Lyman, Patricia Canavan, & Clifford Nichols III, *Handbook on Counter Terrorism Measures: What U.S. Nonprofits and Grantmakers Need to Know* (Berry Day & Howard 2004) at <www.cof.org>.

JOHN A. EDIE & JANE C. NOBER, BEYOND OUR BORDERS: A GUIDE TO MAKING GRANTS OUTSIDE THE U.S. (3d ed. Council on Foundations 2002).

JOHN A. EDIE & JANE C. NOBER, INTERNATIONAL GRANTMAKING: A REPORT ON U.S. FOUNDATION TRENDS, Appendix C (The Foundation Center 1997).

Janne G. Gallagher, *Grantmaking in An Age of Terrorism: Some Thought about Compliance Strategies*, 2004, at <www.cof.org>.

International Grantmaking II, An Update on U.S. Foundation Trends (Council on Foundations and The Foundation Center 2000).

Timothy R. Lyman, Michael G. Considine, & Jennifer L. Sacks, *International Grantmaking after September 11: Dealing with Executive Order 13224 and the USA Patriot Act*, Fall 2002, at <www.usig.org>.

Statutory and Other Authority

I.R.C. § 170(c)(2).

Internet Sites

Letter from the Internal Revenue Service to John A. Edie, Esq., Senior Vice President and General Counsel, Council on Foundations, April 18, 2001, permitting the use of expenditure responsibility for international grants, <www.cof.org/files/Documents/Legal/irsletter.pdf>.

The European Foundation Centre, provides information about foundations and corporate funders active in Europe with the goal of strengthening philanthropy in Europe, <www.efc.be>.

Report on Money Laundering and Terrorist Financing Typologies 2004–2005, <www.fatf-gafi.org/dataoecd/16/8/35003256.pdf>.

International Center for Not-for-Profit Law, resource center that provides information on legal, regulatory, and administrative developments in the nonprofit sector from over 125 countries, <www.icnl.org>.

U.S. Department of the Treasury Revised Anti-Terrorist Financing Guidelines: Voluntary Best Practices for U.S.-Based Charities. February 2006, <www.treas.gov/offices/enforcement/key-issues/protecting/charities-intro.shtml>.

U.S. International Grantmaking provides access to updates on U.S. government statements, articles and laws, and other informational materials and resources. A "must-see" site. <www.usig.org>.

Internet

From the I.R.S.

Cheryl Chasin, Susan Ruth, & Robert Harper, Tax Exempt Organizations and World Wide Web Fundraising and Advertising on the Internet, EOCPE (for FY 2000).

Commentary

Alice M. Anderson & Robert A. Wexler, *What Guidance Is Needed—And Not Needed—For Political and Lobbying Activities on the Internet,* 12 J. TAX'N EXEMPT ORG. 260 (2001).

Susan R. Bills, *Applying Paper Laws to the Virtual Activities of Exempt Organizations,* 12 J. TAX'N EXEMPT ORG. 46 (2001).

Jody Blazek, *The Internet and Tax-Exempt Organizations*, 31 TAX ADVISOR 344 (2000).

Hazel Cameron, *The Nonprofit Phenomenon: Internet Resources for Nonprofit Organizations,* SEARCHER, Feb. 2004, at 33.

Cheryl Chasin, Susan Ruth, & Robert Harper, *Tax Exempt Organizations and World Wide Web Fundraising and Advertising on the Internet,* EOCPE (for FY 2000).

Francis R. Hill, *Donation of Internet Purchase Rebate Qualifies for Section 170 Charitable Contribution,* 42 TAX MGMT. MEMO (BNA) 511 (2001).

Pamela O'Kane Foter, *Looking on the Internet and the Internal Revenue Code's Regulation of Charitable Organizations,* 43 N.Y.L. SCH. L. REV. 567 (1999).

Leeanna Izuel & Leslie Park, *Tax-Exempt Organizations and Internet Commerce: The Application of the Royalty and Volunteer Exceptions to Unrelated Business Taxable Income,* 31 WM. MITCHELL L. REV. 245 (2004).

Darryll K. Jones, *Advertisements and Sponsorships in Charitable Cyberspace: Virtual Reality Meets Legal Fiction,* 70 MISS. L. J. 323 (2001).

Lesli F. Laffie, *Exempt Organization Websites,* 32 TAX ADVISER 220 (2001).

Melissa G. Liazos, *Can States Impose Registration Requirements on Online Charitable Solicitors?,* 67 U. CHI. L. REV. 1379 (2000).

Catherine E. Livingston, *Tax-Exempt Organizations and the Internet, Tax and Other Legal Issues,* 31 EXEMPT ORG. TAX REV. 419 (2001).

Catherine E. Livingston & Amy R. Segal, *Tax-Exempt Organizations and the Internet,* PRAC. TAX LAW, Winter 2000, at 29, Spring 2000 at 13.

Lobbying on the Internet and the Internal Revenue Code's Regulation of Charitable Organizations, 43 N.Y.L. SCH. L. REV. 567 (1999).

Andrew Longstreth *Charity's Guardians: For the Lawyers Who Helped Nonprofits Dodge Legal Problems After September 11, a Background in Interact-Related Regulations Was Suddenly a Useful Talent,* AM. LAW., Dec. 2001, at 35.

Cade Metz, *Your Request Is Granted; We Go Inside the Soup-to-Nuts Web Site for Running Charitable Foundations Online,* PC MAG., Apr. 12, 2005, at 74.

Paul E. Monaghan, Jr., *Charitable Solicitation Over the Internet and State-Law Restrictions* (1996), available at < http://www.charitychannel.com/forums/cyb-acc/resources/monaghan.html>.

Christina L. Nooney, *Tax-Exempt Organizations and the Interact,* 27 EXEMPT ORG. TAX REV. 33 (2000).

Suzanne Ross McDowell, *Nonprofits and the Internet: Tax and Other Legal Issues,* COMPUTER & INTERNET LAW., Oct. 2004, at 18.

Fred Stokeld, *Nonprofit Reps Seek User-Friendly E-Filing System,* 94 TAX NOTES 1094 (2002).

F. LAWRENCE STREET & MARK GRANT, LAW OF THE INTERNET (5th ed. Michie 2001).

Robert A. Wexler & Alice M. Anderson, *Internet Guidance Should Reconcile Old Law With a New Medium,* 12 J. TAX'N. EXEMPT ORG. 187 (2001).

LaVerne Woods & Michelle Osborne, *Healthcare Organizations and the Internet: Impact on Federal Tax Exemption,* 35 J. HEALTH L. 1 (2002).

Case Law

ALS Scan, Inc. v. Digital Serv. Consultants, Inc., 293 F. 3d 707 (D.C. Cir. 2002).

American Charities for Reasonable Fundraising Regulation, Inc. v. Pinellas County, 32 F. Supp. 2d 1308 (M.D. Fla. 1998), *aff'd* in part, *vacated* and *remanded* in part 221 F.3d 1211 (11th Cir. 2000).

GTE New Media Sources, Inc. v. Bell South 199 F. 3d 1343 (D.C. Cir. 2000).

Gorman v. Ameritrade Holding Corp., 293 F.3d 506, 512 (D.C. Cir. 2002).

Vinten v. Jeantot Marine Alliances, S.A., 191 F. Supp. 2d 642 (D.D.C. 2002).

Young v. New Haven Advocate, 315 F.3d 256 (D.C. Cir. 2002).

Statutory and Other Authority

I.R.C. § 170(f), 6113(c), 6115.

Charleston Principles (developed by National Association of Attorneys General and the National Association of State Charities Officials), available from NASCONET at <www.nasconet.org>.

Investment

Bibliography

Paul U. Ali, *Charitable Trusts and Hedge Funds,* 11 J. INT'L TR. & CORP. PLAN. 187 (2004).

Dominic L. Daher, *Unrelated Business Income Tax: Can a "Blocker" Entity Take the "Debt-Financed" Out of Investment Income?,* 17 TAX'N EXEMPTS 46 (2005).

Harvey P. Dale, *Nonprofit Directors and Officers—Duties and Liabilities for Investment Decisions, in* 22 NYU TAX PLAN. 501(C)(3) ORG., Ch. 4 (1994).

Harvey P. Dale & Michael Gwinnell, *Time for Change: Charity Investment and Modern Portfolio Theory,* 3 CHARITY L. & PRAC. REV. 89 (1995).

ROBERT P. FRY, JR. & ROBERT P. FRY, MINDING THE MONEY: AN INVESTMENT GUIDE FOR NONPROFIT BOARD MEMBERS (BoardSource 2004).

ROGER C. GIBSON, ASSET ALLOCATION: BALANCING FINANCIAL RISK (Irwin Professional Publishing 1996).

EDWARD C. HALBACH, JR., *Trust Investment Law in the Third Restatement,* 77 IOWA L. REV. 1151(1992).

Alan S. Halperin & Rachel J. Harris, *Investment Guidelines for Private Foundation Managers,* 30 EST. PLAN. (WGL) 542 (2003).

CHARLES P. JONES, INVESTMENTS: ANALYSIS AND MANAGEMENT (6th ed., John Wiley and Sons 1998).

Michael Klausner, *When Time Isn't Money: Foundation Payout Rates and the Time Value of Money,* STAN SOC. INNOVATION REV., Spring 2003, at 50.

Ronald R. Jordan & Katelyn L. Quynn, *Nonprofit Investment Policies and Procedures* in PLANNED GIVING: MANAGEMENT, MARKETING, AND LAW (3d ed. Jossey-Bass 2004).

John H. Langbein, *Reversing the Nondelegation Rule of Trust Investment Law,* 59 MISSOURI L. REV. 105 (1994).

John H. Langbein, *The Uniform Prudent Investor Act and the Future of Trust Investing,* 81 IOWA L. REV. 641 (1996).

BEVIS LONGSTRETH, MODERN INVESTMENT MANAGEMENT AND THE PRUDENT MAN RULE (Oxford University Press 1986).

Douglas Moore & Ajay Badlani, *Investment Challenges for Private Foundations,* TR. & EST., June 2005, at 46.

Douglas Moore & Mitchell K. Higgins, *Planning and Investing Strategies for Private Foundations,* 15 TAX'N EXEMPTS 156 (2004).

Jane C. Nober, *The Law on Conflicts: Part III: Financial Managers and Investments,* FOUNDATION NEWS & COMMENTARY, Supplement 2005, at 5.

Paul Palmer, et al., SOCIALLY RESPONSIBLE INVESTMENT: A GUIDE FOR PENSION SCHEMES AND CHARITIES (Charles Scanlan ed., 2005).

W. Brantley Phillips, Jr., *Chasing Down the Devil: Standards of Prudent Investment Under the Restatement (Third) of Trusts,* 54 WASHINGTON & LEE L. REV. 335 (1997).

Richard L. Schmalbeck, *Reconsidering Private Foundation Investment Limitations,* 58 TAX L. REV. 59 (2004).

WILLIAM SCHNEIDER, ROBERT DIMEO, & CLARK D. ROBINSON, ASSET MANAGEMENT FOR ENDOWMENTS AND FOUNDATIONS (McGraw-Hill 1997).

William Spitz, Selecting and Evaluating an Investment Manager (Financial Management Guide Book Series, 1) (National Association of College and University Business Officers 1992).

Marlene Givant Star, *Yale Endowment Leaves Tradition Behind,* Pensions and Investments (Apr. 15, 1996).

David F. Swensten, Pioneering Portfolio Management: An Unconventional Approach to Institutional Investment (The Free Press 2000).

Case Law

Carl J. Herzog Foundation v. University of Bridgeport, 699 A. 2d 995, Conn. 1997.

In re Will of James, 223 A.D. 2d 20 (1996).

Statutory and Other Authority

Employee Retirement Income Security Act of 1974 ("ERISA").

Internal Revenue Code § 4944 and the regulations thereunder.

Restatement of the Law of Trusts (Third), American Law Institute (1992).

Uniform Management of Institutional Funds Act (1972) and Uniform Prudent Management of Institutional Funds Act (2006).

Uniform Principal and Income Act, 1997.

Uniform Prudent Investor Act.

Internet Sites

SmithBarney Consulting Group: The Prudent Fiduciary: Understanding the Legal Responsibilities of Charitable Trustees and Directors, <https://www.smithbarney.com/pdf/products_services/consulting_group/Prudent_Fiduciary.pdf>.

Joint Ventures

Bibliography

John D. Colombo, *A Framework for Analyzing Exemption on UBIT Effects of Joint Ventures,* 34 Exempt Org. Tax Rev. 187 (2001).

Thomas M. Dalton, *Structuring Joint Ventures Between For-Profit and Tax-Exempt Entities,* Bus. Entities, Jan./Feb. 2005, at 32.

Gerald M. Griffin, *Redefining Joint Venture Control Requirements: St. David's v. Goliath,* 37 Exempt Org. Tax Rev. 255 (2002).

Darryll K. Jones, *Tax Article: Special Allocations and Preferential Distributions in Joint Ventures Involving Taxable and Tax Exempt Entities,* 31 Ohio N.U. L. Rev. 13 (2005).

Patrick Plunkett & Heidi Neff Christianson, *The Quest for Cash: Exempt Organizations, Joint Ventures, Taxable Subsidiaries and Unrelated Business Income,* 31 WM. MITCHELL L. REV. 1 (2004).

Michael I. Sanders, *Health Care Joint Ventures Between Tax-Exempt Organizations and For-Profit Entities,* 15 HEALTH MATRIX: J. L.-MED. 83 (2005).

Michael I. Sanders, *The Impact of Rev. Rul. 2004-51 on Ancillary Joint Ventures,* 16 TAX'N EXEMPTS 99 (2004).

MICHAEL I. SANDERS, JOINT VENTURES INVOLVING TAX-EXEMPT ORGANIZATIONS (2d ed. Wiley 2002).

Michael I. Sanders, *Update on Joint Ventures,* PAUL STRECKFUS' EO TAX J., Mar./Apr. 2006, at 43.

Pamela C. Smith, *An Empirical Investigation of For-Profit and Tax-Exempt Nonprofit Hospitals Engaged in Joint Ventures,* 29 HEALTH CARE MGMT. REV. 284 (2004).

Gary J. Young, *Federal Tax-Exemption Requirements For Joint Ventures Between Nonprofit Hospital Providers and For-Profit Entities: Form over Substance?,* 13 ANNALS HEALTH L. 327 (2004).

Case Law

Plumstead Theater Soc., Inc. v. Inc. Comm. 74 T.C. 1324 (1980), *aff'd* 675 F.2d 244, (9th Cir. 1982).

Redlands Surgical Services v. Commissioner 242 F. 3d 904 (9th Cir. 2001).

St. David's Health Care System, Inc. v. United States, 439 F.3d 232 (5th Cir. 2003).

Statutory & Other Authority

Internal Revenue Code § 512 (b)(13).

Internet Sites

The Prudent Fiduciary: Understanding the Legal Responsibilities of Charitable Trustees and Directors, available at <www.salomonsmithbarney.com/pdf/products_services/consulting_group/Prudent_Fiduciary.pdf>.

Lobbying

Bibliography

Heidi K. Abegg, *Election Year Issues for Exempt Organizations,* NON-PROFIT LEGAL & TAX LETTER, May 2004, at Special Report 1.

Marcia Avner, THE LOBBYING AND ADVOCACY HANDBOOK FOR NON-PROFIT ORGANIZATIONS: SHAPING PUBLIC POLICY AT THE STATE AND LOCAL LEVEL (Fieldstone Alliance 2002).

Jeffrey M. Berry, *Nonprofits and Civic Engagement*, 65 PUB. ADMIN. REV. 568 (2005).

Rob Boston, *Render Unto Caesar . . . IRS Commissioner Tells Tax-Exempt Churches: Thou Shalt Not Electioneer,* CHURCH & ST., Apr. 2006, at 4.

Lori Brainard & Jennifer M. Brinkerhoff, *Lost in Cyberspace: Shedding Light on the Dark Matter of Grassroots Organizations,* 33 NONPROFIT & VOLUNTARY SECTOR Q. 32S (2004).

Richard Briffault, *The 527 Problem . . . and the Buckley Problem,* 73 GEO. WASH. L. REV. 949 (2005).

GREGORY L. COLVIN & LOWELL FINLEY, THE RULES OF THE GAME: AN ELECTION YEAR LEGAL GUIDE FOR NONPROFIT ORGANIZATIONS (Alliance for Justice 1996).

Douglas H. Cook, THE POLITICALLY ACTIVE CHURCH, 35 LOY. U. CHI. L. J. 457 (2004).

Jason Y. Hall, *Lobbying for Arts and Culture: From the Culture Wars to the Rise of New Issues,* 35 J. ARTS MGMT. L. & SOC'Y 227 (2005).

Gail M. Harmon, Jessica A. Ladel, & Eleanor A. Evans, *Being a Player—A Guide to the IRS Lobbying Regulations for Advocacy Charities.* (The Advocacy Forum 1995).

INDEPENDENT SECTOR, CHARITY LOBBYING: YOU CAN DO IT (2000).

INDEPENDENT SECTOR, PLAYING BY THE RULES: HANDBOOK ON VOTER PARTICIPATION AND EDUCATION WORK FOR 501 (C)(3) ORGANIZATIONS (1998).

LEAGUE OF WOMEN VOTERS, FACE TO FACE: A GUIDE TO CANDIDATE DEBATES (1996).

Gregg D. Polsky & Guy-Uriel E. Charles, *Regulating Section 527 Organizations,* 73 GEO. WASH. L. REV. 1000 (2005).

Jerome Park Prather, *Tax Exemption of American Churches and Other Nonprofits: One election cycle after . . .* 94 KY. L.J. 139–160 (2005–2006).

BOB SMUCKER, THE NONPROFIT LOBBYING GUIDE (2d ed. Independent Sector 1999).

JOHN D. SPARKS, LOBBYING, ADVOCACY AND NONPROFIT BOARDS (National Center for Nonprofit Boards 1997).

TUFTS UNIVERSITY, OMB WATCH, AND CHARITY LOBBYING IN THE PUBLIC INTEREST, STRENGTHENING NONPROFIT ADVOCACY PROJECT: OVERVIEW OF FINDINGS (2002).

Sheila Warren & Rosemary E. Fei, *Politics and Lobbying: Lobbying Clauses in Grant Agreements with Organizational Grantees,* 19 TAX'N EXEMPTS 236 (2006).

Stanley S. Weithorn, *Practitioners' Planning Guide to the New Lobbying Rules for Public Charities,* JOURNAL OF TAXATION (1977).

Stanley S. Weithorn & Douglas F. Allen, *Taxation and the Advocacy Role of Churches in Public Affairs, Baylor University Symposium on the Role of Government in Monitoring and Regulating Religion in Public Life,* J.M. DAWSON INSTITUTE OF CHURCH-STATE STUDIES, Baylor University, 1993.

WORRY-FREE LOBBYING FOR NONPROFITS: HOW TO USE THE 501 (H) ELECTION TO MAXIMIZE EFFECTIVENESS (Alliance for Justice 2003, reprint).

Case Law

American Society of Association Executives v. United States, 195 F.3d 47 (D.C. Cir. 1999).

Christian Echoes Nat'l. Ministry, Inc. v United States, 470 F.2d 849 (10th Cir. 1972).

Haswell v. United States, 500 F. 2d 1133 (Ct. Cl. 1974), *cert. denied* 419 U.S. 1107 (1975).

Regan v. Taxation Without Representation of Washington, 461 U.S. 540 (1983).

Seasongood v. Commissioner, 227 F. 2d 907 (6th Cir. 1955).

Statutory and Other Authority

IRC §§501(h), 527, 4911, 4955.

Internet Sites

Alliance for Justice (www.afj.org), a national association of advocacy organizations working to advance the public interest community's ability to influence public policy.

Charity Lobbying in the Public Interest (http://www.clpi.org/), a project of Independent Sector whose principal purpose is to educate charities about the important and appropriate role lobbying can play in achieving their missions.

Independent Sector (http://www.independentsector.org/), a national leadership forum fostering private initiative for the public good.

IRS, homepage for Internal Revenue Service (http://www.irs.gov/), offers access to forms and publications as well as articles on tax-exempt organizations.

OMB Watch (http://www.ombwatch.org/), monitors activities of the White House Office of Management and Business, budget and governance performance issues, nonprofit advocacy and nonprofit policy and technology.

National Fair Housing Alliance: Lobbying Expenditures Guidance for Non-Profit 501 (c)(3) Organizations (http://www .nationalfairhousing.org/data/Lobbying_Expenditures_501C3.pdf).

Marketing

Bibliography

Alan R. Andreasen, et al., T*ransferring "Marketing Knowledge" to the Nonprofit Sector,* CAL. MGMT. REV., Summer 2005, at 46.

Roger Bennett, *Guest Editorial: Advances in Nonprofit Marketing,* 11 INT'L J. NONPROFIT & VOLUNTARY SECTOR MARKETING 89 (2006).

Jerr Boschee, *Social Entrepreneurship: Transformation of Nonprofit Organizations into Social Purpose Business Ventures,* ACROSS THE BOARD (March 1995 at 20).

Henry N. Butler & Fred McChesney: *Why They Give at the Office: Shareholder Welfare and Corporate Philanthropy in the Contractual Theory of the Corporation,* 84 CORNELL L. REV. 1195 (1999).

J. Gregory Dees, *Enterprising Nonprofits,* HARV. BUS. REV., JAN.-Feb. 1998, at 55.

SIRI N. ESPY, MARKETING STRATEGIES FOR NONPROFIT ORGANIZATIONS (Lyceum 1992).

Angela M. Eikenberry & Jodie Drapal Kluver, *The Marketization of the Nonprofit Sector: Civil Society at Risk?,* 64 PUB. ADMIN. REV. 132 (2004).

Marjorie A. Houston, ed., Marketing the Value of Charitable Gift Annuities: A Strategy for Building Relationships Among Gift Planners, Donors and the CFO, J. GIFT PLAN., Mar. 2005, at 5.

Neil Kotler & Philip Kotler, *Museum Strategy and Marketing* (JOSSEY-BASS 1998).

PHILIP KOTLER & HAROLD T. MARTIN, A GENERIC CONCEPT OF MARKETING, IN INSIGHTS FOR MARKETING MANAGEMENT (Gabriel M. & Betsy D. Gelb, eds., Goodyear 1974).

Philip Kotler & Gerald Zaltman, *Social Marketing: An Approach to Planned Social Change,* J. OF MARKETING, Jan. 1969, at 33.

Ely Levy and Norman I. Silber, *Nonprofit Fundraising and Consumer Protection: A Donor's Right to Privacy,* 15 STAN. L. & POL'Y REV. 519 (2004).

GARY J. STERN, MARKETING WORKBOOK FOR NONPROFIT ORGANIZATIONS, VOL. 1: DEVELOP THE PLAN, (2nd ed. Amherst H. Wilder Foundation 2001).

GARY J. STERN, MARKETING WORKBOOK FOR NONPROFIT ORGANIZATIONS, VOL. II: MOBILIZE PEOPLE FOR MARKETING SUCCESS (Amherst H. Wilder Foundation 1997).

Jeremy Thornton, *Nonprofit Fund-Raising in Competitive Donor Markets,* 35 NONPROFIT & VOLUNTARY SECTOR Q. 204 (2006).

Internet Sites

Free management library, provides information about organizational development to managers of both for-profit and nonprofit organizations, <http://www.managementhelp.org/mrktng/mrktng.htm>.
Action without Boarders (idealist.org) publishes the "Nonprofit FAQ," resources provided by participants in online discussions, <http://www.nonprofits.org/npofaq/keywords/2n.html>.

Membership

Bibliography

Avner Ben-Nev & Theresa Van Hoomissen, *The Governance of Nonprofit Organizations: Law and Public Policy,* 4 NONPROFIT MANAGEMENT & LEADERSHIP 393(1994).
Evelyn Brody, *Entrance, Voice and Exit: The Constitutional Bounds of the Right of Association* 35 U.C.-DAVIS L. REV. 821 (2002).
Zachariah Chafee, Jr., *The Internal Affairs of Associations Not for Profit,* 43 HARV. L. REV. 993 (1930).
HOWARD L. OLECK & MARTHA E. STEWART, NONPROFIT CORPORATIONS, ORGANIZATIONS AND ASSOCIATIONS § 355 at 901 (6th ed. 1994).
Dana Brakman Reiser, *Dismembering Civil Society: The Social Cost of Internally Undemocratic Nonprofits,* 82 OR. LAW REV. 829 (2003).
Dana Brakman Reizer, *Decision-Makers Without Duties: Defining the Duties of Parent Corporations Acting as Sole Corporate Members in Nonprofit Health Care Systems,* 53 RUTGERS L. REV. 979 (2001).
NANCY L. ROSENBLUM, MEMBERSHIP AND MORALS: THE PERSONAL USES OF PLURALISM IN AMERICA (Princeton Univ. Press 1998).
Theda Skocpol, *Advocates Without Members: The Recent Transformation of American Civic Life in American Democracy 461 in* CIVIC ENGAGEMENT (Theda Skocpol & Morris P. Fiorina, eds., 1999).
Alix Slater, *Revisiting Membership Scheme Typologies in Museums and Galleries,* 9 INT'L J. NONPROFIT & VOLUNTARY SECTOR MARKETING 238 (2004).

Case Law

Bernstein v. Alameda-Contra Costa Med. Assoc., 293 P.2d 862 (Cal. App. 1956).

Board of Directors of Rotary International v. Rotary Club of Duarte 481 U.S. 537 (1987).

Boy Scouts of America v. Dale, 530 U.S. 640 (2000).

Chambers of Commerce v. Fed. Election Commission, 69 F.3d 600 (D.C. Cir., 1995).

Dawkins v. Antrobus, 17 Ch. D. 615 (Ct. of App. 1881).

Falcone v. Middlesex County Med. Soc'y, 162 A.2d 324, *aff'd,* 170 A.2d 791 (N.J. 1961).

Fitzgerald v. National Rifle Association, 383 F. Supp. 162 (D.C.N.J. 1.974).

Hurley v. Irish-American Gay, Lesbian and Bisexual Group of Boston 515 U.S. 557 (1997).

Lambert v. Fishermen's Dock Coop., Inc., 297 A.2d 566 (N.J. 1972).

New York State Club Assoc. v. City of New York 487 U.S. 1. (1987).

Owen v. Rosicrucian Fellowship, 342 P.2d 424 (Cal. Ct. App. 1959).

Roberts v. United States Jaycees, 468 U.S. 609 (1984).

Statutory and Other Authority

Revised Model Nonprofit Corporation Act §§ 6.30(a), 7.01–7.30.

Mergers and Consolidations (Other Than Healthcare)

Bibliography

David L. Forst, et al., *No Loss of Exemption and No Gain Recognition on Mergers of Tax-Exempt Organizations,* 103 J. TAX'N 375 (2005).

Garry W. Jenkins, *The Powerful Possibilities of Nonprofit Mergers: Supporting Strategic Consolidation through Law and Public Policy,* 74 S.CAL.L.REV. 1089 (2001).

DAVID LAPIANA, NONPROFIT MERGERS WORKBOOK: THE LEADER'S GUIDE TO CONSIDERING, NEGOTIATING AND EXECUTING A MERGER (Amherst H. Wilder Foundation 2000).

MCLAUGHLIN, THOMAS A.: NONPROFIT MERGERS & ALLIANCES: A STRATEGIC PLANNING GUIDE. (John Wiley & Sons 1998).

ELIOT SPITZER, NEW YORK ATTORNEY GENERAL, A GUIDE TO MERGERS AND CONSOLIDATIONS OF NOT-FOR-PROFIT CORPORATIONS UNDER ARTICLE 9 OF THE NEW YORK NOT-FOR-PROFIT CORPORATION LAW (2004).

Case Law

Rose Ocho Foundation Inc. v. Lebovits 686 N.Y.S. 2d 861 (2d dept. 1999).

Internet Sites

Strategic Solutions, foundation funded initiative dedicated to promoting the understanding and use of strategic restructuring by organizations, <http://www.lapiana.org>.

Minutes

Bibliography

American Society of Corporate Secretaries, *Corporate Minutes: A Monograph for the Corporate Secretary* (2002), available at <www.ascs.org>.

ANTHONY MANCUSO, THE CORPORATE MINUTE BOOK: THE LEGAL GUIDE TO TAKING CARE OF CORPORATE BUSINESS (Nolo Press 2002).

Case Law

U.S. v. Rockford Mem'l Corp., 898 F.2d 1278 (7th Cir. 1990), *cert. denied,* 498 U.S. 920 (2002).

Mission Statements

Bibliography

ANGELICA EMIL, WILDER NONPROFIT FIELD GUIDE TO: CRAFTING EFFECTIVE MISSION & VISION STATEMENTS (Amherst H. Wilder Foundation 2001).

PETER C. BRINKERHOFF, MISSION BASED MANAGEMENT: AN ORGANIZATIONAL DEVELOPMENT WORKBOOK with CD Rom, (2nd ed. The Alliance for Nonprofit Management 2000).

Internet Sites

The Foundation Center, bibliography, and Internet links for information on, and examples of, mission statements, <foundationcenter.org/getstarted/faqs/html/mission_statements.html>.

Nominating Committee

Bibliography

ELLEN COCHRAN HIRZY, NONPROFIT BOARD COMMITTEES: HOW TO MAKE THEM WORK (National Center for Nonprofit Boards 1993).
ELLEN COCHRAN HIRZY, THE NOMINATING COMMITTEE: LAYING A FOUNDATION FOR YOUR ORGANIZATION'S FUTURE (National Center for Nonprofit Boards 1994).

Case Law

Fitzgerald v. National Rifle Assoc., 983 F. Supp. 162 (O.N.J. 1974).

Orientation (Board Training)

Bibliography

PRESENTING: BOARD ORIENTATION (CD AND USER'S GUIDE): AN INTRODUCTORY PRESENTATION FOR NONPROFIT BOARD MEMBERS (BoardSource 2001).
HILDY GOTTLIEB, BOARD RECRUITMENT & ORIENTATION: A STEP-BY-STEP, COMMON SENSE GUIDE (Renaissance Press 2001).
HEALTH RESEARCH AND EDUCATION TRUST, WELCOME TO THE BOARD! AN ORIENTATION FOR THE NEW HEALTH CARE TRUSTEE (American Hospital Publishing 1999).
CYRUS F. FREIDHEIM, PREPARING YOUR NEW DIRECTORS (Directors and Boards Winter 1995).
STEPHANIE R. JOVENER, THE VALUE OF BOARD TRAINING, IN CORPORATE LAW AND PRACTICE COURSE HANDBOOK (Practising Law Institute, Sept./Oct. 1999).

Internet Sites

Ginsler & Associates, Inc., *The Effective Board Member's Orientation Manual, 2000,* <www.ginsler.com/documents/bdman.pdf>.

BoardSource, *Meeting the Challenge: An Orientation to Nonprofit Board Service,* <www.boardsource.org/UserFiles/File/principles.pdf>.

Planned Giving

Bibliography

DEBRA ASHTON, THE COMPLETE GUIDE TO PLANNED GIVING (rev. 3d ed. 2004).

RICHARD D. BARRETT, PLANNED GIVING ESSENTIALS, A STEP-BY-STEP GUIDE TO SUCCESS (2d ed. Aspen 2002).

Jeffrey W. Comfort & Scott R. Lumpkin, *A Practical Approach to Valuing Planned Gifts,* 2004 NATIONAL COMMITTEE ON PLANNED GIVING CONFERENCE PROCEEDINGS 43 (2004).

THE ESTATE TAX AND CHARITABLE GIVING (CONG. BUDGET OFFICE July 2004).

DAVID DONALDSON & CAROLYN OSTEEN, HARVARD MANUAL ON TAX ASPECTS OF CHARITABLE GIVING (8th ed. Ropes & Gray 1999).

Robin R. Ganzert & Charles O. Mahaffey, *Spirit of Sarbanes-Oxley: Relevance of Nonprofit Governance on Planned Giving Fundraising Efforts, in* 2004 NATIONAL COMMITTEE ON PLANNED GIVING CONFERENCE PROCEEDINGS 541 (2004).

GRANT THORNTON, PLANNED GIVING, A BOARD MEMBER'S PERSPECTIVE, (BoardSource, rev. 2003).

Mary C. Hester, *Using Charitable Planned Gifts in Estate Planning to Maximize Tax-Efficient Results,* 104 J. TAX'N 94 (2006).

Ronald R. Jordan & Karelyn L. Quynn, PLANNED GIVING FOR SMALL ORGANIZATIONS (John Wiley & Sons, Inc. 2002).

Thomas J. Ray, Jr., CHARITABLE GIFT PLANNING (ABA Real Property, Probate and Trust Law Section 2006).

Conrad Teitell, *Planned Gifts Under the New Tax Law,* TR. & EST., Sept. 2003, at 46.

JOSEPH P. TOCE, JR. et al., TAX ECONOMICS OF CHARITABLE GIVING 2005/2006 (Warren, Gorham & Lamont 2005).

A.B. TUELLER, PRACTICAL GUIDE TO PLANNED GIVING, 1994 (Taft Group 1993).

STANLEY S. WEITHORN, ALMS AND THE MAN: MATCHING NEW TECHNIQUES TO OLD IDEAS, NEW YORK UNIVERSITY 16TH INSTITUTE ON CHARITABLE ORGANIZATIONS (Matthew Bender & Company, Inc. 1988).

STANLEY S. WEITHORN, CHARITABLE GIVING AS AN ESTATE PLANNING TOOL—THE 8TH ANNUAL UCLA-CEB ESTATE PLANNING INSTITUTE (1986).

Stanley S. Weithorn, *The Charitable Lead Nonreversionary Trust—
An Estate Planner's Dream Come True,* EXEMPT ORG. TAX REV.,
April 2002.

STANLEY S. WEITHORN, SPECIAL TECHNIQUES FOR CHARITABLE
GIVING: MAKING THE MOST OF THE UNUSUAL-44TH NYU
INSTITUTE ON FEDERAL TAXATION, 1986.

STANLEY S. WEITHORN, USING THE CHARITABLE REMAINDER TRUST AS
A SOPHISTICATED CONTRIBUTION TECHNIQUE, 43D NYU INSTITUTE
ON FEDERAL TAXATION, 1985.

STANLEY S. WEITHORN, USING CHARITABLE SPLIT-INTEREST TRUSTS
TO ACHIEVE ESTATE PLANNING GOALS: CASE STUDIES—
UNIVERSITY OF SOUTHEN CALIFORNIA 45TH ANNUAL INSTITUTE ON
FEDERAL TAXATION, JANUARY, 1993.

CYNTHIA WILSON KRAUSE & BETSY A. MANGONE, HOW TO
SUCCESSFULLY NAVIGATE THE PLANNED GIVING PARADIGM SHIFT,
IN 2004 NATIONAL COMMITTEE ON PLANNED GIVING CONFERENCE
PROCEEDINGS 389 (2004).

AL ZIMMERMAN, PLANNED GIVING POLICIES: AVOIDING THE PERILS OF
GIFT PLANNING, IN 2004 NATIONAL COMMITTEE ON PLANNED
GIVING CONFERENCE PROCEEDINGS 613 (2004).

Internet Sites

National Committee on Planned Giving, professional association for
individuals and organizations whose work includes developing
and administering charitable planned gifts, available at
<http://www.ncpg.org>.

Online Compendium of Federal and State Regulations for U.S.
Nonprofit Organizations, Charitable Donations Through Planned
Gifts, available at <http://www.muridae.com/nporegulation/
planned_giving.html>.

Planned Giving Coach, provides free access to marketing ideas,
model letters, policy statements, action plans and gift descrip-
tions, available at <http://www.plannedgivingcoach.com>.

Pledges

Bibliography

Evelyn Brody, *The Charity in Bankruptcy and Ghosts of Donors
Past, Present, and Future,* 29 SETON HALL LEGIS. J. 471 (2005).

Mary Frances Butig, Gordon T. Butler, & Lynne M. Murphy,
*Pledges to Nonprofit Organizations: Are They Enforceable and
Must They Be Enforced?* 27 U.S. F.L.R. 47 (1992).

Lack of Consideration as Baring Enforcement of Promises to Make Charitable Contribution or Subscription: Modern Cases, 86 A.L.R. 4th 241 (1991).

Case Law

Allegheny College v. National Chautauqua Bank, 159 N.E. 173 (N.Y., 1927).

Congregation Kadimah Toras-Moshe v. DeLeo, 540 N.E. 2d 691 (Mass 1989).

Woodmere Academy v. Steinberg, 363 N. E. 2d 1169 (N.Y., 1977).

Political Activities and Organizations

Bibliography

Ellen P. Aprill, *Churches, Politics, and the Charitable Contribution Deduction,* 42 B.C. L. REV. 843 (2001).

Jeffrey M. Berry, *Nonprofits and Civic Engagement,* 65 PUB. ADMIN. REV. 568 (2005).

Rob Boston, *Render Unto Caesar . . . IRS Commissioner Tells Tax-Exempt Churches: Thou Shalt Not Electioneer,* CHURCH & ST., Apr. 2006, at 4.

Richard Briffault, *The 527 Problem . . . and the Buckley Problem,* 73 GEO. WASH. L. REV. 949 (2005).

Johnny Rex Buckles, *Reforming the Public Policy Doctrine,* 53 KAN. L. REV. 397 (2005).

William H. Byrnes IV, *The Private Foundation's Topsy Turvy Road in the American Political Process,* 4 HOUS. BUS. & TAX L.J. 496 (2004).

Gregory L. Colvin, *How Well Does the Tax Code Work in Regulating Politics?* 12 J. TAX'N EXEMPT ORG. (WGL) 66 (2001).

Gregory L. Colvin, *Long-Awaited Clues to IRS Views on Election Rules,* 14 TAX'N EXEMPTS 42 (2002).

Gregory L. Colvin & David A. Levitt, *Political Organization Reporting Requirements Continue to Evolve: Recent Amendments to Internal Revenue Code Section 527,* 39 EXEMPT ORG. TAX REV. 337 (2003).

Douglas H. Cook, *The Politically Active Church,* 35 LOY. U. CHI. L. J. 457 (2004).

DEIRDRE DESSINGUE, POLITICS AND THE PULPIT: A GUIDE TO THE INTERNAL REVENUE CODE RESTRICTIONS ON THE POLITICAL ACTIVITY OF RELIGIOUS ORGANIZATIONS (Pew Forum on Religion & Public Life, 2004).

Alan L. Feld, *Rendering Unto Caesar or Electioneering for Caesar? Loss of Church Tax Exemption for Participation in Electoral Politics,* 42 B.C. L. REV. 931 (2001).

Theodore Garrett, *Federal Tax Limitations on Political Activities of Public Interest and Educational Organizations,* 59 GEO. L. JL. 561 (1971).

Probing the Limits of Section 527 to Design a New Campaign Finance Vehicle, 22 EXEMPT ORG. TAX REV. 205 (1998).

Frances R. Hill, *Softer Money: Exempt Organizations and Campaign Finance,* 32 EXEMPT ORG. TAX REV. 27 (2001).

JOINT COMM. ON TAX'N: DESCRIPTION OF PRESENT-LAW RULES RELATING TO POLITICAL AND OTHER ACTIVITIES OF ORGANIZATIONS DESCRIBED IN SECTION 501(C)(3) AND PROPOSALS REGARDING CHURCHES (2002).

Judith E. Kindell & John Francis Reilly, *Election Year Issues,* EXEMPT ORG. CONTINUING PROFESSIONAL EDU. TECH. INSTRUCTION PROGRAM FOR 2002 § I (2001).

Lloyd H. Mayer, *Political Activities of Tax-Exempt Organizations— Useful Guidance in Rev. Rul. 2004-6,* 100 J. TAX'N 181 (2004).

Robert Paul Meir, *The Darker Side of Nonprofits: When Charities and Social Welfare Groups Become Political Slush Funds* 147 PA L. R. 971 (1999).

Gregg D. Polsky & Guy-Uriel E. Charles, *Regulating Section 527 Organizations,* 73 GEO. WASH. L. REV. 1000 (2005).

Jack B. Siegel, *The Wild, the Innocent, and the K Street Shuffle: The Tax System's Role in Policing Interactions Between Charities and Politicians,* EXEMPT ORG. TAX REV. (Nov. 2006).

Statute, Campaign Finance Reform-Issue Advocacy Organizations— Congress Mandates Contribution and Expenditure Requirements for Section 527 Organizations—Act of July 1, 2000, Pub. L. No. 106230, 114 Stat. 477, 114 HARV. L. REV. 2209 (2001).

Martin A. Sullivan, *More Disclosure from 501(c)'s: Poison Pill a Good Policy,* 29 EXEMPT ORG. TAX REV. 10 (2000).

Case Law

Branch Ministries v. Rossotti, 211 F. 3d 137 (D.C. Ct. of App. 2000).

Christian Echoes National Ministry, Inc. v. U.S. 470 F.2d 849 (10th Cir. 1972).

Federal Election Commission v. Beaumont, 123 S.Ct. 2200 (2003).

McConnell v. Federal Election Commission, 12 U.S. Ct. 619 (Dec. 10, 2003).

Norris v. U.S., 86 F. 2d 379, 382 (8th Cir. 1936, *rev'd on other grounds,* 300 U.S. 564 (1937).

New Faith, Inc. v. Commissioner, 64 T.C.M. 1050 (1992).

U.S. v. Dykema, 666 F.2d 1096, 1101 (7th Cir. 1981) (*cert. denied,* 465 U.S. 983 (1982).

Statutory and Other Authority

I.R.C. §501(h), 162(e), 501(c)(4).

IRS Forms 5768, 8871, 8872, 1120 POL.

Statute, Campaign Finance Reform—Issue Advocacy Organizations-Congress Mandates Contribution and Expenditure Requirements for Section 527 Organizations—Act of July 1, 2000, Pub. L. No. 106230, 114 Stat. 477, 114 HARV L. REV. 2209 (2001).

Internet Sites

National Association for the Education of Young Children Office of Affiliate Relations, Nonprofit Organizations and Lobbying, Political Activity, and Voter Education, available at <www.naeyc.org/affiliates/acb/chapter7.pdf>.

The IRS's Political Organization Home Page, available at <www.irs.gov/charities/political/index.html>.

The IRS's Most Recent Published Guidance on Political Activities, available at <www.irs.gov/pub/irs-drop/rr-04-6.pdf>.

The IRS's Most Recent CPE on Political Activities of 501(c)(4)s, (5)s and (6)s, available at <www.irs.gov/pub/irs-tege/eotopicl03.pdf>.

The IRS's Comprehensive CPE on political Activities, in Q&A format, available at <www.irs.gov/irs-tegetopici02.pdf>.

The Federal Election Commission (note especially the campaign guides and links to laws), available at <www.fec.gov>.

The Campaign Legal Center's home page, available at <campaignlegalcenter.org/index.html>.

The Campaign Legal Center's link pages for reference documents, available at <www.campaignlegalcenter.org/reference.html>.

Bob Bauer's Guide to Campaign Finance Law, available at <softmoneyhardlaw.com>.

Mac Canter's Brief Summary of Relevant Rules, available at <www.exempttaxlaw.com/CM/Articles/articles15.asp>.

Independent Sector's Chart of Relevant Rules, available at <www.independentsector.org/PDFs/campfin.pdf>.

Private Foundations

(See also: Donor-Advised Funds; Supporting Organizations)

Bibliography

Alane L. Boffa, *Disclaimers and Private Foundations,* 36 TAX ADVISER 459 (2005).

Victoria B. Bjorklund, *Charitable Giving to a Private Foundation: The Alternatives, The Supporting Organizations and the Donor-Advised Fund,* 27 EXEMPT ORG. TAX REV. 107 (2000).

LAUREN WATSON CESARE, PRIVATE FOUNDATIONS AND PUBLIC CHARITIES (Tax Management 2003).

Carolyn C. Clark & Glenn M. Troost, *Forming a Foundation: Trust vs. Corporation* 3 PROB. & PROP. 32 (May/June 1989).

COMMONFUND INSTITUTE, THE COMMONFUND BENCHMARKS STUDY ON FOUNDATIONS (2004).

Francesca Di Gregori Boschini, *Private Foundations and Reserved Powers Trusts,* TR. & EST., Apr. 2006, at 46.

JOHN A. EDIE, BEYOND OUR BORDERS: A GUIDE TO MAKING GRANTS OUTSIDE THE U.S. (Council on Foundations 2002).

JOHN A. EDIE, EXPENDITURE RESPONSIBILITY STEP BY STEP (Council on Foundations 2002).

JOHN A. EDIE, Family, Foundations and the Law: What You Need to Know (3d ed., Council on Foundations 2002).

JOHN A. EDIE, FIRST STEPS IN STARTING A FOUNDATION, FIFTH EDITION (Council on Foundations 2005).

Marion R. Fremont-Smith, *Is It Time to Treat Private Foundations and Public Charities Alike?,* 52 EXEMPT ORG. TAX REV. 257 (2006).

Alan S. Halperin & Rachel J. Harris, *Investment Guidelines for Private Foundation Managers,* 30 EST. PLAN. (WGL) 542 (2003).

Jeanne M. Hauch, *The Role of the Charitable and Educational Foundations in Corporate Control Transactions,* 27 U.S.F.L. REV. 19 (1992).

BRUCE R. HOPKINS & JODY BLAZEK, THE LEGAL ANSWER BOOK FOR PRIVATE FOUNDATIONS (Wiley 2002).

BRUCE R. HOPKINS & JODY BLAZEK, PRIVATE FOUNDATIONS: TAX LAW AND COMPLIANCE (2d ed. Wiley 2003).

BRUCE R. HOPKINS & JODY BLAZEK, PRIVATE FOUNDATIONS: TAX LAW AND COMPLIANCE, 2006 CUMULATIVE SUPPLEMENT (2d ed. Wiley 2006).

Michael Klausner, *When Time Isn't Money: Foundation Payout Rates and the Time Value of Money,* STAN. SOC. INNOVATION REV., Spring 2003, at 50.

KATHRYN W. MIREE & JERRY McCOY, FAMILY FOUNDATIONS HANDBOOK (Aspen Publishers 2006).

Viginia G. Richardson & John Francis Reilly, *Public Charity or Private Foundation Status: Issues Under IRC 509(a)(1)-(4), 4942(j)(3), and 507,* EXEMPT ORG. CONTINUING PROFESSIONAL EDUC. TECH. INSTRUCTION PROGRAM FOR FY 2003 § B (2002).

Richard L. Schmalbeck, *Reconsidering Private Foundation Investment Limitations,* 58 TAX L. REV. 59 (2004).

Treasury Department Report on Private Foundations, Printed for Use of the House Committee on Ways and Means. 89th Cong., 1st Sess. (Comm. Print Feb. 2, 1965).

Thomas A. Troyer, *1969 Private Foundations Law: Historical Perspective on its Origins and Underpinnings,* 27 EXEMPT ORG. TAX REV. 52 (2000).

Stanley S. Weithorn, *How to Change Private Foundation Status by Voluntary "Termination" or by "Public Conversion,"* NYU Eleventh Biennial Conference on Charitable Foundations (1973).

Case Law

Coch v. Duke University, 1315 E.2d 909 (N.Car. 1963).

Davison v. Duke University, 1945 E.2d 761 (N. Car. 1973).

Madden v. Commissioner, 74 T.C.M. (CCH) 440 (U.S. Tax Ct. 1997).

Statutory and Other Authority

Form 990PF, <www.irs.gov/pub/irs-pdf/f990pf.pdf>.

IRC §§ 507, 509, 170(b)(1), 4941–4945, 6104(a), 6033.

Internet Sites

Council on Foundations, offering resources, publications, and services to foundations and corporate funders, available at <www.cof.org>.

The Foundation Center, collects, organizes, and communicates information on institutional philanthropy to benefit grantmakers and grantseekers, available at <foundationcenter.org/>.

Website of Philanthropic Research, Inc. contains collection of over 66,000 Form 990-PF's, available at <www.guidestar.org>.

Website of Urban Institute's National Center for Charitable Statistics, contains collection of over 61,000 Form 990-PF's, available at <nccsdataweb.urban.org>.

Private Inurement

(See Intermediate Sanctions)

Bibliography

ABA COORDINATING COMMITTEE ON NONPROFIT GOVERNANCE: GUIDE TO NONPROFIT CORPORATE GOVERNANCE IN THE WAKE OF SARBANES-OXLEY (ABA 2005).

Ellen P. Aprill, *Private Inurement, Private Benefit, and Exempt Purpose: Implications of Airlie Foundation, Inc. v. United States,* 46 MAJOR TAX PLAN. 23 (1994).

Lawrence L. Bell, *Compensation Issues for Nonprofit Organizations—Part II,* J. COMPENSATION & BENEFITS, Mar./Apr. 2005, at 5.

Harvey, Dale, The Crux of Charity: Inurement, Private benefit and Excess Benefit Transactions, unpublished paper delivered on October 28, 2004 at a program sponsored by National Center on Philanthropy and the Law.

BRUCE R. HOPKINS, THE LAW OF TAX-EXEMPT ORGANIZATIONS, §§ 19.1–19.9 (8TH ED.· 2003).

Andrew Megosh, Lary Scollick, Mary Jo Salins, & Cheryl Chasin, *Private Benefit Under I.R.C. 501(c)(3),* INTERNAL REVENUE SERVICE CONTINUING PROFESSIONAL EDUCATION TEXT FOR FISCAL 2001, p. 135 (2001).

Note, "The Inurement of Earnings of Private Benefit" Clause Section 501(c): A Standard Without Meaning?, 48 MINN. L. REV. 1149 (1964).

Rachel Penski, *Note, The Case of CEO Richard Grasso and the NYSE: Proposals for Controlling Executive Compensation at Public Nonprofit Corporations,* 58 VAND. L. REV. 339 (2005).

Brian H. Redmond, *Annotation, Federal Tax Exemption: When Do Earnings of Religious, Charitable, Educational, or Similar Organization Injure to benefit of Private Shareholders or Individuals Without Meaning of 26 USCS § 501(c)(3),* 92 A.L.R. FED. 255 (1996).

REPORT TO CONGRESS AND THE NONPROFIT SECTOR ON GOVERNANCE, TRANSPARENCY AND ACCOUNTABILITY (Panel on the Nonprofit Sector, Independent Sector ed., 2005).

RULES OF THE ROAD: A GUIDE TO THE LAW OF CHARITIES IN THE U.S. (Council on Foundations 1999).

A. L. (Lorry) Spitzer, *Executive Compensation in Nonprofit Health Care Organizations: Who's in Charge?,* 15 HEALTH MATRIX: J. L.-MED. 67 (2005).

Michael Folz Wexler & Alvin J. Geske, *The Private Benefit Rule and Interaction of Excess Benefit Transaction Taxes with Revocation,* 104 J. TAX'N 304 (2006).

Case Law

Church of Scientology of California v. Commissioner, 823 F.2d 1310 (9th Cir. 1987).

United Cancer Council v. Commissioner, 165 F.3d 1173 (7th Cir. 1999).

Western Catholic Church v. Commissioner, 73 T.C. 196 (1979), *aff'd* 631 F.2d (7th Cir. 1980), *cert. denied* 450 U.S. 981 (1981).

Statutory and Other Authority

Internal Revenue Code §§ 415, 501(c)(3), 170(f)(8), 4958, 6115.
Internal Revenue Code Continuing Professional Education Text for Fiscal 2001, p. 135 (2001).
Pub. L. No. 61-5, § 38, 36 Stat. 11, 115 (1909).
G.C.M. 39, 414 (Sept. 25, 1985).

Internet Sites

The Tax Exempt Tool Kit, a publication of the ABA Section of Taxation that provides a basic overview of the various laws and financial responsibilities that apply to small tax exempt organizations, at <www.abanet.org/tax/pubs/tetk.html>.
Risk Management Resource Center, Nonprofit Alert—Intermediate Sanctions Law, 2000, Gammon & Grange, P.C., at <www.eriskcenter.org/assets/pdfs/intermediatesanct.pdf>.

Public Policy

Bibliography

ELIZABETH BORIS & C. EUGENE STEUERLE, PHILANTHROPIC FOUNDATIONS: PAYOUT AND RELATED PUBLIC POLICY ISSUES (Emerging Issues in Philanthropy, Seminar Series, 2004).
David A. Brennen, *Charities and the Constitution: Evaluating the Role of Constitutional Principles in Determining the Scope of Tax Law's Public Policy Limitation for Charities*, 5 FLA. TAX REV. 779 (2002).
David A. Brennen, *The Power of Treasury: Racial Discrimination, Public Policy, and "Charity" in Contemporary Society* 334 U.C. DAVIS L. REV. 389 (2000).
David A. Brennen, *Tax Expenditures, Social Justice, and Civil Rights: Expanding the Scope of Civil Rights Laws to Apply to Tax-Exempt Charities*, B.Y.U.L. REV. 167 (2001).
Arthur C. Brooks, *The Effects of Public Policy on Private Charity*, 36 ADMIN. & SOC'Y 166 (2004).
Johnny Rex Buckles, *Reforming the Public Policy Doctrine,* 53 KAN. L. REV. 397 (2005).
Comment: Taxing Sex Discrimination: Revoking Tax Benefits of Organizations which Discriminate on the Basis of Sex, 1976 ARIZ. L. J. 641 (1976).
Miriam Galston, *Public Policy Constraints on Charitable Organizations,* 3 VA. TAX. REV. 291 (1984).
Martin Ginsburg, *Sex Discrimination and the IRS: Public Policy and the Charitable Deduction,* 10 TAX NOTES 27 (Jan. 14, 1980).

Ober Kaler Attorneys at Law, The Nonprofit Legal Landscape (Thomas K. Hyatt ed., BoardSource 2005).

Robert Paine, *The Tax Treatment of International Philanthropy and Public Policy,* 19 Akron Tax J. 1 (2004).

Georgia A. Persons, *National Politics and Charitable Choice as Urban Policy for Community Development,* 594 Annals Am. Acad. Pol. & Soc. Sci. 179 (2004).

Ronald J. Sider, *Evaluating the Faith-Based Initiative: Is Charitable Choice Good Public Policy?,* 61 Theology Today 485 (2005).

The Will of Bernice Parcahi Bishop, 21 U. of Hawaii L. Rev. 679 (1999) (Symposium Issue on the Bishop Estate Controversy).

Case Law

Association for the Preservation of Freedom of Choice v. Shapiro, 9 N.Y. 2d 376 (1961).

Bob Jones University v. United States, 461 U.S. 574 (1983).

Estate of Colman 317 A. 2d 631 (Pa. 1974).

Legal Servs. Corp. v. Velazquez, 531 U.S. 533; 121 S. Ct. 1043 (2001).

Home for Incurables of Baltimore City v. University of Maryland Medical System Corporation, 797 A.2d 746 (Md. 2003).

McGlatten v. Connally, 338 F. Supp. 448 (D.C. Cir. 1972).

New York State Club Assoc. v. City of New York, 487 U.S. 1 (1988).

Podberesky v. Kirwan 38 F.3d 147 (4th Cir. 1994), *cert. den.* 514 U.S. 1128 (1995).

Statutory and Other Authority

I.R.C. § 4945 (g)(1).

Internet Sites

New York University School of Law, Topics in Philanthropy, Bob Jones University: Defining Violations of Fundamental Public Policy, available at <http://www.law.nyu.edu/ncpl/library/publications/Monograph2000BobJones.pdf>.

U.S. Department of Labor, Office of Small Business Programs (contains information to assist small business companies in complying with rules, regulations, and laws enforced by the U.S. Department of Labor), available at <http://www.dol.gov/osbp/programs/sbrefa.htm>.

Real Property Tax Exemption

Biography

ALFRED BALK, THE FREE LIST: PROPERTY WITHOUT TAXES (Russell Sage Foundation 1971).

William Boak, *Benedictine Sisters of Pittsburgh: The Continuing Development of a Practical Approach to Property Tax Exemption,* 15 WIDENER L. J. 477 (2006).

PROPERTY-TAX EXEMPTION FOR CHARITIES: MAPPING THE BATTLEFIELD. (Evelyn Brody, ed., Urban Institute Press 2002).

John D. Colombo, *Hospital Property Tax Exemption in Illinois: Exploring the Policy Gaps,* 37 LOY. U. CHI. L. J. 493 (2006).

JOHN D. COLOMBO & MARK A. HALL, THE CHARITABLE TAX EXEMPTION (Westview Press 1995).

John D. Colombo & Mark A. Hall, *The Future of Tax Exemption for Nonprofit Hospitals and Other Health Care Providers,* 7 EXEMPT ORG. TAX REV. 395 (1993).

Robert B. Cooter, *Panel VI: Property, Taxation, and Distributive Justice: The Donation Registry,* 72 FORDHAM L. REV. 1981 (2004).

Stacy E. Costello, et al., Allocating Charitable Conservation Easement Deductions to Equity Investors, 19 REAL EST. FIN. J. 43 (2004).

Daniel F. Cullen & Michael T. Donovan, *The Impact of Tax-Exempt Leases on RESOs,* 33 REAL EST. TAX'N 32 (2005).

Joan B. Di Cola, *Alternatives to Donating a Conservation Easement,* EST. PLAN. (WGL), 2004, at 489.

William R. Ginsberg, *The Real Property Tax Exemption of Nonprofit Organizations: A Perspective,* 53 TEMP. L. REV. 291 (1980).

Dan McCall, *Are There Added Preservatives in Section 170(h) of the Tax Code?: The Role of Easements in Historic Preservation,* 39 REAL PROP. PROB. & TR. J. 807 (2005).

Nancy A. McLaughlin, *Increasing the Tax Incentives for Conservation Easement Donations—A Responsible Approach,* 31 ECOLOGY L.Q. 1 (2004).

Lawrence Mendenhall, *Sale of Residential Education Facility's Property,* 48 EXEMPT ORG. TAX REV. 61 (2005).

Phillip M. Purcell, *Gifts of Real Estate to Charitable Remainder Trusts: Issues and Opportunities,* J. GIFT PLAN., Sept. 2004, at 5.

Dana Brakman Reiser, *Enron.org: Why Sarbanes-Oxley will not Ensue Comprehensive Nonprofit Accountability* 384 U.C. DAVIS L. REV. (2004).

Richard Steinberg and Marc Bilodeau, *Should Nonprofit Organizations Pay Sales and Property Taxes* (National Council of Nonprofit Associations 1999).

Peter Swords, *Charitable Real Property Tax Exemption in New York State* (Columbia University Press 1981).

Case Law

Camps Newfound/Owatonna Inc. v. Town of Harrison, 520 U.S. 564 (1997).

Records Retention

Bibliography

ABA COORDINATING COMMITTEE ON NONPROFIT GOVERNANCE, GUIDE TO NONPROFIT CORPORATE GOVERNANCE IN THE WAKE OF SARBANES-OXLEY (ABA 2005).

AMERICAN SOCIETY OF CORPORATE SECRETARIES, RECORDS RETENTION (American Society of Corporate Secretaries 1985).

J. EDWIN DIETEL, ed., RECORDS RETENTION, Vol. 3, CORPORATE COMPLIANCE SERIES (West GroupClark Boardman Callaghan 1993).

Robert Hayhoe, *Canada Revenue Agency Charity Audits and Record-Keeping,* 51 EXEMPT ORG. TAX REV. 237 (2006).

I.R.S. PUBLICATION 4221, COMPLIANCE GUIDE FOR 501 (C)(3) TAX-EXEMPT ORGANIZATIONS (2003).

Suzanne Ross McDowell, *Should Nonprofit Organizations Adopt the Rules of Sarbanes-Oxley?,* 16 TAX'N EXEMPTS 8 (2004).

Paul Ticher, *Data Protection Act,* SOLIC. J. (CHARITY & APP. SUPP.), Spring 2004, at 27.

Herbert N. Watkins, *The Sarbanes-Oxley Act and Nonprofit Organizations,* 52 EXEMPT ORG. TAX REV. 267 (2006).

Statutory and Other Authority

New York Not-For-Profit Corporation Law, Section 520.

Internet Sites

Sample Record Retention Policy, available at <http://www.nonprofitlaw.com/retention.shtml>.

Summary of email records management strategy, available at <http://www.mnhs.org/preserve/records/electronicrecords/eremail.pdf>.

Disaster Recovery Yellow Pages—Information and services related to emergency data recovery & record repair, available at <http://www.disaster-help.com>.

Registration

Bibliography

MARION R. FREMONT-SMITH, GOVERNING NONPROFIT ORGANIZATIONS: STATE AND FEDERAL LAW AND REGULATION (Belknap Press of Harvard University Press 2004).

Case Law

Bensusan Restaurant Corp. v. Richard B. King, 126 F.3d 25 (2d Cir. 1997).

Cybersell, Inc. v. Cybersell, Inc., 130 F.3d 414 (9th Cir. 1997).

GTE New Media Serv. v. Bellsouth Corp., 199 F.3d 1343 (D.C. Cir. 2000).

Inset Sys. Inc. v. Instruction Set Inc., 937 F. Supp. 161 (D. Conn. 1996).

Maritz Inc. v. CyberGold, 947 F. Supp. 1338 (E.D. Mo. 1996).

Mink v. AAAA Development, LLC, 190 F.3d 333 (5th Cir. 1999).

National Awareness Foundation v. Abrams 50 F. 3d 1159 (2d Cir. 1995).

Northern Lights Tech., Inc. v. Northern Lights Club, 97 F. Supp. 2d 96 (D. Ma. 2000).

Panavision International, L.P. v. Toeppen, 141 F.3d 1316, 1321 (9th Cir. 1998).

Quill Corp. v. North Dakota, 504 U.S. 298 (1992).

Zippo Mfg. Co. v. Zippo Dot Com, Inc., 952 F. Supp. 1119 (W.D. Pa. 1997).

Statutory and Other Authority

Rev. Model Nonprofit Corp. Act §§ 1.70, 16.22 (1988).

Internet Sites

The Unified Registration Statement: The Multistate Filer Project. Access to form that consolidates the requirements of all states that require the registration of nonprofit organizations, eliminating the need to make multiple filings. Available at < http://www.multistatefiling.org/>.

Religious Organizations

a. General

Bibliography

Thomas C. Berg, *Christianity and the Secular in Modern Public Life,* 2 U. St. Thomas L. J. 425 (2005).

Charles L. Butler III, *Note, International Law and Religion: Federal Funding to Faith-Based Organizations: Unconstitutional, Wherever the Spirit Moves Them,* 13 Willamette J. Int'l L. & Dispute Res. 27 (2005).

Aaron Cain, *Comment, Faith-Based Initiative Proponents Beware: The Key in Zelman Is Not Just Neutrality, but Private Choice,* 31 Pepp. L. Rev. 979 (2004).

Terrance S. Carter & Jacqueline M. Connor, *Advancing Religion as a Charity: Is it Losing Ground?, Charity Law Bulletin No. 58,* November 10, 2004, *available at* http://www.charitylaw.ca (2004).

James R. Dalton, *Comment, There is Nothing Light About Feathers: Finding Form in the Jurisprudence of Native American Religious Exemptions,* 2005 B.Y.U. L. Rev. 1575.

Emily R. Gill, *Religious Organizations, Charitable Choice, and the Limits of Freedom of Conscience,* 2 Persp. Pol. 741 (2004).

Thomas L. Greaney & Kathleen M. Boozang, *Mission, Margin, and Trust in the Nonprofit Health Care Enterprise,* 5 Yale J. Health Pol'y L. & Ethics 1 (2005).

Steven K. Green, *"A Legacy of Discrimination"? The Rhetoric and Reality of the Faith-Based Initiative: Oregon as a Case Study,* 84 Or. L. Rev. 725 (2005).

Richard R. Hammar, Pastor, Church & Law (3d ed. Christianity Today 2000).

Independent Sector, From Belief to Commitment: The Community Service Activities and Resources of Religious Congregations in the United States (Independent Sector 1993).

Kevin Kearns, et al., *Comparing Faith-Based and Secular Community Service Corporations in Pittsburgh and Allegheny County, Pennsylvania,* 34 Nonprofit & Voluntary Sector Q. 206 (2005).

Christopher C. Lund, *Of Government Funding, Religious Institutions, and Neutrality: Seeing the Charitable-Choice Debate Through the Lens of Arrow's Impossibility Theorem,* 40 Tulsa L. Rev. 321 (2004).

Alexander-Kenneth Nagel, *Charitable Choice: The Religious Component of the US-Welfare-Reform—Theoretical and Methodological Reflections on "Faith-Based-Organizations" as Social Service Agencies,* 53 NUMEN 78 (2006).

Matthew J. Piers, *Malevolent Destruction of a Muslim Charity: A Commentary on the Prosecution of Benevolence International Foundation,* 25 PACE L. REV. 339 (2005).

Laura A. Reese, *A Matter of Faith: Urban Congregations and Economic Development,* 18 ECON. DEV. Q. 50 (2004).

Kathryn A. Ruff, *Note, Scared To Donate: An Examination of the Effects of Designating Muslim Charities As Terrorist Organizations on the First Amendment Rights of Muslim Donors,* 9 N. Y. U. J. LEGIS. & PUB. POL'Y 447 (2005/2006).

Catharine Pierce Wells, *Who Owns the Local Church? A Pressing Issue for Dioceses in Bankruptcy,* 29 SETON HALL LEGIS. J. 375 (2005).

Internet Sites

U.S. Treasury Department, Internal Revenue Service: Tax guide for Churches and Religious Organizations (publication 1828) 2003, available at <http://www.irs.gov/pub/irs-pdf/p1828.pdf>.

Online Discussion Groups—see <http://www.charitychannel.com>— see esp., Charity Law and Christian Dev forums.

b. What Is a Religion?
What Is a Church/Church Structure?

Bibliography

Charles M. Whelan, *Church in the Internal Revenue Code,* 45 FORDHAM L. REV. 885 (1977).

Paul G. Kauper and Stephen C. Ellis, *Religious Corporations and the Law,* 71 MICH. L. REV. 1499 (1973).

1993 (for Fiscal Year 1994) IRS Exempt Organizations Continuing Professional Education Technical Instruction Program Textbook, Defining "Church"—The Concept of a Congregation.

Case Law

American Guidance Foundation, Inc. v. United States 490 F. Supp 304 (1980).

Bubbling Well Church of Universal Love v. Comm'r of Internal Revenue Service, 74 T.C. 531 (1980), aff'd. 670 F.2d 104 (Inc. 9th Cir. 1981). [decided on basis of private inurement rather than church status].

David v. Beason, 133 U.S. 333, 342 (1840).

Founding Church of Scientology v. United States, 412 F2d 1197, 1199 (1969). [decided on basis of private inurement rather than church status].

Lutheran Social Services of Minnesota v. U.S., 758 F.2d 1283 (1985).

Mannix v. Purcell, 46 Ohio St. 102, 24 N.E. 595 (1888).

Presbytery of the Covenant v. First Presbyterian Church of Paris, Inc., Tex. Civ. App., 522 S.W.2d 865, 870.

Torasco v. Watkins, 367 U.S. 488 (1961).

United States v. Seeger, 380 U.S. 163 (1965).

Welsh v. United States, 398 U.S. 333 (1970).

Statutory and Other Authority

Treas. Reg. Section 1.6033-2(h).

Rev. Proc. 91-20, 1991-10 I.R.B. 26 (1991).

Ltr-Rul, IRS Technical Advice Memorandum 9624001, (Nov. 13, 1995).

c. Resolution of Church Disputes

Bibliography

Ira M. Ellman, *Driven from the Tribunal Judicial Resolution of Internal Church Disputes,* 69 CALIF. L. REV. 1878 (1981).

Case Law

Jones v. Wolf, 443 U.S. 595 (1979).

Kedroff v. St. Nicholas Cathedral of the Russian Orthodox Church of North America, 344 U.S. 94 (1952).

Kreshick v. St. Nicholas Cathedral of the Russian Orthodox Church of North America, 363 U.S. 94 (1952).

Presbyterian Church in the United States v. Mary Elizabeth Blue Hull Memorial Presbyterian Church, 393 U.S. 440 (1969).

Rayburn v. General Conference of Seventh-Day Adventists, 772F.2d. 1164.

Serbian Eastern Orthodox Diocese for the United States of America and Canada v. Milivojevich, 426 U.S. 696 (1976) [deference to hierarchical church authority].

Watson v. Jones, 80 U.S. (13 Wall.) 679.

Statutory and Other Authority

California Corporations Code § 9240 (c).

Internet Sites

CareGiver Ministries Christian Conciliation Services, available at <http://www.pastorsnet.com/caregiver_ministries/members/christian_conciliation.html>.

Guidelines for Christian Conciliation, available at <http://www.hispeace.org/html/guidelin.htm>.

d. Exempt Status

Bibliography

Barnett F. Baron, *Treasury Guidelines Have Had Little Impact Overall on U.S. International Philanthropy, but They Have Had a Chilling Impact on U.S.-Based Muslim Charities,* 25 PACE L. REV. 307 (2005).

Tevor A. Brown, *Note Religious Nonprofits and the Commercial Manner Test* 99 YALE L. J. 1631 (1990).

John D. Colombo, *The Role of Access in Charitable Tax Exemption,* 82 WASH. U. L. Q. 343 (2005).

Vaughn E. James, *Reaping Where They Have Not Sowed: Have American Churches Failed to Satisfy the Requirements for the Religious Tax Exemption?,* 43 CATH. LAW. 29 (2004).

Theresa L. M. Man & Terrance S. Carter, *Recent Federal [Canada] Court of Appeal Decisions Revoking Charitable Status of Charities, Charity Law Bulletin No 75,* available at <http://www.carters.ca/pub/bulletin/charity/2005/chylb75.pdf> (2005).

Jill S. Manny, *Governance Issues for Non-Profit Religious Organizations,* 40 CATH. LAW. 1 (2000).

Melissa McClellan, *Note, Faith and Federalism: Do Charitable Choice Provisions Preempt State Nondiscrimination Employment Law,* 61 WASH. & LEE L. REV. 1437 (2004).

Leonard J. Nelson III, *God and Woman in the Catholic Hospital,* 31 J. LEGIS. 69 (2004).

Jerome Park Prather, *Tax Exemption of American Churches and Other Nonprofits: One Election Cycle After Branch Ministries v. Rossotti,* 94 KY. L. J. 149 (2005).

David Pratt, *Focus on . . . Section 457 Exemptions,* J. PENSION BENEFITS, Spring 2004, at 32.

Allan J. Samansky, *Deductiblity of Contributions to Religious Institutions,* 24 VA. TAX REV. 65 (2004).

Melissa Seifer Briggs, *Note, Exempt or Not Exempt: Mandated Prescription Contraception Coverage and the Religious Employer,* 84 OR. L. REV. 1227 (2005).

Carmel Sileo, *No Religious Exemption for Catholic Charities, Says California Court,* TRIAL, May 2004, at 102.

Susan J. Stabile, *Religious Employers and Statutory Prescription Contraceptive Mandates,* 43 CATH. LAW. 169 (2004).

Fred Stokeld & Christopher Quay, *Officials at Law and Faith Conference Discuss IRS Enforcement, Regulations,* 45 EXEMPT ORG. TAX REV. 17 (2004).

Paul J. Weireter, *Vow of Poverty Was Not a Disclaimer,* 36 TAX ADVISER 196 (2005).

Howard W. Wolosky, *Charitable Deduction Claim for Religious Schooling,* PRAC. ACCT., Feb. 2006, at 40.

Case Law

Basic Bible Church v. CIR, 74 T.C. 846 (1980) *aff'd* Granzow v. CIR, 739 F.2d 265 (1984).

The Basic Unit Ministry of Alma Karl Schurig v. CIR, 670 F2d 1210 (1982).

Markus Q. Bishop, et ux. v. United States, No. 3:98mc25/RV (3/18/99).

Bob Jones Univ. v. United States, 461 U.S. 574 (1983).

Church by Mail, Inc. v. C.I.R., 765 F.2d 1387, 1392 (1985).

Church of Scientology of Cal. v. Commissioner, 823 F.2d 1310 (9th Cir. 1987).

Church of the Chosen People v. United States, 548 F. Supp. 1247 (D.C. Minn. 1982).

DeJong v. Commissioner, 309 F.2d 373 (9th Cir., 1962).

Hernandez v. Commissioner, 498 U.S. 680 (1989).

Holy Spirit Assoc. v. Tax Commissioner 55 N.Y. 2d 512 (1982).

Presbyterian & Reformed Publishing Company v. CIR, 743 F.2d 148, 153 (1984).

Scripture Press Foundation v. United States, 285 F.2d 800, (1961) *cert. denied,* 368 U.S. 985 (1962).

United Libertarian Fellowship, Inc. v. Comm'r of Internal Revenue, T.C. Memo. 1993-116, USTC Tax Ct. Dkt. No. 1230689X.

U.S. v. Church of Scientology of Boston, Inc., 933 F.2d 1074 [re church audit procedures act].

U.S. v. Church of World Peace, 775 F.2d 265 [church audit procedures act].

Statutory and Other Authority

I.R.C. §§ 170(b)(1)(A), 170(f)(8), 501, 508, 6033, 7611 (1986).
Treas. Reg. §§ 1,503(3), 1.508-1(a)(3), 301-7611-1.
I.R.S. Form 1023.

Internet Sites

Tax Guide for Churches and Religious Organizations, available at <http://www.irs.gov/pub/irs-pdf/p1828.pdf>.

Basic Tax Aspects for Religious Organizations, Lisa A. Runquist, at <http://runquist.com/ARTICLE_ReligTax.htm>.

e. Lobbying and Political Activity

Bibliography

Rob Boston, *Render Unto Caesar . . . IRS Commissioner Tells Tax-Exempt Churches: Thou Shalt Not Electioneer,* CHURCH & ST., Apr. 2006, at 4.

WILFRED CARON, et al., GOVERNMENT RESTRAINT ON POLITICAL ACTIVITIES OF RELIGIOUS BODIES, IN GOVERNMENT INTERVENTION IN RELIGIOUS AFFAIRS 151 (Dean M. Kelly ed., 1982).

Douglas H. Cook, *The Politically Active Church,* 35 LOY. U. CHI. L. J. 457 (2004).

DEIRDRE DESSINGUE, POLITICS AND THE PULPIT: A GUIDE TO THE INTERNAL REVENUE CODE RESTRICTIONS ON THE POLITICAL ACTIVITY OF RELIGIOUS ORGANIZATIONS (The Pew Forum on Religion and Public Life 2002).

Deirdre Dessingue, *Prohibition in Search of a Rationale: What the Tax Code Prohibits; Why; to What End?,* 42 B.C. L. REV. 903 (2001).

Deirdre Dessingue, *Recognition of Section 501(c)(4) Exemption of Christian Coalition International Raises New Concerns,* PAUL STRECKFUS' EO TAX J., Sept./Oct. 2005, at 5.

Deirdre Dessingue & Wilfred R. Caron, *I.R.C. 501(c)(3): Practical and Constitutional Implications of "Political" Activity Restrictions,* 2 J.L. & POL. 169 (1985).

Deirdre Dessingue Halloran, *Keeping Church Political Activities Within the Constraints of the Code,* 12 J. TAX'N EXEMPT ORG. (WGL) 73 (2001).

Michael Hatfield, *Ignore the Rumors—Campaigning from the Pulpit is Okay: Thinking Past the Symbolism of Section 501(c)(3),* 20 NOTRE DAME J.L. ETHICS & PUB. POL'Y 125 (2006).

Kevin M. Kearney & Deidre Dessingue Halloran, *Federal Tax Code Restrictions on Church Political Activities,* 38 CATH. LAW. 105 (1998).

Jerome Park Prather, *Tax Exemption of American Churches and Other Nonprofits: One Election Cycle After Branch Ministries v. Rossotti,* 94 KY. L. J. 149 (2005).

Fred Stokeld, *Church-State Watchdog Group Again on Trail of Christian Coalition,* 26 EXEMPT ORGANIZATION TAX REVIEW, 195, November, 1999.

Case Law

Branch Ministries, Inc., et al., v. Charles O. Rossotti, 40 F. Supp. 2d 15 (1999), *aff'd* 211 F3d 137 (2000).
Church by Mail, Inc. v. C.I.R., 765 F.2d 1387 (1985); Treas. Reg. Sec. 1.50(c)(3)-(1)(c).
The Christian Coalition v. United States, No. 00-CV-136 (2/25/2000).

Internet Sites

Political Activity Guidelines for Catholic Organizations, at <http://www.usccb.org/ogc/guidelines.shtml>.

f. Ministers, Non-Minister Employees

Bibliography

Kathleen A. Brady, *Religious Organizations and Mandatory Collective Bargaining Under Federal and State Labor Laws: Freedom From and Freedom For,* 49 VILL. L. REV. 77 (2004).
Kristen Colletta & Darya Kapulina, *Note, Employment Discrimination and the First Amendment: Case Analysis of Catholic Charities,* 23 HOFSTRA LAB. & EMP. L. J. 189 (2005).
Laura Christine Henderson, *Comment, Equal Benefits, Unequal Burdens: How the Movement for Gay Rights in the Workplace Is Affecting Religious Employers,* 55 CATH. U. L. REV. 227 (2005).
Melissa McClellan, *Note, Faith and Federalism: Do Charitable Choice Provisions Preempt State Nondiscrimination Employment Law,* 61 WASH. & LEE L. REV. 1437 (2004).
Burgess J. W. Raby & William L. Raby, *Vows of Poverty and the Tax Collector,* 47 EXEMPT ORG. TAX REV. 35 (2005).
Susan J. Stabile, *State Attempts To Define Religion: The Ramifications of Applying Mandatory Prescription Contraceptive Coverage Statutes to Religious Employers,* 28 HARV. J. L. & PUB. POL'Y 741 (2005).
U.S. Treasury Department, Internal Revenue Service: Social Security and Other Information for the Members of the Clergy and Religious Workers (Publication 517).

Case Law

Alford v. United States, 1997 TNT 121-34, 79 AFTR2d Par. 97-1045 (1997). [minister of Assemblies of God was independent contractor].

Bethel Baptist Church v. U.S. 822 F.2d 1334 (3rd Cir. 1987), *cert. denied* 485 U.S. 959 (1988). [withholding social security requirements constitutional].

Bollard v. California Province of the Society of Jesus, 196 F.3d 940 (9th Cir.)(1999).

Corporation of Presiding Bishop of the Church of Jesus Christ of Latter-day Saints v. Amos, 483 U.S. 327, 107 S. Ct. 2862 (1987).

EEOC v. Miss. College, 626 F.2d 477 (CA Miss. 1980).

Eighth St. Baptist Church, Inc. v. United States, 291 F. Supp. 603, 604 (1968), *aff'd.,* 431 F.2d 1193 (1970).

Henry W. Radde, et al. v. Commissioner, T.C. Memo 1997-490 (1997). [minister of United Methodist Church was an employee].

Hutchinson v. Thomas 789 F.2d 392 (6th Cir. 1986) *cert. denied,* 479 U.S. 885.

Kaufmann v. Sheehan, 707 F.2d 355 (8th Cir. 1983).

McClure v. Salvation Army, 460 F.2d 553 (5th Cir.), *cert. denied* 409 U.S. 896, 93 S. Ct. 132, 34 L.Ed. 2d 153 (1972).

N.L.R.B. v. Catholic Bishop of Chicago, 440 U.S. 490 (1979).

N.L.R.B. v. St. Louis Christian Home, 663 F.2d 60 (8th Cir. 1981).

Pacific Union Conf. of Seventh-day Adventists Marshall 434 U.S. 1305.

Rayburn v. General Conference of Seventh-Day Adventists 772 F.2d 1164 (4th Cir.), *cert. denied* 106 S. Ct. 333, 92 L.Ed. 739, 478 U.S. 1020 (1986).

St. Martin Evangelical Lutheran Church v. South Dakota, 451 US 772 (1981). [unemployment tax].

Simpson v. Wells Lamont Corp., 494 F.2d 490 (5th Cir. 1974).

Tony and Susan Alamo Foundation v. Secretary of Labor, 471 U.S. 290, 295 (1985).

United States v. Indianapolis Baptist Temple, et al., 86 AFTR 2d Par.2000-5149 (7th Cir., Aug. 14, 2000).

Statutory and Other Authority

I.R.C. §§ 1402(a)(8), 3102, 3121(b)(8)(A), 3121(w)(1), 3301, 3309(b), 3401(a)(9), 3402(a).

Treas. Reg. §§ 1.1402, 31.3401(a)(9)-1.

Rev. Rul. 80-110, 1980-1 C.B. 190 (1980).

I.R.S. Form 4361, 8274.

Internet Sites

The Catholic University of America—Summary of Federal Laws, Employment, at <http://counsel.cua.edu/fedlaw/Lmra1947.cfm>.

g. Parsonage Allowance

Bibliography

Douglas A. Frazer, *The Clergy, the Constitution, and the Unbeatable Double Dip: The Strange Case of the Tax Code's Parsonage Allowance,* 43 EXEMPT ORG. TAX REV. 149 (2004).

Case Law

C.T. Boyd, Jr. 42 T.C.M. 1136, T.C. Memo 1981-523; Eden v. C.I.R. 41 T.C. 605 (1964).

Flowers v. United States, D.C., 82-1USTC 9114 (1991).

Kirk v. CIR, 425 F.2d 492, 495 (D.C., 1970).

Ling v. U.S. 200 F. Supp. 282 (D.C. Minn. 1961).

Melvin L. Libman, 44 T.C.M. 370, Dec. 39, 161 (M), T.C. Memo 1982-377.

Warnke v. United States, 641 F. Supp. 1083, 1091 (1986).

Warren v. CIR, 114 T.C. No. 23 (5/16/2000).

Larry Whittington, et al. v. IRC, T.C. Memo. 2000-96 (9/21/00).

Statutory and Other Authority

I.R.C. Sec. 107 (1986).

Treas. Reg. 1.107-1(b).

Priv. Ltr. Rul. 8519004 (Jan. 28, 1985).

Rev. Rul. 59-270, 1959-2 C.B. 44 (1952).

Rev. Rul. 72-606, 1972-2 C.B. 78 (1972).

Rev. Rul. 70-549, 1970-2 C.B. 16 (1970).

Internet Sites

U.S. Treasury Department, Internal Revenue Service: Frequently Asked Questions: 4.10 Interest/Dividends/Other Types of Income: Ministers' Compensation & Housing Allowance, at <http://www.irs.gov/faqs/faq4-10.html>.

h. Church Retirement Plans

Statutory and Other Authority

Employee Retirement Income Security Act, 29 USC 1001, 1002 (33), 1003(b)(2), 1321(b)(3) (2002).

IRC Sec. 401, 402, 403, 410(d), 414(c)(5) (1986).

Internet Sites

Ministers and Church Employees, at <http://www.irs.gov/publications/p571/ch05.html>.

Internal Revenue Bulletin: 2004-1 January 5, 2004: Appendix E—
Additional Checklist For Church Plans, at <http://www.irs.gov/irb/
2004-01_IRB/apj.html>.

i. Property Tax Exemptions

Bibliography

Deidre Dessinger, *The Special Case of Churches, in* BRODY, EVELYN,
ed., PROPERTY-TAX EXEMPTION FOR CHARITIES: MAPPING THE
BATTLEFIELD (Urban Institute Press 2002) at 173.

CHARLES WILLIAM ELIOT, VIEWS RESPECTING PRESENT EXEMPTION
FROM TAXATION OF PROPERTY USED FOR RELIGIOUS, EDUCATIONAL
AND CHARITABLE PURPOSES (1874).

William R. Ginsberg, *The Real Property Tax Exemption of Nonprofit
Organizations: A Perspective,* 53 TEMPLE LAW QUARTERLY 291
(1980).

Catharine Pierce Wells, *Who Owns the Local Church? A Pressing
Issue for Dioceses in Bankruptcy,* 29 SETON HALL LEGIS. J. 375
(2005).

Case Law

Walz v. Tax Commissions, 397 U.S. 664, 669 (1970).

j. Sales Tax Exemptions

Case Law

Swaggart v. Calif. Equalization Bd., 493 U.S. 378, 107 L.Ed.2d 796,
110 S. Ct. 688 (1990).

Texas Monthly, Inc. v. Bob Bullock, Comptroller of Public Accounts
of the State of Texas, et al., 488 U.S. 361, 109 S. Ct. 647,
102 L. Ed.2d 714 (1989).

k. First Amendment and Government's Right to Assist/Regulate

Bibliography

*Case Note, Constitutional Law—First Amendment—California
Supreme Court Upholds Compulsory Insurance Coverage of
Contraceptives over Establishment and Free Exercise
Objections—Catholic Charities of Sacramento, Inc. v. Superior
Court, 85 P.3d 67* (Cal. 2004), 117 HARV. L. REV. 2761 (2004).

Charles L. Butler III, *Note, International Law and Religion: Federal
Funding to Faith-Based Organizations: Unconstitutional,
Wherever the Spirit Moves Them,* 13 WILLAMETTE J. INT'L L. &
DISPUTE RES. 27 (2005).

Aaron Cain, *Comment, Faith-Based Initiative Proponents Beware: The Key in Zelman Is Not Just Neutrality, but Private Choice*, 31 Pepp. L. Rev. 979 (2004).

Emily R. Gill, *Religious Organizations, Charitable Choice, and the Limits of Freedom of Conscience*, 2 Persp. Pol. 741 (2004).

Steven K. Green, *"A Legacy of Discrimination"? The Rhetoric and Reality of the Faith-Based Initiative: Oregon as a Case Study*, 84 Or. L. Rev. 725 (2005).

Christopher C. Lund, *Of Government Funding, Religious Institutions, and Neutrality: Seeing the Charitable-Choice Debate Through the Lens of Arrow's Impossibility Theorem*, 40 Tulsa L. Rev. 321 (2004).

John H. Mansfield, *The Religious Clauses of the First Amendments and the Philosophy of the Constitution*, 72 Calif. L. Rev. 847 (1984).

Charles McDaniel, et al., *Charitable Choice and Prison Ministries: Constitutional and Institutional Challenges to Rehabilitating the American Penal System*, 26 Crim. Just. Pol. Rev. 164 (2005).

Melissa McClellan, *Note, Faith and Federalism: Do Charitable Choice Provisions Preempt State Nondiscrimination Employment Law*, 61 Wash. & Lee L. Rev. 1437 (2004).

Erez Reuveni, *Note, On Boy Scouts and Anti-Discrimination Law: The Associational Rights of Quasi-Religious Organizations*, 86 B.U. L. Rev. 109 (2006).

Kathryn A. Ruff, *Note, Scared To Donate: An Examination of the Effects of Designating Muslim Charities As Terrorist Organizations on the First Amendment Rights of Muslim Donors*, 9 N. Y. U. J. Legis. & Pub. Pol'y 447 (2005/2006).

Amy K. Ryder Wentz, *Note, Unreasonable Conditions Impeding Our Nation's Charities: An Unconstitutional Condition in the Combined Federal Campaign*, 53 Clev. St. L. Rev. 689 (2005/2006).

Michael P. Seng, *The Fair Housing Act and Religious Freedom*, 11 Tex . J. on Civ.Lib. & Civ.Rts. 1 (2005).

Susan J. Stabile, *Religious Employers and Statutory Prescription Contraceptive Mandates*, 43 Cath. Law. 169 (2004).

Fred Stokeld, *Virginia High Court to Hear University's Appeal on Exempt Bonds*, 28 Exempt Org. Tax Rev. 200 (May 2000).

Case Law

Agostini v. Felton, 521 U.S. 203 (1997).

Aguilar v. Felton, 473 U.S. 402 (1985).

Board of Educ. V. Allen, 392 U.S. 236 (1968).

Bowen v. Kendrick, 487 U.S. 589, 108 S. Ct. 2562 (1988).

Cantwell v. Connecticut, 310 U.S. 296, 303 (1940).

City of Boerne v. Flores, 521 U.S. 507, 138 L.Ed. 2d 624, 117 S. Ct. 2157 (1997).

Committee for Public Education & Religious Liberty v. Nyquist, 1973, 413 U.S. 756.

Corporation of Presiding Bishop v. Amos, 483 U.S. 327 (1987).

Employment Division, Dept. of Human Resources of Oregon v. Alfred L. Smith, 494 U.S. 872 (1990).

Everson v. Board of Education, 330 U.S. 1 (1947).

Gonzalez v. Roman Catholic Archbishop, 280 U.S. 1 (1929).

Grand Rapids Sch. Dist. v. Ball, 473 U.S. 373 (1985).

Johnson v. Economic Development Corp. of the County of Oakland, (Case No. 99-1884 6th Circuit) (2001).

Lemon v. Kurtzman, 1971, 403 U.S. 602.

Malnak v. Yogi, 592 F.2d 197 (3rd Cir. 1979).

Meek v. Pittenger, 421 U.S. 349 (1975).

Mitchell v. Helms, 530 U.S. 1296 (2000).

Mueller v. Allen, (1983), 463 U.S. 388 (1983).

People v. Worldwide Church of God, 427 Cal. App. 3d 547 (1982) (Cal. Ct. of App. Second District).

School District of the City of Grand Rapids v. Ball, 473 U.S. 373, 105 S. Ct. 3126 (1985).

Sherbert v. Verner, 374 U.S. 398.

Steele et al. v. Industrial Development Bond of the Metropolitan Government of Nashville, et al., No. 3:91-042 (M.D. Tenn, 10/24/00).

Tilton v. Richardson, 403 U.S. 672 (1971).

United States v. Ballard, 322 U.S. 78 (1944).

Watchtower Bible and Tract Society, Inc. v. Village of Stratton, 536 U.S. 150 (2002).

Wisconsin v. Yoder, 406 U.S. 205 (1972).

Statutory and Other Authority

United States Constitution, First Amendment.

Religious Freedom Restoration Act of 1993, 42 USC § 2000bb(a).

Religious Land Use and Institutionalized Persons Act of 2000, 42 USC 2000cc.

Internet Sites

The Beckett Fund for Religious Liberty, at http://www.becketfund.org.

Retreats

Bibliography

Barry S. Bader, Planning Successful Board Retreats: A Guide for Board Members and Chief Executives (National Center for Nonprofit Boards 1991).

Sandra R. Hughes, To Go Forward, Retreat! The Board Retreat Handbook, (BoardSource 1999).

Secrets of Successful Retreats: The Best from the Nonprofit Pros (Carol Weisman ed., Board Builders 2003).

Risk Management

Bibliography

Michael Chernew, et al., *Charity Care, Risk Pooling, and the Decline in Private Health Insurance*, Am. Econ. Rev., 2005, at 209.

Bryan Clontz & Donald F. Behan, *Optimizing Charitable Gift Annuity Risk Management: Collaring the Bear and the Grim Reaper,* J. Gift Plan., Mar. 2004, at 5.

Bryan Clontz & Donald F. Behan, *Optimizing Charitable Gift Annuity Risk Management Part 2: Reinsurance Revisited,* J. Gift Plan., June 2005, at 5.

Paul C. Godfrey, *The Relationship Between Corporate Philanthropy and Shareholder Wealth: A Risk Management Perspective,* 30 Academy Mgmt. Rev. 777 (2005).

Melanie Herman, George L. Head, Peggy M. Jackson, & Toni E. Fogarty, Managing Risk in Nonprofit Organizations (Wiley 2003).

Jerald Jacobs & Daniel Ogden, Legal Risk Management for Associations (American Psychological Association 1995).

Mary Lai, et al., Am I Covered For? (2d ed. Consortium for Human Services, Inc. 1992).

John C. Patterson & Barbara B. Oliver, The Season of Hope: A Risk-Management Guide for Youth-Serving Nonprofits (Nonprofit Risk Management Center 2002).

Sandra B. Richtermeyer & Gary Fleishman, *Planning Strategies to Avoid Intermediate Sanctions,* 36 Tax Adviser 424 (2005).

Risk Management for Nonprofits (2d ed., National Center for Community Risk & Management Insurance 1992).

BYRON STONE & CAROL NORTH, RISK MANAGEMENT AND INSURANCE FOR NONPROFIT MANAGER (First Non Profit Risk Pooling Trial 1988).

CHARLES TREMPER & GEORGE BABCOCK, THE NONPROFIT BOARD'S ROLE IN RISK MANAGEMENT: MORE THAN BUYING INSURANCE (National Center for Nonprofit Boards 1990).

Mervyn F. White, *Essentials of Operational Risk Management, Risk Management Checklist, November 10, 2004,* available at <www.charitylaw.ca.>.

Internet Sites

Nonprofit Risk Management Center (publications), <http://www .nonprofitrisk.org>.

Royalties

Bibliography

Sean Barnett, et al., *UBIT: Current Developments,* EXEMPT ORG. PROFESSIONAL EDUC. TECH. INSTRUCTION PROGRAM FOR 2002 § F (2001).

Richard Holbrook, *The Royalties Exception to Unrelated Business Income: Sierra Club v. Commissioner,* 49 TAX LAW. 517 (1996).

Leeanna Izuel & Leslie Park, *Tax-Exempt Organizations and Internet Commerce: The Application of the Royalty and Volunteer Exceptions to Unrelated Business Taxable Income,* 31 WM. MITCHELL L. REV. 245 (2004).

B. Holly Schadler, *The Courts Point the Way to Royalty Treatment for UBIT Purposes,* 9 J. TAX'N EXEMPT ORG. (WGL) 244 (1998).

Katherine A. Van Ye, *Sierra Club v. Commissioner and the Royalty Exemption to the Unrelated Business Income Tax: How Much Activity Is Too Much?*, 72 WASH. L. REV. 1171 (1997).

Case Law

Common Cause v. Commissioner, 112 T.C. 332 (1999).

Planned Parenthood Federation of America, Inc. v. Commissioner, 77 T.C.M. (CCH) 2227 (1999).

Sierra Club v. Commissioner, 86 F.3d 1526 (9th Cir. 1986).

Statutory and Other Authority

26 U.S.C. 512(b)(2) (1997).

Sarbanes-Oxley Act

Bibliography

ABA COORDINATING COMMITTEE ON NONPROFIT GOVERNANCE, GUIDE TO NONPROFIT CORPORATE GOVERNANCE IN THE WAKE OF SARBANES-OXLEY (ABA 2005).

Dana Brakman Reiser, *Enron.org: Why Sarbanes-Oxley Will Not Ensure Comprehensive Nonprofit Accountability,* 38 U.C. DAVIS L. REV. 205 (2004).

Robin R. Ganzert & Charles O. Mahaffey, *Spirit of Sarbanes-Oxley: Relevance of Nonprofit Governance on Planned Giving Fundraising Efforts, in* 2004 NATIONAL COMMITTEE ON PLANNED GIVING CONFERENCE PROCEEDINGS 541 (2004).

Jane Heath, *Comment, Who's Minding the Nonprofit Store: Does Sarbanes-Oxley Have Anything to Offer Nonprofits?,* 38 U.S.F. L. REV. 781 (2004).

Warwick Hunt, *Sarbanes-Oxley and New Zealand,* CHARTERED ACCT. J. NEW ZEALAND, Nov. 2005, at 1.

Suzanne Ross McDowell, *Should Nonprofit Organizations Adopt the Rules of Sarbanes-Oxley?,* 16 TAX'N EXEMPTS 8 (2004).

Wendy Szymanski, *An Allegory of Good (and Bad) Governance: Applying the Sarbanes-Oxley Act to Nonprofit Organizations,* 2003 UTAH LAW R. NO. 4 1303.

JACK SIEGAL, A DESKTOP GUIDE FOR NONPROFIT DIRECTORS, OFFICERS, AND ADVISORS: AVOIDING TROUBLE WHILE DOING GOOD. (Wiley 2006).

James G. Wiehl, *Roles and Responsiblities of Nonprofit Health Care Board Members in the Post-Enron Era,* 25 J. LEGAL MED. 411 (2004).

Search Firms

Bibliography

Elizabeth M. Fowler, *Recruiting for Nonprofit Boards,* N.Y. TIMES, Sept. 5, 1989, at D8.

Welton Jones, *Art Museum Trustees, Headhunters Labor over Criteria for New Director,* SAN DIEGO TRIBUNE, Nov. 8, 1998, at E1.

Debra Nussbaum, *Earning It: Volunteer Reserves Get Harder To Sell,* N.Y. TIMES, Jan. 14, 1996, at 3:10.

Jeanne B. Pinder, *Big Business: Helping the Helpers,* N.Y. TIMES, Nov. 18, 1998, at G8.

Nancy Polk, *Headhunters Try to Find a Heartbeat in Job Market,* N.Y. TIMES, Dec. 6, 1992, at 13.

Lornet Turnbull, *Search Firm Finds Booming Business Among City Clients,* COLUMBUS DISPATCH, Oct. 20, 1997, at 1D.

Internet Sites

Development Resource Groups, <http://www.drgnyc.com/>.

Goodwin & Co., <http://www.goodwinco.com/>.

The Himmelfarb Group, < http://www.himmelfarbgroup.com/>.

Isaacson, Miller,<http://www.insearch.com/>.

Korn/Ferry International (provides recruitment solutions and management assessments), <http://www.kornferry.com/>.

Spencer Stuart (a management consulting firm specializing in senior-level executive search and board director appointments), <http://www.spencerstuart.com>.

Social Entrepreneurship

(See also Strategic Alliances.)

Bibliography

Dunn Alison & C. A. Riley, *Supporting the Not-for-Profit Sector: The Government's Review of Charitable and Social Enterprise,* 67 MOD. L. REV. 632 (2004).

Linda D. Ketchum, *Social Entrepreneurship: A New Paradigm for Nonprofit Sustainability,* 36 OD PRAC. 3 (2004).

Ronnie L. Korosec & Evan M. Berman, *Municipal Support for Social Entrepreneurship,* 66 PUB. ADMIN. REV. 448 (2006).

Kelly M. Leroux, *What Drives Nonprofit Entrepreneurship?: A Look at Budget Trends of Metro Detroit Social Service Agencies,* 35 AMER. REV. PUB. ADMIN. 350 (2005).

RACHEL MOSHER-WILLIAMS, RESEARCH ON SOCIAL ENTREPRENEURSHIP: UNDERSTANDING AND CONTRIBUTING TO AN EMERGING FIELD (ARNOVA 2006).

Social Investing

Bibliography

Robert P. Fry, Jr. & Robert P. Fry, Minding the Money: An Investment Guide for Nonprofit Board Members (2004).

Maximilian M. Haag, *Hedge Fund Investments of Private Foundations and Educational Endowments,* 50 Exempt Org. Tax Rev. 261 (2005).

Theresa L. M. Man, *Foundations Incurring Debts to Purchase Investments,* available at http://www.carters.ca/pub/bulletin/charity/2006/chylb86.htm (2006).

Douglas Moore & Ajay Badlani, *Investment Challenges for Private Foundations,* Tr. & Est., June 2005, at 46.

Paul Douglas Palmer, et al., Socially Responsible Investment: A Guide for Pension Schemes and Charities (Charles Scanlan ed., 2005).

Lewis D. Salomon & Karen C. Koe, *The Legal Aspects of Social Investing by Non-Profit Fiduciaries,* 66 Univ. of Missouri at Kansas City Law Rev. 213 (1997).

George G. Triantis, *Organizations as Internal Capital Markets: The Legal Boundaries of Firms, Collateral, and Trusts in Commercial and Charitable Enterprises,* 117 Harv. L. Rev. 1103 (2004).

Standing

Bibliography

Rob Atkinson, *Unsettled Standing: Who (Else) Should Enforce the Duties of Charitable Fiduciaries,* 23 Journal of Corporation Law 655 (1998).

Mary Grace Blasko, Curt S. Crossley, & David Lloyd, *Standing to Sue in the Charitable Sector,* 28 University of San Francisco L. Rev. 37 (1993).

George Gleason Bogert: The Law of Trusts and Trustees, Rev. 2d Ed, § 412, 414 (West 1991).

Evelyn Brody, *From the Dead Hand to the Living Dead: The Conundrum of Charitable-Donor Standing,* 41 Ga. L. Rev. (2007).

Ronald Chester, *Grantor Standing to Enforce Charitable Transfers Under Section 405(c) of the Uniform Trust Code and Related Law: How Important Is it and How Extensive Should It Be?* 37 Real Prop., Prob. & Tr. J. 611 (and Related Law: 2003).

Iris J. Goodwin, *Donor Standing to Enforce Charitable Gifts: Civil Society vs. Donor Empowerment,* 58 Vand. L. Rev. 1093 (2005).

Jessica E. Jay, *Third-Party Enforcement of Conservation Easements,* 29 Vt. L. Rev. 757 (2005).

Luis Kutner, *The Desecration of the Furguson Monument Trust: The Need for Watchdog Legislation,* 12 DePaul L. Rev. 217 (1962–63).

Restatement of Trusts, 2nd ed. § 391.

Case Law

Associate Alumni v. General Theological Seminary, 57 N.E. 626 (N.Y. 1900).

Arizonians for Official English v. Arizona, 520 U.S. 43 (1997).

Brzicau v. Trustees of Dartmouth College, 174 N.H. 443 (2000).

Christiansen v. Nat'l Sav. & Trust Co. 683 F.2d 520 (D.C. Cir. 1982).

Consumers Union v. State of N.Y. index no. 118699/02 (N.Y. Sup. Ct. Mar. 6, 2003), *available in* N.Y.L.J., Mar. 12, 2003, p.18.

Greene v. Art Institute of Chicago, 147 N.E. 2d 415 (Ill. App. 1958).

Glenn v. University of Southern California, B151776, 2002 Cal. App. Unpub. LEXIS 8508 (Cal. App. 2002) (unpublished).

Friends World College v. Nicklin, 249 A.D. 2d 393 (2nd Dept., N.Y. 1998).

Carl J. Herzog Foundation, Inc. v. University of Bridgeport, 699A. 2d 995 (Conn. 1997).

Holt v. College of Osteopathic Physicians and Surgeons, 394 P. 2d 932 (Cal. 1964).

Home for Incurables of Baltimore City v. University of Maryland Medical System Corporation, 797 A.2d 746 (Md. 2002).

Hooter v. Edes Home, 579A. 2d 608 (D.C. Cir., 1990).

In re Community Service Society v. Cuomo 561 N.Y.S. 2d 461 (1990).

In re Estate of Duffin, 59 Misc. 2d 987 (1969).

In re Garrison, 137 A.2d 321 (Pa. 1958).

In re Lown, 59 Misc. 2d 987, 301 N.Y.S. 2d 746 (N.Y. Sur. 1969).

In re Sculpture Center, Inc. 2001 N.Y. Misc. 1019 (Sup. Ct. N.Y. 2001).

In re United States Catholic Conference, 885 F.2d 1020 (2d Cir. 1989), *cert. denied,* 495 U.S. 918 (1990). (Abortion Rights Mobilization Case).

Jackson v. Stuhlfire, 547 N.E. 2d 1146 (Mass. App. Ct. 1990).

Jones v. Grant, 344 So. 2d 1210 (Ala. 1977).

L.B. Research and Education Foundation v. UCLA Foundation, 29 Cal. Rptr. 3d 710 (Cal. App. 2005), *rev. denied* 2005 Cal. LEXIS 9658 (Cal. 2005).

Marcus v. Jewish National Fund, 556 N.Y.S. 2d 886 (N.Y. App. Div. 1990).

Matter of Alaimo, 732 N.Y.S. 2d 819 (N.Y. App. Div. 2001).

Matter of Rothko's Estate, 372 N.E. 2d 291 (N.Y. 1977).

McInnes v. Goldthwaite, 52 A.2d 795 (N.H. 1947).

Milton Hershey School and Hershey Trust Company, Trustee; Appeal of Milton Hershey School Alumni Association, 867 A.2d 674 (Pa. Commw. Ct. 2005), *appeal granted,* 2005 Pa. LEXIS 2695 (Pa. Dec. 1, 2005).

Morgan v. Robertson, 609 S.W. 2d 662 (Ark. Ct. App., 1980).

Prentis Family Foundation v. Karmanos Cancer Institute, 698 N.W.2d 900 (Mich. App. 2005), *appeal denied* 2005 Mich. LEXIS 1675 (Mich., Sept. 28, 2005).

Robertson v. Princeton University, Civ. Action No. C-99-02, Mercer County (N.J. Super. Ch. Div., June 20, 2003) (unreported).

Robert Schalkenbach Foundation v. Lincoln Foundation, Inc., 91 P.3d 1019 (Ariz. App. 2004), *rev. denied* 2004 Ariz. LEXIS 125 (Ariz. 2004).

Simon v. Eastern Kentucky Welfare Rights Organization, 426 U.S. 26 (1976).

Smithers v. St. Luke's-Roosevelt Hosp. Ctr., 723 N.Y.S. 2d 426 (App. Div. 2001).

Steeneck v. University of Bridgeport, 668 A.2d 688 (Conn. 1996).

Stock v. Augsburg College 2002 Minn. App. LEXIS 421 (Apr. 16, 2002).

Tennessee Div. of United Daughters of the Confederacy v. Vanderbilt University, 174 S.W.3d 98 (Tenn. App. 2005).

Tennessee Exrel Adventist Health Care System v. Nashville Memorial Hospital, Inc., 914 S.W. 2d 903 (Tenn. Et. App. 1995).

Weaver v. Wood, 680 N.E. 2d 928 (Mass. 1997), *cert. denied* 522 U.S. 1049 (1998).

YMCA v. Covington, 484 A.2d 589 (D.C. 1984).

Statutory and Other Authority

Revised Model Nonprofit Corp. Act §§ 1.70, 6.30.

Strategic Alliances

Bibliography

James E. Austin, The Collaboration Challenge: How Nonprofits and Businesses Succeed Through Strategic Alliances (Jossey-Bass 2000).

James E. Austin, *Principles for Partnership,* Leader to Leader, Fall 2000, at 54.

Ida E. Berger, et al., *Social Alliances: Company/Nonprofit Collaboration,* Cal. Mgmt. Rev., Fall 2004, at 58.

JERR BOSCHEE, THE SOCIAL ENTERPRISE SOURCEBOOK (Northland Institute 2002).

PETER C. BROWN, THE COMPLETE GUIDE TO MONEY MAKING VENTURES FOR NONPROFIT ORGANIZATIONS (The Taft Group 1986).

Carolyn Casselman, *Waltzing with the Muse or Dancing with the Devil: Enhancement Deals Between Nonprofit Theaters and Commercial Producers,* 27 COLUM.-VLA J. ART & L. 323 (2004).

Thomas M. Dalton, *Structuring Joint Ventures Between For-Profit and Tax-Exempt Entities,* BUS. ENTITIES, Jan./Feb. 2005, at 32.

ENTERPRISING NONPROFITS: A TOOLKIT FOR SOCIAL ENTREPRENEURS (J. Gregory Dees et al., eds. 2001).

LEADING BEYOND THE WALLS (Frances Hesselbein, Marshall Goldsmith, & Vain Somerville, eds., Jossey-Bass 1999).

Christine W. Letts, William Ryan, & Allen Grossman, *Virtuous Capital: What Foundations Can Learn from Venture Capitalists,* HARV. BUS. REV., Mar.-April 1997, at 36.

MCKINSEY & COMPANY, DEVELOPING SUCCESSFUL GLOBAL HEALTH ALLIANCES (Bill & Melinda Gates Foundation 2003).

MERGING MISSION AND MONEY: A BOARD MEMBER'S GUIDE TO SOCIAL ENTREPRENEURSHIP (National Center for Nonprofit Boards).

MICHAEL I. SANDERS, JOINT VENTURES INVOLVING TAX-EXEMPT ORGANIZATIONS (2d ed. Wiley 2002).

Pamela C. Smith, *An Empirical Investigation of For-Profit and Tax-Exempt Nonprofit Hospitals Engaged in Joint Ventures,* 29 HEALTH CARE MGMT. REV. 284 (2004).

STRENGTHENING NONPROFIT PERFORMANCE: A FUNDER'S GUIDE TO CAPACITY BUILDING (Amherst Wilder Foundation 2003).

Strategic Planning

Bibliography

MICHAEL ALLISON & JUDE KAY, STRATEGIC PLANNING FOR NONPROFIT ORGANIZATIONS: A PRACTICAL GUIDE AND WORKBOOK (2nd ed. Wiley 2005).

ALAN ANDREASEN & PHILIP KOTLER, STRATEGIC MARKETING FOR NONPROFIT ORGANIZATIONS (5th ed. Prentice Hall 2002).

PETER C. BRINCHERHOFF, MISSION-BASED MANAGEMENT: LEADING YOUR NOT-FOR-PROFIT INTO THE 21ST CENTURY (Alpine Guild 1994).

William A. Brown & Joel O. Iverson, *Exploring Strategy and Board Structure in Nonprofit Organizations,* 33 NONPROFIT & VOLUNTARY SECTOR Q. 377 (2004).

Barry W. Bryan & Vincent Hyman, Strategic Planning Workbook for Nonprofit Organizations (Amherst H. Wilder Foundation 1997).

John M. Bryson, Strategic Planning for Public and Nonprofit Organizations: A Guide to Strengthening and Sustaining Organizational Achievement (3d ed. Jossey-Bass 2004).

Jim Collins, Good to Great: Why Some Companies Make the Leap . . . and Others Don't (HarperBusiness 2001).

Jim Collins, Good to Great and the Social Sectors: A Monograph to Accompany Good to Great (Collins 2005).

J. Gregory Dees, et al., Strategic Tools for Social Entrepreneurs: Enhancing The Performance of Your Enterprising Nonprofit (Wiley 2000).

Peter F. Drucker, How To Assess Your Nonprofit Organization (Jossey-Bass 1993).

Fisher Howe, A Board Member's Guide to Strategic Planning (Jossey-Bass 1997).

Taieb Hafsi & Howard Thomas, *Strategic Management and Change in High Dependency Environments: The Case of a Philanthropic Organization*, 16 Voluntas 329 (2005).

Deborah L. Kocsis & Susan A. Waechter, Driving Strategic Planning, A Nonprofit Executive's Guide (BoardSource 2003).

Neil Kotler & Philip Kotler, Museum Strategy and Marketing (Jossey-Bass 1998).

Thomas A. McLaughlin, Nonprofit Strategic Positioning: Decide Where to Be, Plan What to Do (Wiley 2006).

Richard Mittenthal, *Don't Give up on Strategic Planning: 10 Keys to Success*, Nonprofit World, May/June 2004, at 21.

National Executive Service Corps., Strategic Planning for Nonprofit Organizations (re-released Spring 1999).

Sharon M. Oster, Strategic Management For Nonprofit Organizations: Theory and Cases (Oxford University Press 1995).

Edward J. Pawlak & Robert D. Vinter, Designing and Planning Programs for Nonprofit and Government Organizations (Jossey-Bass 2004).

James A. Phills, Integrating Mission and Strategy for Nonprofit Organizations (Oxford 2005).

Terrie C. Reeves & Eric W. Ford, *Strategic Management and Performance Differences: Nonprofit Versus For-Profit Health Organizations,* 29 Health Care Mgmt. Rev. 298 (2004).

Barbara E. Taylor, Richard P. Chait, & Thomas P. Holland, *The New Work of the Nonprofit Board,* Harv. Bus. Rev., Sept.–Oct. 1996, at 36.

Supporting Organizations

(See also Donor-Advised Funds; Private Foundations.) (Note: since the passage of H.R. 4, the Pension Protection Act of 2006, the provisions of the Internal Revenue Code governing supporting organizations have been significantly revised and expanded. For a discussion of these revisions, see the 2006 publications listed below.)

Bibliography

ABA Section of Taxation, Committee on Exempt Organizations, Comments of ABA Tax Section on S.2020, PAUL STRECKFUS' EO TAX J., Mar./Apr. 2006, at 66.

Victoria B. Bjorklund, *Charitable Giving to a Private Foundation: The Alternatives, The Supporting Organization and the Donor-Advised Fund*, 27 EXEMPT ORG. TAX REV. 107 (2000).

Council on Foundations, *Changes in Intermediate Sanctions for Supporting Organizations (Types I, II, and III)*, available at <http://www.cof.org/> (2006).

Council on Foundations, *Distributions from a Private Foundation to a Supporting Organization*, available at <http://www.cof.org/> (2006).

Alyssa A. DiRusso, *Supporting the Supporting Organization: The Potential and Exploitation of 509(a)(3) Charities*. IND. LAW REV., Vol. 39, March 2006. Available at SSRN: http://ssrn.com/abstract=823085.

Group Offers Draft Guidance on Pension Protection Act Provisions that Affect Charities, 2006 TAX NOTES TODAY 207-13 (2006).

J. Christine Harris, *Lapham Argues Court Missed Bigger Picture*, TAX NOTES 1277 (12/9/2002).

Darryl K. Jones, *Regulating Donor-Advised Funds*, 75 May FLBJ 38 (2001).

Mark Rambler, *Note, Best Supporting Actor: Refining the 509(a)(3) Type 3 Charitable Organization*, 51 DUKE L. J. 1367 (2002).

Sanford J. Schlesinger & Martin R. Goodman, *Supporting Organizations: An Antidote to Lack of Public Funding*, EST. PLAN. (WGL), 2004, at 398.

David A. Shelvin, *Recent Court Decisions Analyze the Rules Governing "Type 3" Supporting Organizations*, 39 EXEMPT ORG. TAX REV. 18 (2003).

Mark Sidel, *The Nonprofit Sector and the New State Activism*, 100 MICH. L. REV. 1312 (2002).

Conrad Teitell, *Public Charities, Advised Funds, Supporting Organizations and Foundations: Selecting Wisely, in* 2004 NATIONAL COMMITTEE ON PLANNED GIVING CONFERENCE PROCEEDINGS 805 (2004).

Gerald B. Treacy, *What's Left of SOs?,* 145 TRUSTS AND ESTATES 10 (2006).

Joel Ugolini, *The Difficulties of Establishing a Supporting Organization When Making Charitable Contributions to a Donor-Advised Fund Program: Lapham Foundation Inc. v. Commissioner,* TAX LAWYER, VOL. 56, NO. 4, 929 (2003).

Merrie Jeanne Webel, *The Supporting Organization: A Beneficial (But Tangled) Alternative for the Directed Donor,* PROBATE AND PROPERTY, March/April (2001).

Frederick B. Weber, *Supporting Organizations: The Less Expensive Alternative to Private Foundations,* ILL. B.J. MARCH (2001).

Case Law

Lapham Foundation v. Commissioner 84 T.C.M. 586 (U.S. Tax Ct. 2002).

Nellie Callahan Scholarship Fund v. Commissioner, 73 T.C. at 637 (2002).

Quarrie v. Commisioner 70 T.C. 182 (1998), *aff'd* 603 Fed., 2d 1274 (7th Cir., 1979).

Cockerline Memorial Fund v. Commissioner, 86 TC 53 (1986).

Roe Foundation Charitable Trust v. Commissioner, 58 T.C.M. 402 (1989).

Change-All Souls Housing Corportation v. U.S., 671 F.2d 463 (Ct. Cl. 1982).

Mabury Trust v. Commissioner, 80 T.C. 718 (1983).

Goodspeed Scholarship Fund v. Commissioner, 70 T.C. 515 (1978).

Cuddeback Memorial Fund v. Commissioner, 84 T.C.M. 623 (2002).

Statutory and Other Authority

Internal Revenue Code § 509(a)(3).

Taxation

(See also relevant specialized entries throughout this volume.)

Bibliography

William D. Andrews, *Personal Deductions in an Ideal Income Tax,* 86 HARV. L. REV. 309 (1972).

Rob Atkinson, *Theories of the Federal Income Tax Exemption for Charities: Thesis, Antithesis, and Syntheses,* 27 STETSON L. REV. 395 (1987).

Chauncey Belknap, THE FEDERAL INCOME TAX EXEMPTION OF CHARITABLE ORGANIZATIONS: ITS HISTORY AND UNDERLYING POLICY (1954), reprinted in 4 Research Papers Sponsored by the Filer Commission on Private Philanthropy and Public Needs 2025, (Filler Commission) (U.S. Treasury Department, 1977).

Boris I. Bittker & George K. Rahdert, *The Exemption of Nonprofit Organizations from Federal Income Taxation,* 85 YALE L. J. 299 (1976).

VICTORIA B. BJORKLUND, JAMES J. FISHMAN, & DANIEL L. KURTZ, NEW YORK NONPROFIT LAW AND PRACTICE: WITH TAX ANALYSIS (Michie 1997).

JODY BLAZEK, TAX PLANNING AND COMPLIANCE FOR NON-PROFIT ORGANIZATIONS (Forms, Checklists, Procedures)(4th ed. John Wiley & Sons 2004).

M. Gregg Bloche, *Health Policy Below the Waterline: Medical Care and the Charitable Exemption 1995,* 80 MINN. L. REV. 299, (1995).

Evelyn Brody, *Charities in Tax Reform: Threats to Subsidies Overt and Covert,* 66 TENN. L. REV. 687 (1999).

Evelyn Brody, *Of Sovereignty and Subsidy: Conceptualizing the Charity Tax Exemption,* 23 J. CORP. L. 585 (1998).

Johnny Rex Buckles, *Reforming the Public Policy Doctrine,* 53 KAN. L. REV. 397 (2005).

NICHOLAS P. CAFARDI & JACLYN FABEAN CHERRY, UNDERSTANDING NONPROFIT AND TAX EXEMPT ORGANIZATIONS (LexisNexis 2006).

John D. Colombo, *Why is Harvard Tax Exempt? (And Other Mysteries of Tax Exemption for Private Educational Institutions),* 35 ARIZ. L. REV. 841 (Winter 1993).

John D. Colombo, *Commercial Activity and Charitable Tax Exemption,* 44 WM. & MARY L. REV. 48 (2002).

Committee on Exempt Organizations of the ABA Section of Taxation, *Exempt Organizations,* 58 TAX LAW. 1095 (2005).

COMPLETE GUIDE TO NONPROFIT ORGANIZATIONS: LAW, TAXATION, OPERATIONAL PLANNING (Penina Kessler Lieber & Donald R. Levy eds., Civic Research Institute 2005).

Nina J. Crimm, *Through A Post-September 11 Looking Glass: Assessing the Roles of Federal Tax Laws and Tax Policies Applicable to Global Philanthropy by Private Foundations and Their Donors,* 23 VA. TAX REV. 1 (2003).

ROBERT J. DESIDERIO, PLANNING TAX-EXEMPT ORGANIZATIONS (LexisNexis 2002).

Developments in the Law-Nonprofit Corporations, 105 HARV. L. REV. 1578 (1992).

Alyssa DiRusso, *Supporting the Supporting Organization: The Potential and Exploitation of 509(a)(3) Charities, 39* IND. L. REV. 207 (2006).

Exempt Organization Tax Review (a monthly publication published by Tax Analysts and available on Lexis).

Peter L. Faber, *The Joint Committee Staff Disclosure Recommendations: What They Mean for Exempt Organizations,* 28 EXEMPT ORG. TAX REV. 31 (2000).

MARION R. FREMONT-SMITH, GOVERNING NONPROFIT ORGANIZATIONS: STATE AND FEDERAL LAW AND REGULATION (Belknap Press of Harvard University Press 2004).

GILBERT M. GAUL & NEIL A. BOROWSKI, FREE RIDE: THE TAX EXEMPT ECONOMY (Andrews Mcmeel Pub. 1993).

Mark P. Gergen, *The Case for a Charitable Contributions Deduction,* 74 VA. L. REV. 1393, 1450 (1988).

Richard Gershon, *Tax Exempt Entities: Achieving and Maintaining Special Status Under the Watchful Eye of the Internal Revenue Service,* 16 CUMB. L. REV. 301 (1986).

MALVERN J. GROSS JR., JOHN H. MCCARTHY, & NANCY E. SHELMON, FINANCIAL AND ACCOUNTING GUIDE FOR NOT-FOR-PROFIT ORGANIZATIONS (7th ed. Wiley 2005).

Mark A. Hall & John D. Colombo, *The Donative Theory of Charitable Tax Exemption,* 52 OHIO ST. L. J. 1379 (1991).

Henry Hansmann, *The Rationale for Exempting Nonprofit Organizations from Corporate Income Taxation,* 91 YALE L. J. 54 (1981).

FRANCES R. HILL, TAXATION OF EXEMPT ORGANIZATIONS (Warren Gorham & Lamont 2002).

FRANCES R. HILL & BARBARA L. KIRSCHTEN, FEDERAL AND STATE TAXATION OF EXEMPT ORGANIZATIONS (Warren Gorham & Lamont 1994).

FRANCES R. HILL & DOUGLAS M. MANCINO, TAXATION OF EXEMPT ORGANIZATIONS (Warren Gorham & Lamont 2002).

BRUCE R. HOPKINS, TAX LAW OF CHARITABLE GIVING (3d ed. Wiley 2005).

BRUCE R. HOPKINS, THE LAW OF TAX-EXEMPT ORGANIZATIONS (8th ed. John Wiley 2003).

Darryll K. Jones, *The Scintilla of Individual Profit: In Search of Private Inurement and Excess Benefit,* VA. TAX REV. 575 (2000).

DARRYLL K. JONES, STEVEN J. WILLIS, DAVID A. BRENNAN, & BEVERLY I. MORAN, THE TAX LAW OF CHARITIES AND OTHER EXEMPT ORGANIZATIONS (Thompson West 2003).

Tanya Marsh, *A Dubious Distinction: Rethinking Tax Treatment of Private Foundations and Public Charities,* 22 VA. TAX REV. 137 (2002).

OBER KALER, THE NONPROFIT LEGAL LANDSCAPE (Thomas K. Hyatt ed., BoardSource 2005).

MARILYN PHELAN, NONPROFIT ENTERPRISES: LAW AND TAXATION (Callaghan, with annual loose-leaf updates 1993).

Report to Congress and the NonProfit Sector on Governance, Transparency and Accountability (Panel on the Nonprofit Sector, Independent Sector ed. 2005).

Allan J. Samansky, *Deductibility of Contributions to Religious Instiutions,* 25 VA. TAX REV. 65 (2004).

John G. Simon, The Tax Treatment of Nonprofit Organizations: A Review of Federal and State Policies in the Nonprofit Sector, in 68 A Research Handbook (Walter W. Powell, ed., 1987).

Senate Finance Committee, *Senate Finance Committee Discussion Draft of Proposals for Reforms and Best Practices in the Area of Tax-Exempt Organizations,* available at <http://www.finance .senate.gov/hearings/testimony/2004test/062204stfdis.pdf> (2004).

C. EUGENE STEUERLE, CONTEMPORARY U.S. TAX POLICY (Urban Institute Press 2004).

Ethan G. Stone, *Adhering To The Old Line: Uncovering The History And Political Function Of The Unrelated Business Income Tax,* 54 EMORY L. J. 1475 (2005).

Martin A. Sullivan, *More Disclosure from 501(c)'s: Poison Pill or Good Policy,* 29 EXEMPT ORG. TAX REV. 10 (2000).

STANLEY S. SURREY & PAUL R. MCDANIEL, TAX EXPENDITURES (Harvard University Press 1985).

Symposium: Health Care And Tax Exemption: The Push And Pull Of Tax Exemption Law On The Organization And Delivery Of Health Care Services, Winter, 2005, 15 HEALTH MATRIX 1 (2005).

Symposium: Religion and Taxation, 42 B.C. L. REV. 733 (2001).

TAX COMPLIANCE FOR TAX-EXEMPT ORGANIZATIONS (Steven D. Simpson ed. Aspen 2005).

PAUL E. TREUSCH, TAX EXEMPT CHARITABLE ORGANIZATIONS (American Law Institute and American Bar Association 1988).

U.S. TREASURY DEPARTMENT, INTERNAL REVENUE SERVICE, EXEMPT ORGANIZATIONS CONTINUING PROFESSIONAL EDUCATION TECHNICAL INSTRUCTION PROGRAM TEXTBOOK (Government Printing Office, prepared annually).

U.S. TREASURY DEPARTMENT, INTERNAL REVENUE SERVICE, TAX EXEMPT STATUS FOR YOUR ORGANIZATION (Publication No. 557 2001).

Carolyn D. Wright, *UCC, IRS Settle Decade-long Exemption Dispute: 501(c)(3) Status Revoked for Three Years,* 28 EXEMPT ORG. TAX REV. 250 (2000).

Case Law

American Campaign Academy v. Commissioner, 92 T.C. 1053 (1989).

Associated Master Barbers & Beauticians of America v. Commissioner, 69 T.C. 53 (1977).

Big Mama Rag v. United States, 631 F.2d 1030 (D.C. Cir. 1980).

Blake v. Commissioner, 697 F.2d 473 (2d Cir. 1982).

Bob Jones Univ. v. United States, 461 U.S. 574 (1983).

Branch Ministries v. Rossotti, 341 U.S. App. D.C. 166 (2000).

Camps Newfound/Owatonna v. Town of Harrison, 520 U.S. 564 (1997).

Goldsboro Art League v. Commissioner, 75 T.C. 337 (1980).

Hernandez v. Commissioner, 490 U.S. 680 (1989).

Hutchinson Baseball Enter., Inc. v. Commissioner, 696 F.2d 757 (10th Cir. 1982).

Regan v. Taxation With Representation, 461 U.S.540 (1983).

Sierra Club v. Commissioner, 86 F.3d.1526 (1996).

St. David's Health Care System, Inc. v. United States 439 F.3d 232 (5th Cir., 2003).

United States v. Brown Univ., 5 F.3d 658 (3d Cir. 1993).

Statutory and Other Authority

Internal Revenue Code, Title 26, see especially Subtitle A (Income Taxes), Chapter 1, Subchapter F (Exempt Organizations); Subtitle B (Estate and Gift Taxes), Chapters 11, 12; Subtitle D (Misc. excise Taxes); Subtitle F (Procedure and Administration); see also associated federal tax regulations contained in the Code of Federal Regulations; and related revenue rulings, private latter rulings, technical advice memoranda, general counsel memoranda, actions on decisions, technical memoranda, field service advice.

Internet Sites

Internal Revenue Service, Tax Information for Charities and Other Nonprofits (including forms and guidance), available at <http://www.irs.gov/charities/>.

National Association of State Charities Officials resources, at <http://www.nasconet.org/>.

Technology

Bibliography

Milton Cerny, *Technology Transfer and the New Economy*, 47 EXEMPT ORG. TAX REV. 39 (2005).

JON PODOLSKY, WIRED FOR GOOD (Jossey-Bass 2003).

Internet Sites

The Nonprofit Technology Enterprise Network (N-TEN): Works to support the diverse people and organizations who help nonprofits employ technology effectively, available at <http://nten.org>.

Terrorism

(See: Disaster Relief and International)

Bibliography

Laila Al-Marayati, *American Muslim Charities: Easy Targets in the War on Terror*, 25 PACE L. REV. 321 (2005).

Sandra T. Barnes, GLOBAL FLOWS, *Terror, Oil & Strategic Philanthropy*, 32 REV. AFR. POL. ECON. 235 (2005).

Victoria B. Bjorklund, et al., *Terrorism and Money Laundering: Illegal Purposes and Activities*, 25 PACE L. REV. 233 (2005).

Terrance S. Carter, et al., *Charities and Compliance with Anti-Terrorism Legislation: A Due Diligence Response*, 19 PHILANTHROPIST 109 (2005).

Terrance S. Carter & Sean S. Carter, *The Implications for Charities of Anti-Terrorism Initiatives on Humanitarian Assistance for Southeast Asia*, available at <http://www.carters.ca/pub/alert/atcla/atcla06.pdf> (2005).

Nina J. Crimm, *High Alert: The Government's War on the Financing of Terrorism and Its Implications for Donors, Domestic Charitable Organizations, and Global Philanthropy*, 45 WM. AND MARY L. REV. 1341 (2004).

Nina J. Crimm, *Post-September 11 Fortified Anti-Terrorism Measures Compel Heightened Due Diligence,* 25 PACE L. REV. 203 (2005).

Terrance S. Carter, *The What, Where and When of Canadian Anti-Terrorism Legislation for Charities in the International Context,* available at <http://www.carters.ca/pub/article/charity/2006/tsc0511.pdf> (2006).

Nina J. Crimm, High Alert, *The Government's War on the Financing of Terrorism and its Implications for Donors, Domestic Charitable Organizations, and Global Philanthropy,* 45 WM. & MARY L. REV. 1341 (2004).

Edgardo Ramos, Timothy R. Lyman, Patricia Canavan, & Clifford Nichols III, *Handbook on Counter Terrorism Measures: What U.S. Nonprofits and Grantmakers Need to Know* (Berry Day & Howard 2004) at <www.cof.org>.

Montgomery E. Engel, *Note, Donating "Blood Money": Fundraising for International Terrorism by United States Charities and the Government's Efforts to Constrict the Flow,* 12 CARDOZO J. INT'L & COMP. L. 251 (2004).

Financial Action Task Force on Money Laundering, Report on Money Laundering & Terrorist Financing Typologies 2003–2004, available at <http://www.fatf-gafi.org> (2004).

Erich Ferrari, *Comment, Deep Freeze: Islamic Charities and the Financial War on Terror,* 7 SCHOLAR 205 (2005).

David Matas, *The New Laws on Terrorist Financing,* 4 ASPER REV. INT'L BUS. & TRADE L. 145 (2005).

Joel G. MacMull, *Note, Removing the Charitable Veil: An Examination of U.S. Policy to Combat Terrorist Funding,* 10 NEW ENG. J. INT'L & COMP. L. 121 (2004).

Jude McCulloch & Sharon Pickering, *Suppressing the Financing of Terrorism,* 45 BRIT. J. CRIMINOLOGY 470 (2005).

Daniel Mitchell, *Fighting Terror and Defending Freedom: The Role of Cost-Benefit Analysis,* 25 PACE L. REV. 219 (2005).

Nicole Nice-Petersen, *Note, Justice for the "Designated": The Process That Is Due to Alleged U.S. Financiers of Terrorism,* 93 GEO. L. J. 1387 (2005).

Joan M. O'Sullivan-Butler, *Combatting Money Laundering and International Terrorism: Does the USA Patriot Act Require the Judicial System to Abandon Fundamental Due Process in the Name of Homeland Security?,* 16 ST. THOMAS L. REV. 395 (2004).

Matthew J. Piers, *Malevolent Destruction of a Muslim Charity: A Commentary on the Prosecution of Benevolence International Foundation,* 25 PACE L. REV. 339 (2005).

Kathryn A. Ruff, *Note, Scared To Donate: An Examination of the Effects of Designating Muslim Charities As Terrorist Organizations on the First Amendment Rights of Muslim Donors,* 9 N. Y. U. J. LEGIS. & PUB. POL'Y 447 (2005/2006).

Amy K. Ryder Wentz, *Note, Unreasonable Conditions Impeding Our Nation's Charities: An Unconstitutional Condition in the Combined Federal Campaign*, 53 CLEV. ST. L. REV. 689 (2005/2006).

John D. G. Waszak, *Note, The Obstacles to Suppressing Radical Islamic Terrorist Financing*, 36 CASE W. RES. J. INT'L L. 673 (2004).

Joseph W. Younker, *Note, The "U.S. Department of the Treasury Anti-Terrorist Financing Guidelines: Voluntary Best-Practices for U.S.-Based Charities": Sawing a Leg off the Stool of Democracy*, 14 TRANSNAT'L L. & CONTEMP. PROBS. 865 (2004).

Statutory and Other Authority

The Victims of Terrorism Tax Relief Act of 2001.

U.S. Treasury Department: Anti-Terrorist Financing Guidelines: Voluntary Best Practices for U.S. Based Charities. (Amended version of Guidelines published in November 2002). Available at <http://www.treasury.gov/offices/enforcement/key-issues/protecting/docs/guidelines_charities.pdf>.

Tort Liability

(See: Charitable Immunity)

Trade Associations

Bibliography

PETER BROWN & DANIEL ABEL, OUTGUNNED: UP AGAINST THE NRA (Free Press 2002).

James Falkins, *Snyder v. American Association of Blood Banks: Balancing Duties and Immunities in Assessing The Third Party Liability of Nonprofit Medical Associations*, 3 DEPAUL J. HEALTH CARE 243 (2000).

JERALD A. JACOBS, ASSOCIATION LAW HANDBOOK (3d ed. American Society of Association Executives 1996).

W. A. Ritch & M. E. Begog, *Strange Bedfellows: The History of Collaborations Between the Massachusetts Restaurant Association and the Tobacco Industry*, 91 AMERICAN JOURNAL OF PUBLIC HEALTH 598 (2001).

Travel Tours

(See: Unrelated Business Income)

Bibliography

Jane C. Nober, *Legal Brief: Encouraging Tourism for Economic Development,* Foundation News & Commentary, Sept./Oct. 2005, at 51.

Statutory and Other Authority

Internal Revenue Code §§ 513(a), 513(c); Treas. Reg. 1.513.7.

Trusts

Bibliography

American Law Institute, Restatement (Third) of the Law of Trusts: The Prudent Investor Rule (1992) and Vol. 2 (ALI 2003).

George G. Bogert & George T. Bogert, The Law of Trusts and Trusters (2d ed., West 1978).

Johnny Rex Buckles, *When Charitable Gifts Soar Above the Twin Towers: A Federal Income Tax Solution to the Problem of Publicly Solicited Surplus Donations Raised for a Charitable Purpose,* 71 Fordham L. Rev. 827 (2003).

Evelyn Brody, *Charity Governance: What's Trust Law Got to Do With It?* 80 Chi-Kent L. Rev. 641 (2005).

David K. Cahoone & Carol Peskoe Schaner, *Everything You Always Wanted to Know About Charitable Lead Trusts, in* 2004 National Committee on Planned Giving Conference Proceedings 653 (2004).

Francesca Di Gregori Boschini, *Private Foundations and Reserved Powers Trusts,* Tr. & Est., Apr. 2006, at 46.

James Fishman, *Improving Charitable Accountability,* 62 Md. L. Rev. 218 (2003).

Richard L. Fox, *A Guide to the IRS Sample Charitable Remainder Trust Forms,* Est. Plan. (WGL), Jan. 2006, at 13.

Austin W. Scott, Jr., Mark L. Ascher, William F. Fratcher, & Austin Wakeman Scott, Scott on Trusts (4th ed. Aspen 1987).

Marion R. Freemont-Smith, *Duties and Powers of Charitable Fiduciaries: The Law of Trusts and the Correction of Abuses,* 14 UCLA L. Rev. 1041 (1966).

Wendy C. Gerzog, *The Collision Between CRTs and the UPC Elective Share*, 52 EXEMPT ORG. TAX REV. 275 (2006).

GEORGE B. JEWELL, CHARITABLE TRUSTS (2005).

Kent C. Kiffner, *Note, Charitable Remainder Annuity Trusts: Why the Internal Revenue Service's Approach Needs Revision*, 54 SYRACUSE L. REV. 739 (2004).

SAMUEL P. KING & RANDALL W. ROTH, BROKEN TRUST: GREED, MISMANAGEMENT AND POLITICAL MANIPULATION AT AMERICA'S LARGEST CHARITABLE TRUST (U. Hawaii Press 2006) (Bishop Estate).

Jennifer L. Komoroski, *Note, The Hershey Trust's Quest to Diversify: Redefining the State Attorney General's Role When Charitable Trusts Wish to Diversify*, 45 WM. & MARY L. REV. 1769 (2004).

Christopher Quay, *Exit Strategies for Charitable Donations and Charitable Remainder Trusts*, 51 EXEMPT ORG. TAX REV. 221 (2006).

John G. Simon, *American Philanthropy and the Buck Trust*, 21 U. OF SAN FRANCISCO L. REV. 641 (1987).

THOMAS J. RAY, JR., CHARITABLE GIFT PLANNING (ABA 2006).

Sanford J. Schlesinger & Martin R. Goodman, *Back To Basics: A Primer for Charitable Remainder Trusts*, EST. PLAN. (WGL), Mar. 2005, at 9.

Lisa M. Schreiber, *Split-Interest Trusts*, 2002, SOI BULL., Winter 2004/2005, at 89.

Stanley S. Weithorn, TRUSTS WITH CHARITABLE INTERESTS, REAL PROPERTY, PROBATE AND TRUST JOURNAL, Winter, 1969.

Stephen Wilmot, *Foundation Trusts and the Problem of Legitimacy*, 12 HEALTH CARE ANALYSIS 157 (2004).

Case Law

Brigham v. Peter Bent Brigham Hosptial 124 F. 513 (1st Cir. 1904).

Mercury Bay Boating Club v. San Diego Yacht Club 76 NY2d 256 (1990).

Nixon v. Lichtenstein, 959 S.W. 2d 854 (Mo. App. 1997).

Unrelated Business Income

(See: Commercial Activity, Royalties, Taxation, Travel Tours)

Bibliography

ABA Section of Taxation, Committee on Exempt Organizations, *Comments of ABA Tax Section on S.2020*, PAUL STRECKFUS' EO TAX J., Mar./Apr. 2006, at 66.

John D. Colombo, *Commercial Activity and Charitable Tax Exemptions,* 44 WM. & MARY L. REV. 487 (2002).

JOHN D. COLOMBO, *A Framework for Analyzing Exemption and UBIT Effects of Joint Ventures,* 34 EXEMPT ORG. TAX REV. 187 (2001).

HARVEY P. DALE, ABOUT THE UBIT . . . , 18TH NYU CONF. TAX PLAN. 501(c)(3) ORG. Ch. 9 (1990).

Daniel Halperin, *The Unrelated Business Income Tax and Payments from Controlled Entities,* 51 EXEMPT ORG. TAX REV. 25 (2006).

Henry B. Hansmann, *Unfair Competition and the Unrelated Business Income Tax,* 75 VA. L. REV. 605 (1989).

BRUCE HOPKINS, THE TAX LAW OF UNRELATED BUSINESS FOR NONPROFIT ORGANIZATIONS (Wiley 2006).

Darryl K. Jones, *When Charity Aids Tax Shelters*, 4 FLA. TAX REV. 769 (2001).

Faith Stevelman Kahn, *Pandora's Box: Managerial Discretion and the Problem of Corporate Philanthropy,* 44 UCLA L. REV. 579 (1997).

Catherine E. Livingston & Amy R. Segal, *Tax-Exempt Organizations and the Internet,* PRAC. TAX LAW., Winter 2000, at 29.

Catherine E. Livingston & Amy R. Segal, *Tax-Exempt Organizations and the Internet (Part 2),* PRAC. TAX LAW., Spring 2000, at 13.

Suzanne Ross McDowell, *Taxation of Unrelated Debt-Financed Income,* 34 EXEMPT ORG. TAX REV. 197 (2001).

Suzanne Ross McDowell, *What You Need to Know About the Unrelated Debt-Financed Income Rules,* 14 TAX'N EXEMPTS 206 (2003).

J. Patrick Plunkett & Heidi Neff Christianson, *The Quest for Cash: Exempt Organizations, Joint Ventures, Taxable Subsidiaries and Unrelated Business Income,* 31 WM. MITCHELL L. REV. 1 (2004).

Margaret Riley, *Unrelated Business Income Tax Returns, 2000, with a Decade in Review, 1991–2000,* SOI BULL., Spring 2004, at 135.

R. C. Sansing, *In Search of Profits: Measuring Income From the Unrelated Commercial Use of a Tax-exempt Organization's Assets,* 76(2) ACCOUNTING REVIEW 245 (2001).

Ethan G. Stone, *Adhering to the Old Line: Uncovering the History and Political Function of the Unrelated Business Income Tax,* 54 EMORY L. J. 1475 (2005).

John Strefeler & Leslie Hiller, *Exempt Organizations: A Study of Their Nature and the Applicability of the Unrelated Business Income Tax,* 12 AKRON TAX J. 223.

Case Law

Hi-Plains Hosp. v. United States, 670 F.2d 528 (5th Cir. 1982).

National Collegiate Athletic Ass'n v. Commissioner, 914 F.2d 1417 (10th Cir. 1990).

Sierra Club, Inc. v. Commissioner, 86 F.3d 1526 (9th Cir. 1996).

United States v. American College of Physicians, 475 U.S. 834 (1986).

Zeta Beta Tau Fraternity, Inc. v. Commissioner, 87 T.C. 421 (1986).

Statutory and Other Authority

I.R.C. §§ 511–514, 502.

Volunteers

(See: Tort Liability)

Bibliography

Perry Applebaum & Ryder, Samara, *The Third Wave of Tort Reform: Protecting the Public or Pushing the Constitutional Envelope?* 8 CORNELL J. L. & PUB. POL. 591 (1999).

Kenneth W. Biedzynski, *The Federal Volunteer Protection Act: Does Congress Want to Play Ball?* 23 SETON HALL LEGIS. J. 319 (1999).

Eleanor Burt & John Taylor, *Striking the Regulatory Balance in the Unique Case of the Voluntary Sector,* 24 PUB. MONEY & MGMT. 297 (2004).

William J. Chriss, *House Bill 4 Symposium Issue: House Bill 4 and Other New Legislation: Homeowners Insurance, Architects & Engineers, and Immunity for School & Charity Workers and Volunteer Firefighters,* 46 S. TEX. L. REV. 1201 (2005).

SUSAN J. ELLIS, MAXIMIZING VOLUNTEER RESOURCES (National Center for Nonprofit Boards 1999).

SUSAN J. ELLIS, VOLUNTEER MANAGEMENT AUDIT (Energizer 2003).

CAROLYN FARB & ROBIN LEACH, THE FINE ART OF FUNDRAISING: SECRETS FOR SUCCESSFUL VOLUNTEERS (Emmis Books 2006).

LINDA L. GRAFF, BETTER SAFE: RISK MANAGEMENT IN VOLUNTEER PROGRAMS & COMMUNITY SERVICE (Linda Graff & Associates 2003).

JEAN BALDWIN GROSSMAN & KATHRYN FURANO, MAKING THE MOST OF VOLUNTEERS (Public/Private Ventures 2003).

David Hartmann, *Volunteer Immunity: Maintaining the Vitality of the Third Sector of Our Economy,* 10 BRIDGEPORT L. REV. 63 (1989).

Alfred R. Light, *Conscripting State Law to Protect Volunteers: The Odd Formulation of Formulization in "Opt-Out" Preemption,* 10 SETON HALL JOURNAL OF SPORTS LAW 9 (2000).

Linda Lysakowski, Nonprofit Essentials: Recruiting and Training Fundraising Volunteers (Wiley 2005).

Myles McGregor-Lowndes & Linh Nguyen, *Volunteers and the New Tort Law Reform,* 13 Torts L. J. 41 (2005).

Laurie Mook, Jorge Sousa, Susan Elgie, & Jack Quarter, *Accounting for the Value of Volunteer Contributions,* Nonprofit Management & Leadership (2005) 15 (4), 401–415.

Andrew Watts, *Fundraising Code: Volunteer Fundraising Is Now Protected by New Codes,* Solic. J. (Charity & App. Supp.), Spring 2005, at 20.

Statutory and Other Authority

Volunteer Protection Act of 1997, 42 U.S.C. §§ 14501, 14505 (1997).

About the Acting Editor-in-Chief

Lisa A. Runquist is a principal in the law firm of Runquist & Associates, with offices in California. She has 30 years of experience representing nonprofit organizations. She is AV-rated (highest rating given by Martindale-Hubbell) and is the first winner of the Outstanding Lawyer Award, a Nonprofit Lawyers Award presented by ABA Business Law Section. She has authored numerous publications on nonprofit and religious organizations, most recently, *The ABC's of Nonprofits,* published in 2005, and is active in nonprofit and exempt organization committees of both the American Bar Association and the State Bar of California.